T0204671

THE USMCA

NAFTA RE-NEGOTIATED AND ITS BUSINESS IMPLICATIONS

IN A NUTSHELL®

SIXTH EDITION

RALPH H. FOLSOM
Professor of Law, University of San Diego

W. DAVIS FOLSOM
Distinguished Professor of Economics,
University of South Carolina Beaufort

WEST
ACADEMIC
PUBLISHING

© West, a Thomson business, 1999, 2004, 2008
© 2012 Thomson Reuters
© 2014 LEG, Inc. d/b/a West Academic
© 2020 LEG, Inc. d/b/a West Academic
      444 Cedar Street, Suite 700
      St. Paul, MN 55101
      1-877-888-1330

West, West Academic Publishing, and West Academic are trademarks of West Publishing Corporation, used under license.

Printed in the United States of America

ISBN: 978-1-64020-132-3

PREFACE

NAFTA 1994 and its re-negotiated 2018/2019 successor, the USMCA, remain essential to business operations in North America. No lawyer or business person in Canada, Mexico or the United States can escape the significance of these free trade agreements. They blend national legal and business cultures and traditions.

One issue is what to call the new trilateral North American agreement. The Trump administration prefers the name "United States-Mexico-Canada Agreement" (USMCA). Canada prefers New NAFTA and/or CUSMA in English or ACEUM in French. Mexico calls it T-MEC in Spanish. For purposes of this book, we generally call the 2018/2019 agreement the USMCA.

In many ways, NAFTA's arrival in 1994 was a watershed moment for international trade. NAFTA law and its business impact greatly influenced a host of other free trade agreements around the globe. See R. Folsom, *Free Trade Agreements: From GATT 1994 through NAFTA Re-Negotiated* (West Academic Publishing). The USMCA in turn is influencing U.S. trade negotiations with the EU, Japan and others.

We initially collaborated with pleasure on *Understanding NAFTA and Its International Business Implications*, an interdisciplinary publication written just after NAFTA 1994 came online. A professional book, *NAFTA Law and Business* followed thereafter.

It has been a genuine pleasure to jointly prepare this Nutshell on *The USMCA, NAFTA Re-Negotiated and Its Business Implications*. In it, we attempt to evaluate NAFTA's impact since its inception, as well as the future implications of its re-negotiation.

We hope that students, lawyers, government officials and people in business will find this Nutshell a useful introduction. In preparing it, we have attempted to address the interests not only of North Americans, but also persons located outside the region who are concerned about the externalities of USMCA trade, technology and foreign investment law.

Following the established Nutshell style most citations are omitted. This style creates a book that reads easily and has been widely used in law and business schools. Selected Internet citations have been provided throughout and in the Web Resources index that follows this Preface.

For a global Nutshell on trade law and policy, see R. Folsom, *International Trade Law including Trump and Trade*. Your comments and suggestions concerning any of these books are most welcome.

RALPH H. FOLSOM
rfolsom@sandiego.edu

W. DAVIS FOLSOM
davisfolsom@gmail.com

San Diego and Beaufort, 2020

ACKNOWLEDGMENTS

Ralph wishes to thank his brother Davis for extensively tutoring him on the economics and business impact of NAFTA 1994 and USMCA 2018/2019. This tutoring opened many doors of understanding. Davis wishes to thank Ralph getting him started on book publishing and trying to present legal matters in plain English.

Lastly, we very much appreciate the outstanding support of West Academic Publishing.

Professor Ralph Folsom has also authored the Nutshells on:

European Union Law including BREXIT

International Trade Law including Trump and Trade

Foreign Investment Law including Investor-State Arbitrations

International Business Transactions (co-author).

WEB RESOURCES

U.S. Government Resources:

    https://ustr.gov/trade-agreements

NAFTA 1994 Secretariat:

    www.nafta-sec-alena.org/

NAFTA 1994 Investor-State Arbitrations:

    www.naftaclaims.com

    www.state.gov/s/l/c3439.htm

North American Agreement on Labor Cooperation (NAALC, 1994):

    https://www.dol.gov/agencies/ilab/trade/agreements/naalcgd

North American Agreement on Environmental Co-operation (NAAEC,1994):

    www.cec.org

USMCA:

    https://ustr.gov/trade-agreements

OUTLINE

TABLE OF CASES

References are to Pages

TABLE OF CASES

References are to Pages

THE USMCA

NAFTA RE-NEGOTIATED AND ITS BUSINESS IMPLICATIONS

IN A NUTSHELL®

SIXTH EDITION

CHAPTER 1
WHY TRADE AT ALL?

For generations, readers fortunate enough to grow up with access to *National Geographic* were treated to stories about trade among different societies. Sometimes the stories were about present-day caravans traversing Rajasthan or trekking in the Himalayas. Other times the stories were about trade in the past. While treasure hunters focus on gold and silver, *National Geographic* writers reported the mundane trade items the ship was carrying; spices, grains, animals and other items. Whether in the 2nd or 21st century, trade has been an important part of economic activity of people.

If trade was not good for people, it would have ended long ago. The basic benefits of trade include greater choice, availability of goods and services that could not be produced locally, and expanded total output based on comparative advantage. Without trade the alternative would be self-sufficiency, whether individual, family, community or country self-sufficiency. Consider the resources and skills you and your family have today. If you had to survive on just your family's skills, the natural resources you control, and the capital resources you have, how long would you last? What would your standard of living be like?

As these words were written, a hurricane was approaching South Carolina. We hoarded water, wine, gasoline and propane, had too much in our freezer, needed to test our back-up generator, and find oysters and crabs in the creek. Fortunately, we have neighbors and friends who will look out for and share with each other. Still we are vulnerable, fourteen feet above sea level on an island with bridges that may close. If the hurricane hits hard, our choices will be limited, money will be almost useless to get our needs met and our standard of living will decline because our ability and access to trade will be reduced, hopefully only temporarily!

Countries, like individuals and families, have found trade beneficial. This chapter provides a brief review of trade as part of the economic output of a country, clarification of trade deficits versus balance of trade, and the theoretical basis of trade.

TRADE AS PART OF GDP

Often, when trade negotiations takeover the headlines it seems like trade is the only economic activity in a country. Trade is important; however, it is only on part of the total economic activity in a country. Economists measure the output of an economy using Gross Domestic Product (GDP). GDP is the total market value of final goods and services produced in a country in a period of time, usually a year. GDP includes goods *and* services that are exchanged in the marketplace and therefore does not include goods or services that are produced and consumed by households or, as demonstrated after Hurricanes Harvey, Sandy, Florence, and Irma, given to others. Which is why most economists anticipate GDP will "take a hit" after hurricanes as households depend on government, families, and charities rather than consumer spending in the marketplace. The following quarter, however, will likely include a boost as households and businesses receive insurance payments and spend to replace lost and damaged assets.

Note that GDP includes only final goods and services, and excludes primary or intermediate goods to avoid double accounting of output. Also, GDP is a measure of goods and services produced as opposed to consumed.

Having briefly described what GDP is, two obvious questions are: Why bother measuring it and what is it composed of? Why bother came out of the Great Depression when President Roosevelt asked advisors how they would know if their economic intervention programs were working. Professor Simon Kuznets developed the Gross Domestic Product model and later received the Nobel Prize for his work. Today, economists use two approaches developed by Kuznets to measure GDP, the income approach or the expenditures approach. The income approach measures total economic activity by the flow of income it generates, including wages, rents, profits and interest income. The aggregate expenditures approach, the more widely quoted method, measures GDP as the sum (with adjustments) of consumer expenditures, business investment, government spending, and net international trade, otherwise shown as $AE = C+I+G+(X-M)$.

TRADE DEFICITS, CURRENT ACCOUNT BALANCE, AND TRADE BALANCE

Net trade, total exports minus total imports, is clearly the most important component of GDP to anyone studying NAFTA or USMCA. This leads to the use of a variety of trade terms including bilateral trade, trade deficits, current account balance or trade balance. Trade deficits occur when a country's imports exceed its exports. President Trump frequently cited what he called huge and expanding trade deficits with Mexico and Canada as evidence that NAFTA was a "bad deal", "the worst trade agreement ever negotiated", and threatened to terminate the accord.

One observer suggested Mr. Trump views world trade deals as adversarial and zero-sum with other countries as rivals competing for their share of the trade "pie", not as trading partners enjoying mutually beneficial exchange. From the perspective of trade as a zero-sum game, running a trade deficit with another country would suggest that the United States is losing and is engaged in a "bad deal." But a trade deficit with Canada or Mexico is a bilateral trade deficit, not the overall balance of trade. Trying to balance U.S. trade with its two NAFTA partners would create goals to manage trade, offset certain imports with commensurate value exports, and negotiating outcomes rather than negotiating the rules of trade.

A common analogy used to challenge the idea of balanced bilateral trade is to consider a microeconomic example, a typical household. Almost all workers run a trade surplus with their employer while running a trade deficit with the various merchants and service providers they do business with. The only way a household could have balanced trade would be to only buy goods and services from our employers. (This transpired in nineteenth century "company stores" which often provided limited choices and high prices for workers.) Attempting to balance bilateral trade would similarly reduce choices for consumers, reduce competition and restrict the benefits of trade; namely expansion of the potential output of an economy sometimes referred to as "increasing the size of the pie."

While recent political debate has focused on bilateral trade, trade deficits refer to a country's overall "merchandise trade balance" and/or the "current account balance". The merchandise trade balance includes only the goods exported from and imported to a country while the current account also includes trade in services and all receipts and payment from investments including foreign debt payments. (In spring 2017, the media reported an exchange between President Trump and Canadian Prime Minister Justin Trudeau in which the President claimed the U.S. had a huge trade deficit with Canada but the Prime Minister said the U.S. had a small trade surplus with Canada. The President was quoting merchandise trade statistics while the Prime Minister spoke in current account terms including trade in services.)

Merchandise trade is more visible, particularly to consumer/voters, but the current account balance is a more comprehensive measure of trade. Trade data, including changes before and after NAFTA will be discussed later in this book but, one other trade term needs to be defined, "trade balance" or "balance of trade". Balance of trade is a summary of a country's economic exchanges with the rest of the world. Balance of trade, by definition, must balance or be equal, but different components of the balance of payments can have net positive or negative balances. The three most important components of the balance of trade are, as described earlier, the merchandise account, the current account, plus the capital account.

Since the United States has had a current account deficit for over thirty years, three things can and at various times have occurred. First, foreigners can exchange their excess dollars for their own currency. This increases the supply of dollars as well as demand for other currencies, causing the value of the dollar to fall in world currency markets. A decreasing dollar will, *ceteris paribus,* make U.S. imports more expensive and exports cheaper to foreigners, reducing the current account deficit.

Second, foreigners can use the excess dollars to make direct investments in the United States. Often, foreign creditors purchase upscale homes, condos, hotels or resorts. Frequently they buy competing firms or firms with access to critical technology. Also, in recent years, many American farmers have been approached by Asian investors. The controversial EB-5 visa program, where foreigners invest $500,000 to $1,000,000 in an American enterprise and create new jobs, would be considered foreign direct investment.

Third, foreigners can use the excess dollars to purchase financial assets, stocks, bonds issued by U.S. companies and increasingly U.S. Treasury securities. This is known as portfolio investment. For decades, foreigners have invested heavily in U.S. debt, holding approximately 20 percent of U.S. Treasury securities. Alarmists fear this could lead to economic blackmail and one of the ironic twists in USMCA rhetoric was the frequent political criticism of trade deficits with Mexico, Canada, and South Korea but less mention of the largest U.S. trade deficit-country, China.

Because foreign trade partners have often used excess dollars to purchase U.S. investments and securities the value of the dollar has remained relatively stable and the capital account, has been positive. Basically, merchandise and current account deficits have been offset by capital inflows. These financial assets represent claims against future income and output from the United States. If, or when, investment options in the United States appear less attractive to global alternatives, capital account inflows will decline and the balance of trade will adjust through shifts in currency values and/or current account balances.

Domestically, running a current account deficit might be a political/economic concern. Policies that increase savings and reduce consumption (including reduced government budget deficits) could alleviate a trade imbalance. While many factors including trade and currency policies influence a country's overall trade balance, countries like China, Japan, and Germany all have relatively higher savings rates than the United States and positive net trade balances.

COMPARATIVE ADVANTAGE, MODERN TRADE THEORY

For centuries economists have attempted to develop theories to explain and predict trade behavior. Why does international specialization and exchange occur? What determines which goods and services are exported or imported? How does international trade affect the overall economy of a country? Because NAFTA involved expanding trade between two industrialized economies and one developing economy it presented particularly interesting opportunities to observe the theory of comparative advantage in action.

Early trade theory, or pure theory, predicted trade occurred because of price differentials for products between countries. Pure theory included the assumptions that there were no artificial barriers to trade, competitive markets existed, and only goods (not resources) were traded between countries.

In the 1840s, British economist David Ricardo developed the principle of comparative costs, leading to the theory of comparative advantage. While absolute costs are costs measured in some standard unit, usually a country's currency, comparative costs are costs expressed in relationship to the costs of producing some other goods, resulting in a ratio. The principle of comparative costs states that a country will tend to export those goods for which the comparative costs are lower domestically than abroad and import those products which have higher comparative costs at home than abroad. Comparative advantage recognizes the opportunity costs or highest-valued alternative use of resources that is foregone when making a decision.

In USMCA discussions one writer described the hypothetical decision of a pediatrician, who would likely be an excellent nanny, but instead hires someone else for that task and works in her profession. With her skills and training the opportunity cost of taking care of children would be the lost income as physician. Similarly, in early 2017, as USMCA negotiations began, Ford Motor Company initially announced it would expand production in Mexico, then changed its plans to expanding capacity in the United States and, finally, decided it would instead use its scarce resources to increase production in China. It is hard to say whether these changes were due to pressure from Washington, shifts in corporate priorities, new corporate leadership, or host country economic incentives but, as the law of comparative advantage suggests, individuals, households, firms, and countries tend to allocate scarce resources to the expected highest valued outcome. Ricardo also promoted other benefits of free trade. "It binds together, by one common tie of interest and intercourse, the universal society of nations throughout the civilized world."

Ricardo's theory predicted countries will tend to export products for which they have a comparative advantage and import those for which they do not. One critical question was why do prices vary among countries? In an open competitive market environment, prices will be set by the equilibrium of international supply and demand. At the internationally determined price there will be only so much domestic quantity demanded. If domestic supply exceeds this amount then the remainder will be exported, and likewise if domestic quantity demanded exceeds supply the difference will be imported. However, domestic prices are determined in domestic currency while world equilibrium prices may be determined in other currencies. The domestic equivalent of the world price for a particular good then depends on exchange rates. But exchange rates (assuming no intervention) change to equalize aggregate exports and imports, not the level of trade in an individual product of a country. For example, readers familiar with U.S. energy markets will recognize how dramatically domestic/international supply and demand have changed since NAFTA's inception. This topic will be discussed in a later chapter.

The level of international trade then involves a balancing of many forces including domestic supply and demand, international supply and demand, changing resource market prices and exchange rates. Swedish economists Eli Heckscher and Bertil Ohlim developed a theorem bearing their names to examine more closely the cause of trade. According to the Heckscher-Ohlim theorem, the relative factor endowments of a country are the major determinant of comparative cost differences. Empirical studies have both supported and challenged Hechscher and Ohlim's conclusions. Newer theories have suggested that demand considerations, economies of scale, and technology may play more important roles in explaining the economics of international trade.

Modern trade theory suggests that international differences in factor supplies, production functions, and the pattern of demand (both domestic and international) are the major causes of trade. Using Computable General Equilibrium (QCE) analysis, economists build databases to reflect macroeconomic outputs and then "shock" the model to quantify the impact of changes in trade barriers. While USMCA is being heralded as a major improvement over NAFTA, most analysts predict relatively small changes in regional output and income. Though widely used by the Congressional Research Service (CRS) and others, QCE models, like all economic analysis, depends on the quality of the database, and assumptions made by modelers. Databases are quantitative descriptions of what happened in the past. If "conditions", including resources, technology, labor, and political, remain relatively constant models using past data can estimate the economic impact of changing regulations.

With regard to trade, TPP-12 analysts assumed that reduced trade barriers would result in more firms becoming exporters in response to reduced costs of trade. While reduced costs of trade benefit existing multinational corporations, they may not be sufficient to induce to smaller, domestic companies to expand beyond national borders. Similarly, will increased intellectual property (IP) protections, as written in USMCA and TPP-12, result in increased investment and exports? Economists are still debating whether increased IP protection increases competition, reducing prices and expansion based on comparative advantage or reduces competition by increasing costs and impeding the technology advancement and application.

Modern trade theory incorporates "endogenous growth models", reflecting the fact that reduced trade barriers affect the level of economic growth over time through the impact on investment, savings, and labor productivity. More experienced, smarter workers along with applied research and development result in a dynamic loop, reinforcing the impact of initial changes from the pre-freer trade status quo. Numerous multinational corporations initially outsourced simple production and assembly operations to low-cost countries only to find their subcontractors becoming the source of expertise in improving quality and/or efficiency in second and third generation product development.

PERFECT AND NOT SO PERFECTLY COMPETITIVE MARKETS

In the previous section it was noted that trade theory assumes that competition exists in product and factor markets. But what is competition? Does competition exist in international trade markets and, if not, how does the lack of competition impact international trade?

While virtually every business owner will state that their market is highly competitive, economists distinguish perfect competition as having distinct qualities. These include numerous, independently operating buyers and sellers of the same product. Each firm's output is only a small part of the total market supply. Therefore, each firm's decision of whether to produce or how much to produce, will not affect the market price. Competitors also have access to market information on which to base their decisions and there is ease of entry into and exit from markets. Finally, perfect competition assumes there are no externalities, costs or benefits for third parties not involved in the market exchange.

In a perfectly competitive market, supply and demand will determine the equilibrium price. Firms are "price takers" producing up to the level of the marginal costs just equal to the market price, resulting in economic efficiency. In addition, firms in the industry will only earn "normal" profits, a level sufficient to keep resources in a particular business activity but not great enough to attract new competitors or so low as to discourage existing businesses. Above normal profits, sometimes called excess or economic profits, get noticed. For example, during a particularly good agricultural year, the *Wall Street Journal* reported a farmer telling a car dealer that he wanted a new truck, exactly like the one he had. When asked why, the farmer said he did not want to attract attention. In perfectly competitive markets, specialization and trade will cause prices for products and resource to equalize over time in global markets, eliminating any initial economic profits, and enhancing economic efficiency.

Even before the NAFTA agreement, trade was growing rapidly, faster than the general rate of economic growth throughout the world. In addition to decreased trade barriers, improved and less costly global telecommunications and computer technology have provided greater access to information, facilitating international trade and competition, increasing the number of industries to which the perfectly competitive model is applicable.

In the real world, there are still numerous barriers preventing or reducing competition including less than perfect knowledge of market choices among both consumers and producers, government taxes and subsidies altering market prices, and multiple non-tariff barriers (NTBs) making it difficult to enter international markets. Often markets contain a few large firms whose actions influence market prices. In other markets some firms' products are differentiated from other competitors allowing them a degree of market power. In these imperfect markets, firms are "price makers" rather than "price takers." Legendary investor Warren Buffett is often quoted as saying "In business I look for economic castles protected by unbroachable moats." As stated earlier, while almost every business person will say their market is highly competitive, quietly they will admit that they would prefer markets where they can prevent competitors from bridging their moats.

Another, theoretically important, aspect of competition is contestable market theory. Before NAFTA, some economists proposed the idea that the agreement might increase the number of markets that act competitively without greatly expanding the number of firms. Contestable market theory suggests that the potential for competition has the same effect as actual competition, reducing prices to marginal costs and eliminating economic profits. The idea of contestable markets is analogous to business' fear of new competitors. Before NAFTA there was considerable fear among businesses in certain industries including U.S. textiles and auto manufacturing, and Mexican retail industries. As will be discussed in a later chapter, many of their fears proved justified. Likewise, contestable market theory also applies to labor markets.

ALTERING THE COMPETITIVE LANDSCAPE

As stated in the last section, taxes and subsidies influence prices and the basis of competition in a market. NAFTA's primary purpose was to end tariffs, a tax on imports, among the three countries but it did not eliminate subsidies, the source of many claims of unfair competition among the NAFTA partners. In the spring of 2017, the U.S. imposed a 20 percent "anti-subsidy" tariff on Canadian softwood lumber coming into the country. This dispute goes back to 1982 with each country claiming the other unfairly subsidizes their timber industries. More recently, President Trump, claiming some countries unfairly subsidize producers, used laws designed to protect industries critical to U.S. national security to impose global tariffs on imported steel and aluminum. Domestic steel and aluminum producers, including multinational firms with operations within the United States, were the major beneficiaries. U.S.-based fabricators of products containing steel and aluminum, along with their consumers, took a hit. In May of 2019, seeking to achieve ratification of USMCA, President Trump rescinded tariffs on Canadian and Mexican steel and aluminum.

Subsidies come in many forms with many names. What are the differences among an economic development incentive, export promotion program, and corporate welfare? It, like beauty, depends on the eye of the beholder! Is a new interstate highway an infrastructure investment or a manufacturing subsidy? In the U.S., labeling something as "welfare" can lead to intense political name-calling, but proclaiming something to be an economic development investment will likely generate much less political wrangling.

In 2017, one of the largest "investments" was Wisconsin's $3 billion package to lure Foxconn electronics manufacturer to the state. Incentives included exemption from state and local sales taxes, tax credits, and the state borrowing funds to rebuild a nearby interstate highway. One journalist pointed out the factory would likely employ a significant percentage of workers who live in nearby Illinois while the incentives are being offered by Wisconsin. Foxconn later announced, because they could not find enough qualified workers locally, it would hire engineers from China. After building only one small part of the plant, the company changed plans for what would be produced in Wisconsin and has moved slowly in the direction of fulfilling its commitments. One analyst suggested it would take at least 25 years for the state to break-even, while another noted that in less than that time, whatever Foxconn plans to produce at the factory will be obsolete.

Again, in theory, free trade agreements expand the competitive landscape and should increase choices and reduce prices, but often the benefits are hard to quantify while the costs are visible and concentrated. Harvard economist, Dani Rodrik and others have criticized mainstream economists for ignoring the negative consequences of trade including some industries and communities who lose out to foreign competition. Rodrik argues that supporters of free trade fear that any criticism would empower protectionist responses from opponents of free trade, suggesting open discussion of the pros and cons of trade would "empower the barbarians." Also, many trade economists note that the biggest supporters of free trade often oppose "safety net" provisions such as trade adjustment assistance (TAA) to address the "cons" that come with trade.

New studies have found the depressing effects of sudden exposure to foreign competition can lower wages and employment for extended periods of time, challenging the standard theoretical assumption that workers would easily adapt and adjust to changes in the marketplace. When NAFTA was being negotiated, Rodrik warned that globalization would drive a wedge between workers who had the skills and mobility to adapt and prosper in the global economy and those that did not. Leading economists acknowledged that increased trade with Mexico, a relatively lower-wage country would widen the gap between highly skilled and less-skilled workers in advanced countries like the United States and Canada, but often they minimized the significance of these effects.

While supporting free trade, Rodrik is critical of "hyperglobalization" which he defines as wrestling control of commerce from individual governments and handing it to global institutions such as the World Trade Organization. His critics argue a global forum like the WTO offers smaller countries a better opportunity to negotiate with large, powerful countries than they would have in bilateral negotiations. If international trade did not benefit societies it would have disappeared centuries ago, but, as will be discussed in Chapter 5, the impact of NAFTA has varied by industry, region, and country, and not always as theory would suggest.

CHAPTER 2

PRE-NAFTA, CUSFTA

PART A: NORTH AMERICAN ECONOMIC RELATIONS

NAFTA 1994 was not just about free trade in goods and services. It also incorporated major developments in the law of intellectual property, foreign investment and dispute settlement. Its companion agreements on North American cooperation regarding the environment and labor law, on the other hand, have proven largely cosmetic and of modest influence regionally and almost none internationally.

Economically speaking, NAFTA was about the diminution of boundaries among Mexico, Canada and the United States. The political borders, including immigration and customs controls, between these countries remain firmly in place. In other words, NAFTA had little (if any) agenda beyond economics. It was a simple agreement, with limited goals and means, its economic scope ran wide and deep. NAFTA helped make the combined Gross Domestic Product (GDP) of Canada, Mexico and the United States exceed one-quarter of the world's GDP. Together versus separate, the NAFTA partners have been a considerable force in global trade.

CANADA AND THE UNITED STATES

Integrating the economies of Canada, Mexico and the United States is a theme that has reverberated throughout North American history. Canada and the United States, for example, have been discussing free trade for nearly two centuries. In the years after the United States Revolution, Canadians were concerned that they might be annexed. Indeed, one of the first acts of the United States was to invade British Canada. Defeat of the U.S. forces ensured, ultimately, the creation of Canada as a nation.

Free trade with the United States became a preferred alternative whenever annexation raised its ugly head. Such forces reached their peak in the mid-1800s when Lord Elgin, Governor of Canada under British rule, successfully negotiated a free trade agreement with the United States. This agreement, the Elgin-Marcy Treaty of 1854, established free trade for nearly all goods and also provided for mutual access to fisheries. This was, of course, the period of the Civil War in the United States which ultimately caused the U.S. to abrogate the Elgin-Marcy Treaty in 1866. This was done because Great Britain had generally exhibited sympathies with the South and in particular had permitted Confederates to construct and repair ships in British Canada.

Canada obtained independence from Britain in 1867 by Act of Parliament. The United States and the Dominion of Canada periodically considered renewing free trade relations after the Civil War. Late in the Nineteenth Century these negotiations broke down and both nations enacted highly protective tariffs intended to foster local manufacturing. In 1911, the United States took the initiative and proposed free trade. An agreement was actually reached which the United States Congress ratified, but manufacturing interests in Canada successfully defeated it in the Canadian Parliament.

The trend towards protectionism continued throughout the 1920s and 1930s as both Canada and the United States sought to remedy their economic depressions through trade restraints. Freer trade between the countries was not revived until 1935 when Congress adopted the Reciprocal Trade Agreements Act. Under this Act, President Roosevelt negotiated a substantial reduction in tariffs applicable to Canada-U.S. trade. This agreement was part of Roosevelt's broader "good neighbor policy." This policy even led to secret talks about free trade after World War II. Yet another agreement for free trade was reached, but Canadian Prime Minister King removed his support at the last minute and thus killed the deal.

In the ensuing decades, Canada and the United States participated in the General Agreement on Tariffs and Trade (GATT 1947). This participation diverted both countries from free trade initiatives while generally enhancing trade opportunities through tariff reductions. As long as the GATT provided a reasonably successful alternative, there was little movement in the direction of free trade. One exception, however, was the United States-Canada Automobile Pact of 1965. Broadly speaking, the Auto-Pact permitted free trade in new automobiles and original equipment automotive parts. Over time, the Auto-Pact led to substantial integration of the Canadian and U.S. automotive industries.

The GATT continued to provide an alternative to free trade through the Tokyo Round of negotiations (1973–1979). The Tokyo Round attempted for the first time to reduce nontariff trade barriers. It was not until the Uruguay Round of GATT negotiations commenced in 1986 that Canada and the United States had cause to become concerned about improving their trade relations. This concern arose quickly because the Uruguay Round negotiations seemed endless and fraught with controversy. It appeared that there might not even be a successful conclusion to the Uruguay Round.

This prospect, perhaps more than others, pushed negotiations on free trade and investment between Canada and the United States in the 1980s.

Each nation appreciated that their willingness to agree to free trade would act as a spur to the Uruguay Round negotiations in which they had vested interests. In addition, it did not hurt that President Reagan was in power and that he found a conservative ally in Canadian Prime Minister Mulroney. Both countries also recognized that the European Community, having launched in 1987 its campaign for a Europe without internal frontiers, was on the verge of creating the world's largest integrated market. A Canada-U.S. agreement would raise the ante in this rivalry.

In sum, after decades of nearly agreeing to free trade, all of the stars were properly aligned for agreement between Canada and the United States. The Canada-United States Free Trade Agreement (CUSFTA) took effect January 1, 1989. There was very little expectation at that time that CUSFTA would ultimately be expanded to include Mexico. Indeed, the CUSFTA Agreement made no provision for accession of new members. Nevertheless, as we now know, the NAFTA Agreement arrived in 1994 and traces many of its provisions to CUSFTA (outlined below).

MEXICO AND THE UNITED STATES

United States trade relations with Mexico prior to NAFTA were quite different from those with Canada. There were no repeated attempts and experiments at free trade across the border. Moreover, Mexico did not participate in the GATT until 1986. The history of Mexican-U.S. trade relations was instead much more confrontational and protectionist. Mexican independence from Spain in 1821 was followed by periods of conflict with the United States. Texas became the center of controversy in the 1830s.

By 1846, in what Mexicans call the "War of North American Invasion," U.S. forces occupied Mexico City. This war resulted in the 1848 Treaty of Guadalupe Hidalgo. Under this treaty, Mexico conveyed roughly one-third of its lands to the United States including large parts of what are now the states California, Arizona, New Mexico, Utah, Colorado and Nevada. Even to this day, the Treaty of Guadalupe Hidalgo remains a deeply felt loss to most Mexicans.

In the years after the Mexican-American War, Mexico entered a period of instability. In 1876, however, Porfirio Diaz took power and he dominated Mexico until 1911. It was under his iron rule that foreign investors obtained major concessions in railroads, mining and petroleum. Apart from commodities, there was relatively little trade between Mexico and the United States during this time.

The Diaz regime was repressive and led to economic extremes. While the Mexican elite, foreign investors and the Roman Catholic Church did well, most Mexicans were hungry and resentful. This resentment exploded in 1910 for a period of seven years during the Mexican Revolution. Many deaths preceded the adoption in 1917 of a new constitution for the Federal Republic of Mexico. Dr. Guillermo Margadant, Mexico's distinguished legal historian, has referred to the 1917 constitution as "a multilateral declaration of war, directed against the large land holders, the bosses, the clergy and mining companies".

This constitution, much amended over time, influenced a variety of provisions in the NAFTA agreement. Apart from agrarian and land reform, foreigners were a principal focus of revolutionary change in Mexico. In 1938 President Cardenas nationalized all foreign oil company interests in Mexico. In many ways, including symbolically, this nationalization was perceived as a declaration of Mexican economic independence. PEMEX, the state oil and gas monopoly of Mexico, is a direct descendant of the 1938 nationalization.

After World War II, Mexico pursued a policy of import substitution and foreign investment controls. The goal of this policy was to raise tariff and other trade barriers on imports to levels that caused Mexican suppliers to prevail. Behind this protective wall, Mexican industry was sheltered from world competitive forces. Government involvement in the economy grew. While Mexico is not a member of OPEC, the rise in oil prices in the 1970s financed development and paid for the costs of economic isolation. They also greased the wheels of corruption at a level that was shocking even by Mexican standards. In 1981, when oil prices fell dramatically, the Mexican holiday from reality was over.

In rapid succession Mexico's peso was severely devalued, trading in dollars was suspended, Mexico's banks were nationalized, and payment on its national debt became doubtful. Under the influence of the International Monetary Fund, and increasingly out of a perception of self-interest, Mexico abandoned its policy of import substitution. It adopted instead the goal of export promotion and embraced for the first time in its history global trade law by joining the GATT in 1986. This was a watershed decision for Mexico and certainly a prerequisite to participation with Canada and the United States in North American free trade.

When Canada and the United States agreed to free trade in 1989, Mexico's President Salinas looked at his alternatives. He first turned towards Europe, but found little interest in an economic partnership across the Atlantic. President Salinas then expressed a desire to negotiate a free trade agreement with the United States. He was influenced in part by the popularity of the idea among the Mexican people, a popularity that remains strong to this day. President George H.W. Bush, without extensive consultations with Canada, agreed.

From the United States perspective, separate free trade agreements with Canada and Mexico were an option. From the Canadian perspective, however, participation in trilateral North American free trade negotiations was essential. The Canadians were afraid that some of their hard won CUSFTA benefits might be diluted if they failed to join in the negotiations. Their participation was thus initially defensive, but over time they realized that NAFTA 1994 offered the chance to revisit and take up issues of importance to Canada.

Professor Michael Gordon astutely observed that the United States agenda for NAFTA went beyond what was negotiated in the agreement. See 56 *Modern L.Rev.* 157 (1993). He suggests that the U.S. had and continues to have unwritten NAFTA objectives concerning Mexico. Broadly speaking these are goals of "containment" of what he refers to as the "Mexican Problem." The first objective is the hope that an open and growing Mexican economy will help stem the tide of illegal migration to the United States. On this theme, President Salinas is said to have remarked that the U.S. had a choice, either to take Mexican goods under NAFTA or Mexican people without it.

Professor Gordon also suggests that the U.S. had and has long-term interests in Mexico's abundant energy reserves. This agenda item found its way into the agreement, but certainly not with the terms and conditions preferred by the United States. See Chapter 3. Thirdly, Professor Gordon believes that the U.S. feared the concentration of power in Mexico. Politically this fear focused on decades of single party rule. Economically this fear centered on extreme disparities in wealth. Concentration of power in Mexico has always (as Porfirio Diaz learned and Chiapas illustrates) provided a ready recipe for violence and revolt. The United States hoped that mixing NAFTA into the recipe might reduce the risk of instability south of the border. This agenda item was never put in writing and barely spoken when NAFTA took shape.

MERGING ECONOMIES

NAFTA 1994 was primarily about the integration of the Canadian, Mexican and United States economies. Each of these economies had different characteristics, but on balance and taken together they were quite complementary. The United States, of course, is the giant in the middle with over 330,000,000 people driving an extremely consumer-oriented, high-tech economy. The United States has a post-industrial society where services comprise the large majority of economic activity. Computers, telecommunications, banking, insurance, engineering and fast food are just some of the wide-ranging services for which the U.S. is well known. Keeping the massive U.S. economy going requires importation of many commodities, including energy. The United States is an energy-dependent nation. In 1994, one reason for the complementarity of the North American economies was the fact that Canada and Mexico have energy surpluses.

Canada has approximately 35,000,000 people, most living along the United States border, in what is geographically the third largest nation in the world. Canada possesses great natural resources and the exportation of these resources has always been a key ingredient in its economy. Canada is also an industrial nation, producing a wide range of goods including automobiles under the 1965 Canada-United States Auto Pact. Comparatively speaking, Canada has more of a producer-driven economy.

The Province of Ontario, located roughly in the center of Canada north of the Great Lakes, is the economic powerhouse of the nation. Canada's western provinces and Quebec along with the Maritime Provinces in the east have long harbored a certain resentment of the economic and financial power exercised by Ontario. It is perhaps not surprising therefore that CUSFTA and NAFTA have been more popular in the east and west of Canada than in the central and more economically dominant province of Ontario.

Mexico has a developing economy. This contrasts sharply with the mature economies of its northern neighbors. More than 110,000,000 Mexicans, many of them struggling to rise out of poverty, hoped that NAFTA would help them realize their economic aspirations. Poverty in Mexico, especially among subsistence farmers hit among other causes by NAFTA free trade, has been growing.

Since the peso devaluation in 1994–95, and the arrival of inexpensive U.S. farm products (notably corn), more than millions of Mexicans have entered extreme poverty (defined as earning less than $2 a day). Workers living in moderate poverty ($3 a day) have also been increasing rapidly in number. Both groups, taken together, now constitute roughly two-thirds of all Mexicans. These trends, and the desperation and instability that accompany them, encourage migration to the United States and generally push down Mexican wages.

Mexico's energy exports dominate its trade relations and national budget. Every $1 change in the price of oil equates with roughly $1 billion in national revenues. Some 40% of the Mexican federal government's budget is derived from oil revenues. Mexico relies heavily upon foreign investment capital, more than half of which comes from the United States. Comparatively speaking, Mexico's large, inexpensive and increasingly skilled labor force is a principal asset. Mexican "maquiladoras" (assembly plants, often using U.S. and foreign components) initially expanded production under NAFTA 1994, employing over two million persons making electronics, clothing, auto parts, medical devices, furniture, automobiles, appliances and the like.

But after China's WTO entry in 2001, some producers moved their assembly plants to Asia. By 2019, however, rising Chinese labor and transport costs caused some plants to return to Mexico. Supply chain management is easier and faster in Mexico, and "just-in-time" assembly strategies can more readily be undertaken. Production costs in China and Mexico are now roughly the same. All that said, when Ford was deliberating where to build a new plant for its Focus in 2017, it leaned first to Mexico but in the end chose China and its vast domestic market, intending to ship cars to North America. Alas, as demand for sedans declined, Ford declared in 2018 that the Focus would no longer be made anywhere in the world.

It is often difficult to appreciate from inside the United States how economically *dependent* Canada and Mexico are upon the United States market. Both nations ship the large majority of their exports to the United States. United States investors dominate in Canada with U.S.-owned subsidiaries playing a critical role in Canada's industrial economy. United States investors are less visible in Mexico, in part because restrictive foreign investment controls have historically been pursued.

If anything, NAFTA increased the dependence of the Canadian and Mexican economies upon the United States, which now runs sizeable trade deficits with Mexico. Given such dependence, it is understandable that Canada and Mexico viewed NAFTA as a kind of insurance policy. At least prior to President Trump, NAFTA diminished the risk that the United States might in a worst-case scenario erect tariff or other trade and investment barriers damaging their economies. In dealing with the giant in the middle, there is a certain alliance of Canadian and Mexican interests.

DIFFERENT LEGAL TRADITIONS

The economic integration of North America under the NAFTA agreement depended upon law for its implementation. Each country brought with it different legal traditions that affected the operational reality of NAFTA. Certain common legal themes resonated, however. Canada, Mexico and the United States are, for example, all federal states. But their federalism is by no means uniform. Mexico probably has the most centrist tradition of federalism. Although there has been some relaxation of the federal government's powers in modern Mexico, most Mexican states are relatively powerless. Thus, in implementing NAFTA, legal activity at the federal level in Mexico usually suffices.

In contrast, Canada has a weak federal tradition. This is why inter-provincial economic agreements exist, for example the British Columbia-Alberta Trade, Investment and Labour Mobility Agreement of 2007. Among other areas, the federal government shares labor and environmental law jurisdiction with the provinces. This meant that implementation in Canada of the side agreements on North American Labor and Environmental Cooperation was dependent upon provincial action. Such implementation arrived slowly. It was not until 1997, for example, that the Labor Cooperation Agreement actively applied anywhere in Canada.

The United States, with a strong federal power balanced against a history of states' rights, lies in the middle of these traditions of federalism. State regulation of products and services freely traded under NAFTA sometimes resulted in significant barriers. That is one reason why the NAFTA Implementation Act of 1993 provided (for the first time under any U.S. trade agreement) that the states must be informed and permitted to participate in trade matters affecting their interests. While the states could not alter NAFTA law, which was supreme, they were entitled to significant procedural rights to participate in the defense of state laws that were challenged. See Section 102(b)(1)(B) of the NAFTA Implementation Act.

Other legal traditions impact NAFTA more obliquely. In Mexico and in Quebec there are strong Civil Law traditions originating in continental Europe. These traditions contrast with the Common Law heritage found generally in the United States and English-speaking Canada. In Quebec and Mexico, for example, one can find a range of Civil Law Codes and comparatively weak traditions of precedent.

The tradition of judicial lawmaking found in Common Law legal systems is much diminished in Mexico and to a lesser extent in Quebec. It is thus perhaps not surprising that United States courts in interpreting NAFTA law were more willing to aggressively reject the NAFTA agreement and its

Implementation Act. For example, the U.S. Court of International Trade ruled that the country of origin marking requirements specified by NAFTA Implementation Act did not supplant traditional United States legal doctrine in that area.

A third legal tradition that provides some contrast between the three North American partners is as much political as constitutional. Both Canada and the United States have mature multiparty democracies and strong commitments to the rule of law. Mexico, on the other hand, was ruled by a single party (the Partido Revolucionario Institucional or PRI) for about 70 years. Indeed, Mexico had the dubious distinction of possessing the longest running single party government on the globe. This often made it difficult to distinguish between the party and the state.

However, starting in the late 1990s, significant political change arrived in Mexico as competing parties captured a number of state governorships, control of Mexico City, and control collaboratively of the Mexican Congress. The PRI lost power in Mexico's 2000 presidential elections, lost again in 2006, but returned to power in 2012, only to lose again in 2018. All of this change has been influenced by the spotlight that NAFTA focused upon Mexican politics since 1994.

More generally, the NAFTA spotlight contributed to the challenge of ruling Mexico by law. It is always important to remember that Mexico is a developing nation not just in an economic sense but also in terms of its legal system. It is no secret that political and legal corruption can be found in Mexican government. Prior to NAFTA, corruption in Mexico was that of a distant neighbor. Since 1994 the increased visibility of corrupt practices under the NAFTA spotlight has arguably helped Mexico improve its rule of law. While there is nothing in the NAFTA agreement that requires such developments, it appears to be a byproduct of North American integration.

Dean Stephen Zamorra has suggested that Mexican law is undergoing "Americanization." See 24 Law & Policy in International Business 391 (1993). Multiparty politics and growing integrity in the Mexican legal system are certainly part of that process. But as Dean Zamora emphasizes, there are important cultural differences at work. For example, Mexican society stresses cooperation and is communitarian, while U.S. society stresses competition and glorifies individual freedom.

In Mexico's culture, people may feel more comfortable with authoritarian styles of government than competitive and responsive models of democracy. Similarly, in the economic sector, the cooperative, authoritarian tradition of "El Pacto" between business, government and labor violates free market principles. El Pacto agreements have held down prices and wages as part of inflation control programs. Dean Zamora suggests that pushing U.S.-style solutions on Mexico without acknowledging its different cultural bases may not only be imperialistic, but also counterproductive in the sense that the solutions will not work.

THE PRIVATE SECTOR

The preceding sections are focused upon the history and growth of intergovernmental trade relations, economies and legal traditions in North America. This section turns to the private business sector and its historical relationships prior to NAFTA. Two broad and significant trends emerge from this picture.

In Canada, with its dependence upon U.S. corporate investment, a large number of so-called "branch plants" were established. These branch plants were often subsidiaries of U.S. multinational corporations created for Canada's small market because of tariff and other trade restraints. Such plants provided significant employment opportunities to Canadians, but their economies of scale were limited and therefore typically the costs of production in the Canadian market were higher than in the United States.

One of the pronounced trends under NAFTA was the closure of Canadian branch plants by U.S. corporations. Many U.S. companies have folded their Canadian production needs into their United States manufacturing facilities. This generated some highly visible unemployment and hostility to NAFTA in Canada.

A second historical trend prior to NAFTA involves Mexico. In Mexico, since the 1960s, but particularly since the devaluation of the Mexican peso in 1982, assembly plant production centers have proliferated. These are known as "maquiladoras" and they provide for Mexico an enormous source of hard currency earnings and employment. Many maquiladoras are owned by U.S. companies. Others are owned by Mexican, Japanese and Korean investors. They have taken advantage of Mexico's inexpensive labor by shifting production of assembly goods to maquiladoras. Over a million Mexicans, many of them younger women, are employed in assembly plants making electronics, automotive parts, furniture, and apparel among other labor-intensive products and services (such as sorting grocery coupons and operating phone banks).

While the devaluation of the peso in 1995 contributed significantly to increased growth in assembly plant operations, the rapid growth of less expensive assembly plants in China and Asia has hurt Mexico's maquiladoras. And, since 2001, China's exports to Canada and the United States permanently enjoy normal (MFN) tariff status. Hence NAFTA's free trade benefits were to a degree overcome. Maquiladora employment peaked in 2001, but has been rebounding in recent years.

Mexico, quite understandably, wished to preserve the maquiladora program that existed prior to NAFTA. Canada and the United States, on the other hand, were concerned that foreign companies might use maquiladoras as "export platforms" into the NAFTA free trade area. Under the agreement, a compromise was reached which encouraged continued use of Mexican maquiladoras and allows free trading of maquiladora products provided those goods met the rules of origin that governed NAFTA 1994 trade.

In other words, maquiladora products can be free traded only if they are deemed "North American." Classic Japanese "screwdriver plants" using primarily Asian components, for example, did not qualify for free trade. Resolving issues of product origin thus became a central legal concern for attorneys and their clients. See Chapter 3. Virtually all maquiladora producers had in place strategies for compliance with the NAFTA rules of origin so that their products could be freely traded.

CONCLUSION

This brief historical perspective on CUSFTA and NAFTA has hopefully prepared you for the more detailed law of North American integration that follows. It is important to remember that these agreements emerged from different contexts and traditions that help explain their contents and implementation. History also gives us, rightly or wrongly, a sense of the expectations and hopes of the parties and economic actors seeking to benefit from NAFTA and the USMCA.

BOUNDARIES OVER TIME

Wall or no wall, NAFTA and the USMCA reduce the importance of boundaries in North America. The border between the United States and Canada totals 5,527 miles, and the Mexico-United States border is 2,013 miles. The map of North America presented below by Professor Davis Folsom and the adjacent list of events in history that influenced the current boundaries are instructional starting points. This list provides a sampling of the major historical events that have affected the political geography of North America.

NORTH AMERICAN BOUNDARY CHANGES

1.   Treaty of Utrecht, 1713. France cedes Hudson Bay and Newfoundland to Britain.

2.   Treaty of Paris, 1763. France cedes Quebec and lands east of the Mississippi River to Britain.

3.   Treaty of Paris, 1783. Britain cedes mid-west claims to United States.

4.   Louisiana Purchase, 1803. United States buys areas west of the Mississippi River from France.

5.   Convention of 1818. Defines boundary between British Canada and the United States as the 49th parallel from Lake of the Woods to the Rockies.

6.   Adams-Onis Treaty, 1819. Defines northern boundary of Spanish claims to North America; Spain cedes Florida to the United States.

7.   1820s. Chiapas becomes part of Mexico.

8.   Webster-Ashbury Treaty, 1842. Defines the Maine-New Brunswick boundary.

9.   Annexation of Texas, 1845. Adds southern Texas to the United States.

10.   Oregon Treaty, 1846. Extends the 49th parallel as the boundary between the United States and Canada from the Great Lakes to the Pacific Ocean.

11.   Treaty of Guadalupe-Hidalgo, 1848. Mexico cedes California, Arizona and parts of New Mexico, Nevada, Colorado and Utah to the United States.

12.   Gadsden Purchase, 1853. Mexico sells land on Arizona border for $10 million.

13.   Alaska Purchase, 1867. The United States buys Alaska from Russia.

14.   International Commission, 1903. Defines Alaska-Canada border.

PART B: CANADA-U.S. FREE TRADE

North American economic integration began in earnest when Canada and the United States concluded a broad free trade and foreign investment agreement in 1989. Without intending to do so, the Canada-United States Free Trade Agreement (CUSFTA) laid the foundations for NAFTA. In the United States, CUSFTA was almost a non-event. In Canada, the agreement was much contested. Special Parliamentary elections focused on CUSFTA kept the Mulroney government in power, which was critical to Canadian ratification of the agreement.

NAFTA did not repeal the Canada-United States Free Trade Agreement. The CUSFTA agreement continued and still continues to govern selected areas of trade (as specified in NAFTA and the USMCA). Officially, the United States and Canada "suspended" their 1989 agreement. **If NAFTA failed or either Canada or the United States withdrew from it, CUSFTA would come out of suspended animation and continue to bind the two countries.** There is no comparable arrangement for the United States and Mexico.

Understanding the CUSFTA agreement is important because it served as the model upon which NAFTA was built. In some areas, the terms of NAFTA were identical or nearly so. In others, minor or major changes were made which are best understood as attempts at improving upon the early experience of free trade and expanded foreign investment. NAFTA and the USMCA insights can still be drawn from CUSFTA even as it lies in suspended animation.

The Canada-United States Free Trade Agreement was limited in its scope and purposes. Nevertheless, the CUSFTA agreement is lengthy and relatively complex. It is comprised of eight Parts that are divided into a total of twenty-one Chapters. Each chapter is comprised of various Articles and accompanying Annexes. Above all CUSFTA was a pragmatic agreement.

CORE COMMITMENTS—FEDERALISM, SUPREMACY AND NONDISCRIMINATION

Chapter One of the Agreement contains a listing of CUSFTA objectives. Internal trade barriers on goods *and* services are to be eliminated, fair competition facilitated and investment opportunities liberalized. Effective procedures to administer CUSFTA, to resolve disputes, and cooperation to expand and enhance the benefits of the agreement were also listed as objectives.

In realizing these objectives, Canada and the U.S. promised to "ensure that all necessary measures are taken in order to give effect to [CUSFTA's] provisions, including their observance by state, provincial and local governments" (Article 103). This obligation was a major commitment, particularly for Canada since it has a relatively weak federal system with the provinces retaining considerable power. Binding the two federal governments to free trade was relatively simple. Binding their political subdivisions has proven more difficult.

Canada and the United States affirmed their existing 1989 bilateral and multilateral trade agreements. They self-servingly declared their agreement consistent with Article 24 of the original (pre-Uruguay Round) General Agreement on Tariffs and Trade (GATT 1947). Article 24 governs the establishment of free trade areas by GATT signatories, and CUSFTA did indeed ultimately pass examination by a GATT working party. See R. Folsom, *International Trade Law including Trump and Trade* in a Nutshell.

If there are inconsistencies between CUSFTA and then existing trade agreements, CUSFTA is supreme (Article 104). Under this supremacy rule, for example, conflicts with the GATT 1947 agreement would apparently result in regional rules prevailing. This potential was somewhat minimized via incorporating by reference into CUSFTA various GATT provisions, including the 1979 Procurement Code and Articles III, XI and XX of the GATT 1947. *Id.*

There are a number of specific exceptions to CUSFTA supremacy, some limited in scope, if conflicts arise with any of the following agreements: (1) The GATT rules on antidumping and countervailing duties; (2) the GATT rules on balance of payments problems; (3) the OECD Code of Liberalization of Capital Movements; (4) the Income Tax Convention between Canada and the U.S.; and (5) the International Monetary Fund Agreement. In addition, it is generally specified that CUSFTA is *not* supreme on agriculture, emergency trade relief, wine and spirits, trade in goods, energy, tariff waivers and investment matters. These exceptions had less impact than their numbers imply.

Canada and the United States broadly promised to grant "national treatment" on investment and trade matters. Each side thus agreed to treat the other's investors and traders in the same manner as their own, a general promise not to discriminate on the grounds of nationality. In addition, Article III of the GATT 1947 agreement, along with its interpretative notes, was specifically incorporated into CUSFTA. Article III stipulates national treatment for goods on taxation, fees and charges, distribution or sale requirements, transport rules, and domestic sourcing (among other matters). *Id*. Furthermore, the existing GATT interpretations of Article III were to be applied under CUSFTA. Several Article III disputes subsequently went to binding arbitration under Chapter 18 of CUSFTA (below).

A state or provincial treatment rule was also created. Regarding like, directly competitive or substitutable goods, treatment that is no less favorable than the most favorable treatment that the state or province grants to any goods is required. Hence, unlike at the federal level, this rule was not one of identical treatment, but a variation on most-favored-nation (MFN) treatment. The states and provinces were obliged to treat goods from the other country in the best manner they treated goods coming from anywhere, including their own state or province. Arguably, this duty provided greater protection from nondiscrimination than simply national treatment.

TRADE IN GOODS

Part Two of the 1989 Canada-United States Free Trade Agreement, covered in Chapters 3 through 12, governs free trade in goods. This central goal must be measured against a history of substantial free trade in goods prior to 1989. Canada, for example, had been exporting more than 75 percent of its goods to the U.S. on a duty-free basis prior to the CUSFTA agreement. Most goods were entering the United States at an average 5 percent tariff. Hence, tariffs were not really a significant trade relationship.

Both countries were much more concerned with nontariff trade barriers (NTBs), such as health, safety, environmental and technical product regulations. NTBs sometimes excluded goods totally from either market and each country sometimes applied international trade remedies to limit the cross-border flow of goods. With its commanding dependency on access to the U.S. market, this Part of the CUSFTA agreement was critical to Canada. Conversely, the United States was ready to make concessions on trade in goods in order to obtain benefits on trade in services, technology and cross-border investment.

TARIFFS AND QUOTAS

Canada and the United States agreed to a phased elimination of the tariffs applicable to their trade in goods. Article 401 created a schedule for import tariff removals starting in 1989 and ending in 1998. This schedule was not subsequently altered by NAFTA. Schedule A goods immediately became duty free on January 1, 1989. Schedule B goods became duty free after 5 years of 20 percent annual reductions on January 1, 1993. Schedule C goods became duty free on January 1, 1998 after 10 years of 10 percent annual reductions. Schedule C goods included the most tariff-sensitive, such as agricultural products, textiles and clothing. Thus, at this writing, President Trump notwithstanding, trade between Canada and the United States is largely free of tariffs.

Export taxes (tariffs) were prohibited at the outset of the CUSFTA agreement. Canada and the U.S. also agreed not to employ "customs user fees" which function like tariffs. The United States phased out its existing fees as applied to Canadian goods. In addition, private sector requests for accelerated tariff reductions ahead of the timelines in the CUSFTA Schedules were allowed. Companies and industries filed a surprising number of petitions for acceleration with their governments. Canadian and United States officials then met and decided which tariffs to reduce on an accelerated basis. Considerable acceleration in tariff removals were achieved under CUSFTA and this innovative process continued under NAFTA.

The CUSFTA agreement, unlike the customs unions of Europe and MERCOSUR, did not embrace the creation of a common external tariff. In other words, the United States and Canada retained their own tariffs on goods entering their markets. Goods from the rest of the world are still, even after NAFTA

1994 and USMCA 2018, subject to United States or Canadian (not CUSFTA, NAFTA or USMCA) tariffs.

Nevertheless, certain external tariff tensions were addressed in CUSFTA. These primarily concerned foreign goods that entered Canada or the United States and were subsequently shipped to the other country. The widespread practice of "drawback" under customs law was the main issue. The refunding of tariffs that manufacturers pay on imported goods after they are exported, or incorporated or consumed in the production of goods subsequently exported, is the essence of drawback. Drawback can take the form of waivers or reductions in such duties. Either way, manufacturers have lower costs because of the customs refund. Supporters of drawback argue that the imported goods have really not come to rest, merely passed through, and therefore should be beneficially tariffed.

Canada and the United States recognized that drawbacks created problems for their free trade agreement. Manufacturers obtaining them could sell at lower costs than competitors not benefiting from drawback. To solve this problem, Canada and the United States agreed to all but eliminate drawbacks on goods they trade, and were scheduled have done so by 1996. However, this commitment was notably altered by the NAFTA agreement of 1994. See Chapter 3.

Another external tariff tension that CUSFTA remedied was waivers of tariffs triggered by "performance requirements." Such requirements were primarily found in Canadian law. Often, a Canadian manufacturer had to incorporate a minimum amount of Canadian content, purchase or substitute Canadian goods, and maintain minimum export percentages. Manufacturers meeting Canadian performance requirements were recipients of drawback or tariff waivers as an investment incentive. This resulted in an unfair advantage for Canadian manufacturers competing under CUSFTA with United States companies that did not obtain comparable benefits. Article 405 of CUSFTA prohibited new or expanded tariff waivers based upon performance requirements (i.e., a "standstill" was stipulated). For all but Auto Pact goods, tariff waivers were eliminated in 1998.

Regarding trade quotas and their equivalents, Canada and the United States agreed to apply Article XI of the GATT 1947. Most quotas were banned, excepting notably agricultural, fishery or marketing quotas. Several Article XI disputes were arbitrated under Chapter 18 of CUSFTA.

THE ORIGIN OF GOODS

Free trade agreements like CUSFTA, NAFTA and the USMCA have a critical problem. Since Canada and the United States did not establish a common external tariff, other nations in theory could ship their goods into the country with the lowest tariff and then benefit from free trade. If so, third party goods could "free ride" on CUSFTA. To prevent this, Canada and the United States crafted rules to decide which goods came from their countries and allowed only those goods to be freely traded. All other goods are subject to national tariffs and trade restraints as they cross the border.

The CUSFTA "rules of origin" became one of the most complex and controversial of the agreement's provisions. Canada and the United States, with different legal traditions in this area, undertook a path-breaking set of rules of origin. To start, they agreed that all goods "wholly obtained or produced" within either or both of their nations could be freely traded. Since this rule applies mainly to minerals, agricultural goods and fish, it was not difficult to fulfill.

Manufactured goods, not so clearly Canadian or United States in origin, were another story. In the global economy, with multinationals producing goods and parts in many nations, it is hard to ascertain which products come from where. In the United States, the origin of goods has typically been decided under the doctrine of "substantial transformation." See *Anheuser-Busch Brewing Assn v. United States,* 207 U.S. 556 (1908). If in the process of manufacture, a material or part was "substantially transformed" into a new product, then its foreign origin was lost. The material or part so transformed originates as a matter of U.S. law in the country of transformation.

Unfortunately, the doctrine of substantial transformation in U.S. customs law has many imprecisions. Canada and the United States, having adopted the Harmonized Tariff System (HTS) of classification of goods, moved in a different direction. Under Article 301 of CUSFTA, they agreed as a general rule that whenever items of third-party origin were transformed to a degree that their tariff classification under the HTS changed, then those items originated in Canada or the United States. But packaging, combining or diluting goods of third-party origin was insufficient. The core CUSFTA rule of origin was therefore linked to changes in HTS tariff classifications. This approach embodied the idea but provided more precision than the doctrine of substantial transformation. For more on the HTS system, see R. Folsom, *International Trade Law including Trump and Trade* in a Nutshell.

Canadian legal traditions and priorities were the primary source of additional CUSFTA "content" rules of origin. The CUSFTA content rules of origin applied only to trade in selected (but quite a large number) goods. These rules generally had to be satisfied *in addition to* the basic rule of change in tariff classification. In a few instances, the content origin of the goods sufficed for free trade.

Canada and the United States agreed, in most circumstances, on a 50 percent CUSFTA content rule. The value of materials originating in Canada or the United States plus the direct cost of processing performed in either or both countries had to exceed 50 percent of the value of the goods crossing the border. Only if this content rule was satisfied could many goods be freely traded under CUSFTA. Thus companies whose economic contribution to the region was less significant could not participate in free CUSFTA trade.

The 50 percent CUSFTA content rule of origin proved difficult to apply. In one noted case, it became especially controversial regarding Honda automobiles. See Cantin and Lowenfeld, 87 *Amer. J.Int'l Law* 375 (1993). The dispute centered on how to treat third party content that was "rolled up." Honda-U.S. exported auto engines with 10 percent third party content to Honda-Canada. Since the value of the engines was 90 percent United States in origin, when Honda-Canada installed the engines in its automobiles, it "rolled up" (treated as American) the 10 percent third party content when it subsequently shipped the autos to the United States.

Canada took the position that the engines were 100 percent American in origin. But U.S. Customs ruled that the 10 percent third-party engine value could not be rolled up in this manner, which meant that overall the autos did not meet the 50 percent CUSFTA content rule. They therefore could not be freely traded and were subject to United States tariffs. The *Honda* case reverberated in the NAFTA negotiations. Important changes were later made in the North American rules of origin for automobiles. See Chapter 3.

Special rules of origin for textiles and clothing were created under CUSFTA and then tightened under NAFTA. Demanding "fabric-forward" production requirements were stipulated so as to exclude third party textile goods from CUSFTA free trade. Certain fabrics (like silk) were exempt from these special CUSFTA origin requirements.

PRODUCT STANDARDS

Canada and the United States focused on technical product standards as nontariff trade barriers in Chapter 6 of their agreement. Unusually, and importantly, Chapter 6 did not apply to state, provincial or local governments. The GATT Code on Technical Barriers to Trade of 1979 was affirmed by the two countries. This Code provided that technical standards and product certification systems could not be used to create obstacles to trade, and foreign goods had to be treated no less favorably on standards than domestic goods. Coverage of process and production methods (PPMs) was omitted from the 1979 Code.

Under CUSFTA, "standards-related measures" (SRM) (including production processes) and "product approval procedures" were subject to free trade goals (Article 603). If the demonstrable purpose of standards was to achieve legitimate domestic objectives without excluding goods fulfilling those objectives, then CUSFTA's terms were met. Otherwise, a disguised obstacle to Canada-United States trade might occur and breach the treaty. Regarding each other's standards and certification systems, Canada and the United States generally granted mutual recognition. This approach meant that most goods certified as meeting technical standards by Canada or the United States could be freely traded.

A separate and detailed Chapter 7 was created for agricultural, food and beverage products. For these goods, a unification or harmonization approach was adopted for both standards and inspection procedures. In further contrast, CUSFTA's harmonized "sanitary and phytosanitary" (SPS) rules were made binding on state, provincial and local governments.

FREE TRADE EXCEPTIONS

Article 1201 of CUSFTA incorporated Article XX of the GATT 1947 agreement. Article XX creates general exceptions to the free movement of goods. These exceptions, however, may not be used in ways constituting "a means of arbitrary or unjustifiable discrimination" or "a disguised restriction on international trade."

The exceptions to international free trade in goods found in Article XX of the GATT include restraints of trade justified on grounds of public morals, protection of human, animal or plant life or health, compliance with laws and regulations which are compatible with the GATT, prison labor, and protection of national historic or artistic treasures. Article XX also exempts international restraints of trade undertaken to conserve natural resources (jointly undertaken with restraints on the domestic sector), to adhere to intergovernmental commodity agreements or domestic price stabilization programs, and in response to supply shortages.

Canada attempted to invoke Article XX to conserve Pacific salmon and herring as exhaustible natural resources by means of "landing" requirements. A CUSFTA dispute settlement panel ruled against Canada, finding that these requirements were enacted to restrain trade as well as conserve the species (CDA–89–1807–01). The panel doubted that the alleged conservation benefits were sufficiently large to justify the commercial inconvenience of landing *all* salmon and herring caught in Canada's Pacific waters. Despite this ruling, and CUSFTA Commission efforts at compromise, Canada has continued to impose limited landing requirements as Canadian fisherman assert excessive catches by U.S. boats.

A second group of CUSFTA general exceptions to free trade, borrowed from GATT 1947, deal with "national security." Article 2003 of CUSFTA was essentially lifted from Article XXI of the GATT 1947 agreement. Under it, restrictions on the flow of security-related information, actions to protect national security interests (such as non-proliferation of nuclear weapons), and United Nations peace and security obligations were recognized exceptions to CUSFTA free trade.

However, there was a special agreement regarding energy goods. Such goods could not be restricted except as necessary to: (1) Supply the Canadian or United States military when facing domestic armed conflicts; (2) fulfill critical defense contracts; (3) implement nuclear non-proliferation agreements; or (4) respond to direct threats of disruption in the supply of nuclear defense materials. This proviso reinforced the general CUSFTA commitments made to free trade in energy discussed below.

CANADIAN CULTURAL
INDUSTRIES EXCLUSION

Canada has a long history of supporting cultural industries through investment, financial, tax and other governmental acts. The 1989 free trade and foreign investment agreement between Canada and the United States excluded "cultural industries" from its scope. This exclusion has been retained under NAFTA *and* the USMCA. The Canadian cultural industry exclusion covers the entire gamut of the NAFTA and USMCA agreements. It applies to goods, services, investment, intellectual property, and dispute settlement.

The argument for this exclusion is not to keep American culture out of the market, but instead to assure a Canadian presence as well. Indeed, Canada maintains that it has neither attempted nor succeeded in keeping out American cultural products and services. That certainly seems right. Over 90 percent of Canada's movie screens and more than 80 percent of its news and TV broadcasts are U.S. controlled. Books of U.S. origin occupy 60 percent of all Canadian shelf space and U.S. magazines take 80 percent of the English-language market.

Cultural industries are defined those engaged in publishing, distributing or selling:

- Books, periodicals and newspapers (except their printing or typesetting);

- Films or videos; audio or video music recordings; or printed or machine-readable music;

- Public radio communications;

- Radio, television and cable TV broadcasting; and

- Satellite programming and broadcasting network services (Article 2012).

One practical effect of securing the cultural industries exclusion has been to insulate Canada's broadcasting regulations from regional scrutiny. In Canada, content requirements and airtime rules are an important means by which the Canadian Radio-Television and Telecommunications Commission (CRTC) restricts the amount of foreign broadcast material. Current broadcasting regulations employ a quota system mandating Canadian content for a minimum of 60 percent of all programming and 50 percent of prime time. Comparable quotas apply to films, broadcast TV, cable TV and satellite transmissions. "Canadian content" is calculated under a points system traditionally requiring that the producer be Canadian and that at least 6 of 10 key creative positions be filled by Canadians. In addition, most production and distribution expenses must be paid to Canadians.

The requirements for radio are similar and focus on the nationality of the composer and performer, and the location and performance of the selection. The government also provides subsidies and tax incentives for national broadcasting enterprises which have financial difficulty in complying with content quotas. Furthermore, investment regulations effectively limit U.S. ownership or control of Canadian cultural enterprises. For example, Canada refused to permit Borders to open a super-bookstore in Toronto even after securing a Canadian partner as a majority owner. Ironically, although these economically driven rules ensure a national presence in broadcasting, they do not guarantee Canadian cultural content.

All that said, technology has greatly diminished the effectiveness of Canada's audio-visual content rules. Satellite transmission and Internet streaming have made particular inroads. There is a thriving gray market for dishes aimed at U.S. satellites receiving services paid via a U.S. billing address. More broadly, the Internet has undermined Canada's cultural industry trade restraints in ways that mostly avoid even the most determined regulator. Canadian limits on access to Netflix titles, for example, have been widely circumvented by obtaining U.S. Internet addresses via virtual private networks (VNP) installed on Canadian computers and other devices.

In contrast, there is no cultural industry exclusion under NAFTA or the USMCA applicable to Mexico-United States trade and foreign investment. Integration of U.S.-Mexican cultural industries is occurring. In 1996, for example, the United States and Mexico reached agreement allowing companies in either country to compete for provision of satellite services, including direct-to-home and direct broadcast services. Each country retains the right to impose "reasonable" ownership, content and advertising regulations, but Mexico (unlike Canada) will not impose local content requirements.

There are exceptions and qualifications to the general exclusion of Canadian cultural industries from CUSFTA, NAFTA and USMCA free trade. Tariff reductions were specified under CUSFTA for film, cassettes, records, cameras, musical instruments and the like. Additional tariff reductions were agreed to in NAFTA. Responding to a United States complaint about Canadian cable TV "pirates," copyright royalties must be paid when U.S.-sourced free transmissions are retransmitted to the Canadian public by cable. In addition, no alteration or non-simultaneous retransmission of such broadcasts is permitted without the permission of the copyright holder. Likewise, no retransmission of cable or pay TV can occur without such authorization.

Occasionally, United States investors may acquire a Canadian cultural industry company by merger or acquisition. If ordered to divest, the U.S. investor must be paid open market value by Canada. Canada, for example, forced Simon & Shuster to divest a Canadian textbook publisher to a Canadian company, which subsequently went bankrupt. No other parties being interested, the Canadian government was obliged to buy the textbook publisher, and sold it back to Simon & Shuster.

CANADIAN CULTURAL INDUSTRIES
EXCLUSION—U.S. RESPONSES

Canada's cultural industry exception comes with a price. The United States can unilaterally implement retaliation for cultural industry protection. The U.S. can undertake "measures of equivalent commercial effect" against acts that would have been "inconsistent" with CUSFTA but for the cultural industries exclusion (Article 2005.2). There is no need to utilize CUSFTA's dispute settlement procedures prior to retaliation, which can be anything except a violation of the free trade agreement. The United States could, for example, pursue "Section 301" investigations and unilateral retaliation under the Trade Act of 1974. See R. Folsom, *International Trade Law including Trump and Trade* in a Nutshell. Each year the United States Trade Representative must identify new Canadian acts, policies and practices affecting cultural industries.

Both Canada and the United States have sought to minimize the potential for cultural industry disputes through negotiations. The "successful" resolution of the Country Music Television (CMT) dispute in 1995 is often cited as an example. CMT of Nashville had, in the absence of a Canadian competitor, been licensed as a Canadian cable TV distributor. When a competitor emerged, CMT's license was revoked by the CRTC. CMT then petitioned the USTR for Section 301 relief, and an investigation was commenced. Intergovernmental negotiations resulted in the creation of a partnership of the two competitors, which was then licensed by the CRTC.

Cultural industry disputes have also been diverted from CUSFTA by using the World Trade Organization as an alternative forum. In March of 1997, a WTO Dispute Settlement Panel ruled that Canada's taxes, import regulations and postal subsidies concerning magazines (and advertising) violated the GATT 1994 agreement (WT/DS31/AB/R (1997)). This longstanding dispute centered on *Sports Illustrated*. Canada was seeking to protect and ensure "Canadian issues" of periodicals and prevent the export of its advertising revenues. The United States overcame culturally-based Canadian policies by electing to pursue WTO remedies, although Canada's compliance was disputed. In May of 1999, a settlement was reached. United States publishers may now wholly-own Canadian magazines. In addition, Canada will permit U.S. split-run editions without Canadian editorial content. Such editions may contain Canadian advertisements not in excess of 12 percent by lineage (rising to 18 percent).

Professor Oliver Goodenough has thoughtfully analyzed Canada's preoccupation with culture. See 15 *Ariz. J. Int'l & Comp. Law* 203 (1998). He believes that the cultural industry exclusion reflects a weak national identity and that a principal purpose is to rally Canadians around their flag in a "recurring pageant of threat and defense." Professor Goodenough notes that the "war" against Hollywood is primarily protective of Anglophone Canada. Francophone Canada, with a healthy cultural identity, has already demonstrated resilience to U.S. and Anglophonic Canadian influences.

Reaching into the literature on "culture transmission theory," Professor Goodenough finds that most foreign influences will "bounce off" healthy cultures without government intervention or, at the very least, compartmentalize such influences in ways which separate them from hearth and home. He concludes that Canada is "defending the imaginary to death" and if it continues to press its cultural protection policies: "[I]t will indeed be to the death, a death brought about not by 'invasion' from the south, but by the incomparably better claims to culturally-based nationhood possessed by Francophone Quebec and by the First Nation Peoples. Rather than acting as a rallying cry for national preservation, cultural protection provides the intellectual basis for a break-up of Canada."

PROCUREMENT

The GATT Procurement Code of 1979, along with past (1986) and future (1995) amendments, was incorporated by reference into CUSFTA. The agreement, however, surpassed the Code as it existed in 1989 in several important ways. The number of goods eligible for free procurement trade was increased, the value of eligible contracts decreased to $25,000 U.S. and its equivalent in Canadian dollars, and a general rule of most-favored-treatment for goods with at least 50 percent cost-based CUSFTA origin was established. Canada and the United States also agreed to create opportunities to challenge procurement awards before administrative authorities, a remedy followed in NAFTA, the 1995 WTO Procurement Code and the USMCA.

TEMPORARY IMPORT RESTRAINTS

In a step well ahead of the rest of the world, Canada and the United States agreed to dramatically reduce their rights to take unilateral, temporary action against import surges. When such surges cause or threaten serious injury to domestic producers of similar or competing products, Article XIX (the "escape or safeguards clause") of the GATT permits taking relief in the form of tariffs, quotas, voluntary trade restraints or other protection measures. Nations impacted by such relief can retaliate equivalently. Canada and the United States significantly limited each other's right to pursue *bilateral* escape clause relief. After 1997, CUSFTA totally eliminated bilateral escape clause relief except with the other's unlikely consent. This ban continued in effect under NAFTA, but was softened under the USMCA.

A different type of escape clause relief (known as "global actions") could be undertaken when the trade involves third parties. If global actions were taken under the GATT, neither Canada nor the United States may restrict imports from the other unless they are "substantial" and "contributing importantly" to injury or its threat (Article 1102). However, several WTO Appellate Body rulings cast doubt on the legality of excluding or favoring Canada or Mexico in global escape clause proceedings. See

U.S.-Lamb Meat from New Zealand, WT/DS 177/ AB/R (May 16, 2001).

While the huge amount of trade between Canada and the United States is not always harmonious, CUSFTA virtually took Canada-United States trade out of escape clause proceedings. In contrast, NAFTA established a number of escape clauses to insure against the possibility of import surges from Mexico. Temporary import restraints were even subject to a special "understanding" supplementing NAFTA 1994. See Chapter 3.

WINE, BEER AND SPIRITS

The barriers to trade in alcoholic beverages between the United States and Canada presented a complex regulatory maze. Beer was so difficult that little agreement was reached and existing restraints were retained on both sides of the border. Wine and spirits were dissected under Chapter 8 of CUSFTA and these rules remained in force under NAFTA.

Nondiscriminatory national treatment and most-favored sub-national treatment on licensing the sale of wine and spirits was required. Wine and spirits licensing had to be undertaken using normal commercial considerations without causing disguised barriers to trade. Prompt, fair and objective appeals from administrative boards were to be made available to applicants from either side of the border. Furthermore, pricing decisions by public distributors had to be nondiscriminatory, but could reflect actual cost-of-service differentials between handling domestic and imported wines or spirits. Canadian price mark-ups above those levels were removed between 1989 and 1995.

Regulations governing the distribution of wine and spirits are also subject to general national and most-favored treatment rules. Certain traditional exceptions continue in force. For example, Ontario and British Columbia oblige private sellers to favor wines originating in their provinces. And Quebec requires food stores to sell wine bottled in that province. Canada did eliminate longstanding blending requirements on U.S. bulk distilled spirits, and the exclusive right to sell products labeled Bourbon Whiskey and Canadian Whiskey was recognized. Under NAFTA, exclusivity was also extended to Tennessee Whiskey and Mexican Tequila and Mezcal.

The extensive CUSFTA dismantling of restrictive trade regulations governing wine and spirits contrasts with the coverage of beer. Restrictive and discriminatory beer practices in effect on October 4, 1987 were retained. Only new restraints had to conform to the national and most-favored treatment obligations. Notably, Canada and the United States reserved their GATT 1947 rights and obligations for wine, spirits *and* beer. The GATT subsequently provided a venue to challenge some of the trade restraints on beer preserved by CUSFTA. See GATT Doc. DS17/R (Oct. 16, 1991); BISD395/206 (June 19, 1991). Ontario, for example, maintained "warehouse charges" and "environmental" taxes that mostly hit U.S. beer. The United States at one point slapped a 50 percent tariff on Ontario beer. By filing GATT complaints and engaging in negotiations, both countries largely succeeded in removing restraints of trade on beer. Hopefully this will at last resolve the Canadian-U.S. "beer wars."

ENERGY

Canada exports large amounts of oil, gas, coal, electricity and uranium to the United States. This helps meet the energy-hungry needs of the United States. The CUSFTA 1989 provisions on trade in energy goods contained in Chapter 9 were unusually significant. Similar provisions were retained under NAFTA, but there was a dispute about their meaning if an energy crisis occurs. See Chapter 3.

The Canadian National Energy Board (NEB) regulates trade in energy goods by licensing surplus exports. The NEB has the power to regulate the prices of Canadian energy imports and exports, determining whether prices are "just and reasonable." The United States perceived this price regulation as constituting minimum export price controls. Article 902(2) of the CUSFTA agreement bans such price controls. CUSFTA also disallows charging higher than domestic prices for energy exports. Furthermore, since Canada taxes the export of energy goods, Article 903 prohibits discriminatory taxation. Export taxes and fees are permissible only if they are imposed domestically, and Canada adjusted export taxes on energy as a consequence.

Perhaps most importantly for the national security of the United States, Canadian law authorizes the NEB to restrain energy exports in times of crisis, as

Canada did during the world oil shocks of the 1970s. Article 904(a) of CUSFTA is less than a model of clarity but seems to remove this authorization as it might apply to exports to the United States. Canada appeared instead obliged in a crisis to maintain the prior proportion of exports to domestic production. The standard proportions among the various energy exports to the United States had apparently also to be maintained. The only exception to these duties was if sharing under the International Energy Program is imposed. The USMCA dropped these controversial provisions. See Chapter 6.

MOTOR VEHICLES

Under their bilateral Auto Pact of 1965, Canada and the United States substantially embraced free trade in new automobiles and OEM parts. The Auto Pact was retained under CUSFTA (and NAFTA) subject to some changes. Tariffs on auto parts traded between Canada and the United States were extinguished. Canada's historic blockage of the importation of used vehicles from the United States was also eliminated. The United States adopted the more rigorous 50 percent regional content test of origin found in CUSFTA, but permitted manufacturers to average their value content over 12 months.

On the Canadian side, the Auto Pact was limited under CUSFTA to the Big Three and by special exception CAMI (a General Motors-Suzuki joint venture). No other manufacturers (including various Japanese companies) could acquire preferential Auto

Pact status. They and other manufacturers had to meet the general CUSFTA rule of origin content requirements. Canada further agreed to abolish tariff refunds and waivers for non-Auto Pact producers. But Canada retained its sales to production performance ratio obligations and various "Canadian value-added" content rules for Auto Pact companies.

By 1998 the United States and Canada had removed virtually all tariffs on automotive goods.

SERVICES

The United States, with many highly competitive service providers, sought a general commitment to free trade in services from Canada. Chapters 14 and 17 of CUSFTA make it clear that the U.S. failed to obtain free trade in services as a general rule. Substantial free trade in "covered" services was all that could be agreed upon. Annex 1408 of the CUSFTA agreement lists the services subject to its free provision rules. This list included some glaring omissions, such as transportation, that were not remedied until NAFTA.

Service providers and service seekers acquired benefits under CUSFTA. The "provision" of covered services included the right to be located in one country and service clients in the other. Provision embraced production, distribution, sale, purchase, marketing, delivery and use of covered services. Provision also included access to and use of domestic distribution systems. Beneficiaries could establish a "commercial presence" to facilitate covered services, such as establishing a sales agency or branch office in the other country. The right to invest in order to provide covered services was also protected. Indeed, virtually *any* activity associated with the provision of covered services was allowed, including the organization, control, operation, maintenance and disposition of companies, branches, agencies, offices or other facilities to conduct business as well as borrowing money and handling property.

Who could provide services was clarified in Article 201 of CUSFTA. Canadian and United States nationals *and* enterprises principally carrying on business in either country were the main beneficiaries. Such businesses had to be incorporated or otherwise constituted under Canadian or United States laws. The Agreement's focus on principal place of business meant that Canadian or U.S. businesses owned or controlled by individuals or companies from other nations benefited from free trade in CUSFTA-covered services. Denial of these third-party benefits was possible only if the service was provided "indirectly." This exception functioned like a rule of origin. It ensured that only service providers with substantial businesses in Canada or the United States could partake of free trade.

Cross-border CUSFTA service providers and seekers received "no less favorable" treatment than nationals and enterprises under Canadian and United States laws. For each federal government, national treatment was the general rule. Each state, province or local government was obliged to grant most-favored treatment to service providers and seekers. Ironically, while California could give less than most-favored treatment to New York service providers, it could not do so to Canadians. Since CUSFTA's beneficiaries included enterprises principally carrying on business in Canada or the United States, third party subsidiaries qualified for national and most-favored services treatment.

There were significant exceptions to the CUSFTA standards for service providers. Canada and the United States indefinitely retained (in their 1989 form) inconsistent statutes and regulations. Furthermore, Article 1402.3 allowed for deviations in treatment for prudential, fiduciary, health and safety or consumer protection reasons. Any such different treatment had to be "equivalent in effect" to that applied domestically for the same reasons. No deviation could require the establishment of a commercial presence in order to provide services in the other country. And, borrowing from GATT 1947 language relating to goods, no deviation (including tax laws), could serve as a means to "arbitrary or unjustifiable discrimination" or a "disguised restriction" on CUSFTA trade in services.

Canada and the United States retained their own licensing and certification systems for services. They agreed that these systems should "relate principally to competence or the ability to provide" covered services. (Article 1403) Licensing and certification could not discriminatorily impair or restrain access. Existing inconsistent statutes and regulations were indefinitely retained, but no new licensing or certification statute or regulation could require a commercial presence, arbitrarily discriminate, or disguise a trade restraint.

FINANCIAL SERVICES

The provisions of Chapter 17 of CUSFTA reflect the complexity and sensitivity of the financial services sector. For purposes of Chapter 17, "financial services" were defined so as to exclude securities underwriting and sales of insurance policies. Insurance services were generally a covered service under Chapter 14 of CUSFTA.

Each country made commitments to alter specific statutes and regulations to benefit the other's financial sector. These commitments were retained under NAFTA. Canada made commitments on financial services in three key sectors:

(1)　Greater U.S. ownership of Canadian banks;

(2)　Deregulation of U.S.-controlled foreign bank subsidiaries; and

(3)　Reduced application of Canada's foreign investment control laws.

The United States also made three major commitments on financial services:

(1)　Permission for U.S. banks to underwrite Canadian debt;

(2)　Extension of future U.S. Glass-Steagall Act (48 Stat. 162) amendments to Canadian-controlled financial institutions; and

(3) A promise not to restrict interstate branching rules.

The Canadian commitments allow United States residents and U.S. companies controlled by such persons to acquire Canadian banks and federally regulated trust, loan and life insurance companies. However, no one person could own more than 10 percent of a Schedule A bank class of securities. Limits on the total domestic assets of banking subsidiaries controlled by U.S. citizens or permanent residents were removed, as were restraints on the transfer of loans from subsidiaries to their parent companies. Moreover, new branches of U.S.-controlled banking subsidiaries could be opened without getting the approval the Minister of Finance. More broadly, Canada agreed not to apply its investment review powers over U.S. financial institutions in a manner that would be inconsistent with the "aims" of Chapter 17.

The United States commitments permit federally regulated U.S. banks to underwrite and market the debt of Canada, its political subdivisions, and the debt of Canadian agencies backed by full faith and credit. This authority is an exception to the general prohibition against U.S. banks dealing in securities contained in the Glass-Steagall Act of 1933. Canadian public debt has been more readily sold in the United States as a consequence. If the U.S. amends the Glass-Steagall Act or its regulations at any future time (which it has now done), Canadian-controlled financial institutions must be given equal treatment. For these limited purposes, a financial institution controlled directly or indirectly by persons who ordinarily reside in Canada suffices. In the event of federal regulation of interstate branches, the United States agreed not to adopt or apply any laws that would be more restrictive on Canadian banks than those in force at the state level on October 4, 1987.

These commitments notwithstanding, Canada and the United States publicly expressed mutual dissatisfaction with treatment of financial institutions in the other's country. Both promised no reduction in existing rights and privileges, except if the benefits from future deregulation of financial markets are not extended to each other absent "normal regulatory and prudential considerations." Canada and the United States now give each other notice and an opportunity to comment on proposed financial regulations. Consultation between the Canadian Department of Finance and the U.S. Treasury Department is frequent. Such consultations generally displace regional dispute settlement procedures.

FOREIGN INVESTMENT

Chapter 16 of CUSFTA 1989 governed laws, regulations and policies generally affecting cross-border investment by Canadian or United States investors. However, financial services, cultural industries, transportation services, government procurement and services not covered by CUSFTA did not benefit from Chapter 16. CUSFTA created a rule of national treatment at the federal level and most-favored treatment at lower levels of government. Such rules covered establishing new businesses, acquiring or selling existing ones, and conducting business operations.

The foreign investment rules of CUSFTA applied *only* to United States and Canadian nationals, governments and enterprises they controlled. This differed from CUSFTA free trade in services which benefited third party providers established or principally doing business in Canada or the United States. Nevertheless, it was forbidden to require that shareholders include nationals of either country. Nor could investors be forced due to nationality to divest a qualified investment.

Perhaps most importantly, Canada undertook to amend its 1985 Investment Canada Act (ICA). The ICA normally applied to foreign acquisitions of Canadian businesses worth more than 5 million Canadian dollars. CUSFTA did not suspend the ICA's application to U.S. acquisitions of existing Canadian businesses, but it did alter the thresholds triggering Canadian review. Only direct acquisitions or sales of Canadian firms subject to CUSFTA that exceed $150 million Canadian dollars could be reviewed by Canada's investment authorities. Indirect acquisitions of Canadian businesses were not reviewable unless they fell in the economic sectors excluded from CUSFTA. These commitments were continued under NAFTA.

The United States could not trigger dispute settlement about any Canadian decision under the ICA regarding an acquisition by a U.S. investor.

Significantly from the point of view of existing U.S. investors in Canada, the $150 million threshold also triggers a "right of exit." Canadian investments below that amount can be sold to non-Canadians without ICA review.

Performance requirements were a central focus of CUSFTA's investment rules. They could not be imposed as a condition to allowing or operating an investment. Article 1603 prohibited (for CUSFTA investors) performance requirements on exports, obligations to substitute or purchase local goods or services, and domestic content minimums. Even so, certain types of performance requirements (notably employment, technology transfer, or research and development obligations) were permissible for CUSFTA investors. With third party investors, any performance requirement could be used, provided this did not have a "significant impact" on trade between Canada and the United States.

Direct or indirect nationalization or expropriation of investments held by each other's investors was banned by CUSFTA. The only exception was for nondiscriminatory public purposes in accordance with due process of law and upon payment of prompt, adequate and effective compensation at fair market value. Cross-border CUSFTA investors were free to transfer their profits, dividends, royalties, fees, interest and other earnings or proceeds from the sale or liquidation of their investments. Canada or the United States could prevent such transfers (acting equitably, without discrimination and in good faith) under their bankruptcy, insolvency, creditors' rights, securities, criminal, currency transfer reporting, tax withholding or court judgment enforcement laws. New tax or subsidy rules were allowed provided they did not arbitrarily or unjustifiably discriminate between Canadian or U.S. investors, or function as a disguised restriction on the CUSFTA benefits of those investors.

Note that there were no provisions allowing foreign investors to file claims against governments for damages as a result of alleged violations of rights created under CUSFTA. Such remedies became a controversial focus of dispute settlement under NAFTA. See Chapter 3.

MOVEMENT OF BUSINESS PERSONS

Chapter 15 of CUSFTA governed *temporary* entry for business persons engaged in trading goods or services, or cross-border investors. Similar provisions can be found under NAFTA 1994. Four groups of persons were granted preferential treatment: (1) Business visitors; (2) professionals; (3) traders and (substantial) investors; and (4) intra-company transferees. In the event of disputes concerning the entry of business persons, all available appeals in Canada or the United States had to be first pursued. Only if there was a pattern of restrictive practices was dispute settlement under Chapter 18 of CUSFTA an option.

All four categories were exempted from labor certification or employment validation tests demonstrating in advance that a local person could not fulfill the needs that these business persons temporarily met. On the other hand, all such business persons had to meet the standard national security, public health and safety requirements for entry. Except for business visitors, employment authorization prior to entering the other country was required. Tens of thousands of Canadian professionals took advantage of CUSFTA to head south for employment in the United States.

CUSFTA DISPUTE SETTLEMENT

Dispute settlement under NAFTA replaced comparable procedures first established under CUSFTA. Chapter 18 of CUSFTA employed consultations and, if necessary, arbitration to settle most kinds of disputes. Chapter 19 of CUSFTA utilized special binational panels to resolve antidumping and countervailing duty disputes. All of the CUSFTA dispute settlement decisions, including those cited in this chapter, can be obtained at www.nafta-sec-alena.org.

None of CUSFTA's dispute settlement procedures were mandatory. For example, disputes that could be resolved under CUSFTA, the GATT 1947 agreement, or the GATT Tokyo Round Codes could be pursued in either forum. Practically speaking, forum shopping as between Chapters 18 and 19 and the GATT (now WTO) was perfectly acceptable. However, once an avenue of relief was chosen by the complaining party, the dispute had to be resolved there exclusively.

One reason behind this legitimization of forum shopping was the sorry state of GATT 1947 and GATT Code dispute settlement procedures in 1989.

"Working-groups" or panels composed of experts who were not from the nations in dispute issued a "report." This report made findings of fact, rendered conclusions of law, and made remedial recommendations which were forwarded to the GATT Council. Lengthy, cumbersome and subject to a consensus vote in the GATT Council, GATT dispute settlement in 1989 was not really binding as each nation could negate the panel's ruling. Even if the process worked, compliance was essentially voluntary.

The GATT (now WTO) does offer political advantages as a dispute settlement forum. Its membership of about 165 nations frequently means that others will join in the dispute, thus raising visibility and pressure. This was true for CUSFTA in 1989 and remained true under NAFTA 1994. However, NAFTA complicated the forum selection process. See Chapter 3.

CHAPTER 18 DISPUTE SETTLEMENT

Dispute settlement under Chapter 18 of the CUSFTA agreement applied in most instances, but notably not concerning financial services. The Canada-United States Trade Commission (TC) was the center of the Chapter 18 dispute settlement process. International trade representatives of Canada and the United States or their designees constituted the CUSFTA Trade Commission, which was aided by Secretariats in Ottawa and Washington, D.C. There were three stages to Chapter 18 dispute settlement: (1) Bilateral

Consultations; (2) Trade Commission Review; and (3) Binding Arbitration.

The CUSFTA Trade Commission was after 1994 largely been supplanted by the NAFTA Trade Commission. The CUSFTA Commission provided a forum to discuss CUSFTA disputes. Consultations always preceded Commission deliberations. Questions of implementation, interpretation, application, allegedly inconsistent action, or "nullification and impairment" of benefits expected under the CUSFTA agreement fell within its jurisdiction. The CUSFTA Commission had the power to delegate its responsibilities to ad hoc committees and working-groups. It could also obtain the advice of nongovernmental individuals or groups. The Commission promulgated its own rules and procedures and functioned by cooperative consensus.

Notice as far in advance as possible was required of any proposed law with the potential to materially affect the operation of CUSFTA. With or without notice, Canada and the United States undertook to consult in good faith and "make every attempt" at a mutually satisfactory resolution. A meeting of the CUSFTA Trade Commission became mandatory only if no resolution was had within 30 days. The Commission then sought to resolve the dispute promptly, relying at its discretion on mediators acceptable to both sides.

For most disputes the CUSFTA Commission could refer the matter to binding arbitration only by mutual agreement. If no consensus was reached to refer the dispute to arbitration, the fallback was to appoint a panel of experts. Only in disputes concerning emergency escape clause proceedings was binding arbitration mandatory. The Commission could set the terms for arbitration of CUSFTA disputes, but unless it directed otherwise an arbitration panel was established following the provisions of Article 1807. Under Article 1807, two panelists were chosen by each side with the fifth member (absent agreement) chosen by lot. A list of qualified panelists was established by the Commission. The confidential arbitration panel set its own procedural rules, including a hearing and the right of reply.

An innovative provision of CUSFTA 1989 authorized the submission of memoranda by the governments of Canada and the United States acting jointly if possible, or singly if not, to courts or administrative tribunals in either country. Such submissions could only concern issues of interpretation, but they could be requested by a national court or tribunal entertaining CUSFTA issues in litigation. This little used request authority resembled somewhat the advisory ruling procedure followed in Europe as between national courts and the European Court of Justice. Memoranda on interpretative issues could be submitted whenever the governments of Canada or the United States considered it meritorious.

A related authority can be found in Chapter 20 of the NAFTA agreement. Article 2020 authorizes the NAFTA Commission to forward "agreed interpretations" to national judicial and administrative bodies. If no agreed interpretation can be reached, individual member state opinions can be submitted. All such submissions are *not* binding upon the national court or tribunal considering how to interpret NAFTA.

ARBITRATION DECISIONS
UNDER CHAPTER 18

Chapter 18 of CUSFTA resulted in five binding arbitrations. Other trade disputes were taken to the GATT, and some contentious issues resolved during the NAFTA and Uruguay Round negotiations.

In the first Chapter 18 arbitration panel, the United States complained against Canadian landing requirements for fish (mostly salmon) caught in their waters. A prior GATT panel ruling against Canadian fish export controls had led to the landing requirements. The CUSFTA arbitration panel ruled with one dissent in favor of the United States argument that the requirements unfairly increased the burden of exporting Canadian fish in violation of GATT Article XI and were not exceptions under GATT Article XX, discussed above (CDA–89–1807–01). Canada accepted the panel's findings. A mutually satisfactory settlement was then reached, but salmon fishing in the Northwest remains a remarkably divisive issue to this day.

The second arbitration panel under Chapter 18 upheld United States limits on the sale of undersized lobsters. By a split vote, argued under GATT Articles III and XI which were incorporated by reference into the CUSFTA agreement, the panel decided that since both Canadian and United States lobsters were affected there was no unlawful trade restraint (USA–89–1807–01). The third CUSFTA panel upheld, contrary to a U.S. Customs Service ruling, Canada's practice of including certain interest payments in the costs of production of automobiles (USA–92–1807–01). This issue arose when Canada determined CUSFTA content in ascertaining origin under Article 304. The panel followed the Vienna Convention of the Law of Treaties in interpreting CUSFTA even though the United States is not a party to that Convention.

The fourth arbitration panel generally agreed with Canada's interpretation of Article 701.3 of the CUSFTA agreement (CDA–92–1807–01). Minimum pricing of durum wheat for sale to the United States was at issue. This dispute was surrounded by U.S. perceptions of unfair subsidization of Canadian wheat exports. Once again, the Vienna Convention was invoked to interpret CUSFTA. Canadian wheat exports have remained the center of considerable controversy, trade complaints and intergovernmental memoranda of understanding imposing tariff rate quotas.

The fifth and final CUSFTA arbitration panel concerned Puerto Rico's refusal to allow entry of "improperly certified" long-life milk from Quebec (USA–93–1807–01). Articles III and XI of the GATT were at issue. This panel generally supported the U.S. position that it was entitled to enforce its standards against Canadian goods. The panel suggested that if both countries were essentially using the same inspection standards then entry should have been allowed as a matter of good faith so as to avoid nullification and impairment of CUSFTA trade benefits. Ongoing equivalency discussions between the two trade partners were recommenced.

CHAPTER 19 DISPUTE SETTLEMENT

Dispute settlement under CUSFTA Chapter 19 was limited to two types of international trade law actions: antidumping and countervailing duty proceedings. Both are GATT-authorized and regulated. See R. Folsom, *International Trade Law including Trump and Trade* in a Nutshell.

Such proceedings are typically commenced at the request of industries that face import competition and can ultimately result in the imposition of special tariffs on imported goods. Antidumping duties apply to imported goods or services sold at below home country prices (price discrimination) that injure or threaten domestic industries. Countervailing duties apply to imported goods that have benefited from export or specific domestic governmental subsidies and have injured or threaten national industries.

Antidumping actions challenge private sector activities while countervailing duty actions question governmental acts. The amount of tariff duties possible is the margin of the dump or the level of subsidy determined to exist. Many antidumping duty proceedings (the most prevalent) are "settled" when the exporter agrees to raise its prices. See the *Tomatoes Dispute* in Chapter 3. Countervailing duty disputes may also be settled by intergovernmental accords. See the *Softwood Lumber Dispute* (below).

Antidumping and countervailing duty actions had been frequently used by the United States to impede entry of Canadian goods. Chapter 19 thus attempted to respond to critical Canadian concerns.

Canada and the United States had long acknowledged through the GATT the unfairness of dumping and subsidy practices. Unlike the European Union, they were unwilling to eliminate internal utilization of these trade remedies. GATT Codes on antidumping and countervailing duties provided the basic ground rules, but GATT dispute settlement was inadequate in the 1980s. Most importantly, Canada was distrustful of lengthy judicial reviews and law in U.S. courts of administrative antidumping and countervailing duty determinations. Prime Minister Mulroney actually walked away from the CUSFTA negotiating table to emphasize their concerns. The end result was a unique form of dispute settlement under Chapter 19 of CUSFTA that was largely replicated in NAFTA *and* for Canada (but not Mexico) under the USMCA, procedures which exist nowhere else in the world.

Under Chapter 19, binational panels of mutually approved experts (mostly international trade lawyers and law professors) ultimately decided antidumping and countervailing duty disputes. Prior to CUSFTA, the final resolution of such disputes had been in the national courts. Each country selected two panelists with an additional panelist chosen by mutual agreement. Each side had four opportunities to reject the other side's proposed panelists. No cause for rejection was required. A majority of the panelists had to be lawyers in good standing.

The administrative proceedings of Canada and the United States determining the existence of dumping or a countervailable subsidy remained in place. These decisions are made by the International Trade Administration (Commerce Dept.) in the United States and by the Deputy Minister of National Revenue for Customs and Excise in Canada. Likewise, the domestic proceedings used to decide if there has been material injury (or its threat) to a domestic industry were also retained. These decisions are made by the U.S. International Trade Commission and the Canadian Import Tribunal.

All Chapter 19 proceedings were pursued under the laws of Canada and the United States, neither of which was substantively changed by CUSFTA 1989. The critical change was the remarkable surrender of judicial sovereignty accomplished by Chapter 19. After CUSFTA, all final national administrative determinations in antidumping or countervailing duty proceedings were only "appealable" by all interested parties to a quasi-judicial binational CUSFTA panel.

When an antidumping or subsidy proceeding came before a CUSFTA panel, the legal principles that would have been used by a court in the importing country controlled. For binational panels reviewing final U.S. determinations this meant that U.S. Supreme Court and Federal Circuit Court of Appeal (but not Court of International Trade) decisions were binding precedent. By its terms, CUSFTA provided that previous panel decisions were not to be treated as precedent. NAFTA and the USMCA also retain these rules.

There were no new CUSFTA standards for review. With much controversy, each panel proceeded to apply the different standards of judicial review traditionally found in the law of Canada and the United States. For example, Canada's standards of review under the Federal Court Act § 28(1) are failure to observe principles of natural justice, jurisdictional abuse, errors in law, and pervasive, capricious or insupportable erroneous findings of fact. The standards of the U.S. Tariff Act of 1930 §§ 516A(b)(1)(A) and (B) are findings or conclusions unsupported by substantial evidence in the record or otherwise not in accordance with law.

There were over fifty CUSFTA Chapter 19 panel decisions, with more than two-thirds of them reviewing U.S. antidumping and countervailing duty determinations. Not surprisingly, trade in steel products garnered first place in the pursuit of market protection. The U.S. steel industry, in particular, has a long history of resorting to antidumping and countervailing duties to obtain shelter from import competition. Many observers have noted that the mere filing of AD and CVD complaints can produce some breathing room for domestic industries.

Most Chapter 19 panel decisions under CUSFTA were rendered in less than a year. Technically, these decisions either affirmed the final determination under review or, reversing, referred the determination back to the relevant administrative tribunal. It was up to that tribunal to take appropriate action. If it did not, and a second panel review took place, the agency was typically instructed to act in a not inconsistent manner by the second or (infrequently) third panel. The only further review, a final appeal by Canada or the United States (not the interested parties) of a panel decision, could come before an "Extraordinary Challenge Committee" (ECC). Such Committees were composed of three mutually acceptable judges.

ECC review of binational Chapter 19 panel decisions was intended to be truly extraordinary. In fact, there were only three such reviews (see below) between 1989 and 1994. All of them were raised by the United States. Many believe these challenges were politically motivated, in part to persuade Congress to extend fast track trade agreements authority to the President and in part to assuage key private sector interests. Challenges to CUSFTA (and NAFTA) panel decisions were allowed only in limited circumstances such as if a panel member engaged in gross misconduct, was biased, or had a serious conflict of interest. Challenges could also be raised if the panel departed seriously from a fundamental rule of procedure or it manifestly exceeded its powers, authority or jurisdiction. The challenger has the duty to prove that the error alleged materially influenced the panel's decision and threatened the integrity of the review process.

BINATIONAL PANEL AND EXTRAORDINARY CHALLENGE COMMITTEE DECISIONS UNDER CHAPTER 19

Chapter 19 dispute settlement under CUSFTA in the five years prior to NAFTA was voluminous. With a few exceptions, most analyses of these decisions suggest an objective and not terribly politicized process. But the ability of binational panels to expertly rule under Canadian and United States law has been hotly contested. A prominent U.S. judge involved in the infamous *Softwood Lumber* dispute wrote a blistering dissent. See ECC–94–1904–01–USA (Wilkey, J.) excerpted in part in Chapter 3. Some administrative determinations had to be repeatedly reviewed by CUSFTA panels before compliance was achieved. One must wonder whether Chapter 19, which was intended to reduce trade tensions and suspicions, did not instead intensify Canada-U.S. antidumping and countervailing duty disputes.

Appeals to CUSFTA Extraordinary Challenge Committees demonstrated limited opportunities for relief. For example, the first Extraordinary Challenge Committee decision concerned U.S. countervailing duties on Canadian exports of pork (ECC–91–1904–01–USA). The initial binational panel decision questioned the substantiality of the evidence supporting the International Trade Commission's domestic injury determination. Upon reconsideration, the ITC found a threat of material injury to the U.S. domestic pork industry for a second time. A second binational panel decision ruled that the ITC had exceeded its notice for the proceedings, and issued specific evidentiary instructions to the ITC.

The ITC's next decision bitterly denounced the second binational panel's ruling. The ITC asserted that the panel's decision violated fundamental principles of CUSFTA and contained egregious errors of U.S. law. Nevertheless, the ITC acquiesced. It determined no threat of material injury expressly (and only) because of the binding nature of the CUSFTA panel's decision. The United States Trade Representative alleged gross error and sought review by Extraordinary Challenge Committee of the panel's *Pork* rulings. The Committee unanimously held that there was no gross error even if some of the panel determinations might not have followed U.S. rules of evidence. The Committee did caution panels not to rely on evidence not appearing in the record of the national proceedings.

The second extraordinary challenge concerned exports of live swine from Canada (EEC–93–1904–01–USA). Once again, the Committee unanimously ruled against the challenge, although it did acknowledge that the panel may have made errors of law.

SOFTWOOD LUMBER DISPUTE

The bitterly disputed binational panel decisions on U.S. countervailing duty actions against Canadian exports of softwood lumber did not conclude with the third Extraordinary Challenge Committee proceeding in 1994 from which Judge Wilkey so

vigorously   dissented.   Trade   tensions   and
negotiations continued. Canada, the victor before the
Challenge Committee, appeared to realize that it
might lose the next time around if changes in U.S.
countervailing duty law were recognized. Indeed,
these changes were undertaken specifically for that
purpose. In 1996, a "settlement" was reached.

The 1996 Softwood Lumber Agreement applied to
Alberta, British Columbia, Ontario and Quebec. It
committed Quebec, for example, to raising its
"stumpage" (timbering) fees. British Columbia (the
largest exporter) promised to impose taxes on
shipments of lumber to the U.S. above designated
levels starting at 9 billion board feet. In addition, the
Canadian federal government promised to impose
taxes if exports exceed 14.7 billion board feet. The
U.S. government and forest industry, in turn,
pledged not to commence a countervailing duty
action for 5 years so long as the agreement was
followed.

In 2001, the 1996 Agreement lapsed and U.S.
countervailing duties on Canadian lumber were
renewed, followed by Canadian challenges under
NAFTA and within the WTO. Billions of dollars in
U.S. antidumping and countervailing duties on
Canadian lumber were collected. In 2006, a second
Softwood Lumber Agreement was achieved. Canada,
then with about 34 percent of the U.S. softwood
lumber market, agreed to impose rising export taxes
if prices fall below specified trigger levels. About 80
percent of the duties previously collected were
returned to Canadian producers. The Second

Agreement was to be "dispute-free" for a minimum of three years. Nevertheless, the U.S. commenced arbitration proceedings before the London Court of Arbitration (LCIA) in 2007 and 2009 challenging the adequacy of Canadian implementation of the Agreement. Several LCIA rulings subsequently found Canada in breach of the 2006 Agreement. The 2006 Agreement was extended to October 2015.

To this day, softwood lumber disputes continue. Indeed, the Trump administration levied countervailing duties on Canadian lumber in 2017 prior to commencing re-negotiation of NAFTA. Canada promised compensation to its exporters, and filed yet another dispute under NAFTA and before the WTO.

The legal and political controversy surrounding Chapter 19 panel decisions under CUSFTA sometimes blurs their practical consequences for tariffs and trade between the two countries. A careful reconstruction of that impact has been undertaken by a leading international trade attorney. See Mercury, 15 *N.W. J. Int'l Law & Bus.* 525 (1995). This study demonstrates that Canadian exporters were disproportionate beneficiaries in terms of CUSFTA Chapter 19 outcomes.

QUEBEC

The Canadian Constitution of 1982 was adopted by an Act of the British Parliament. As such, the Act and Constitution of 1982 are thought to bind all Canadian provinces including Quebec. That province, however, has never formally ratified the Constitution of

Canada. Since 1982 a series of negotiations have attempted to secure Quebec's ratification, and all have failed miserably.

Prior to CUSFTA in 1987, for example, the "Meech Lake Accord" was reached. This agreement recognized Quebec as a "distinct society" in Canada. What the practical consequences of this recognition would have been will never be known. Quebec's adherence to the Meech Lake Accord was nullified when Manitoba, New Brunswick and ultimately Newfoundland failed to ratify the Accord. A second set of negotiations led in 1992 to the Charlottetown Accord which also acknowledged Quebec as a distinct society with its French language, unique culture and Civil Law tradition. This time a national referendum was held and its defeat was overwhelming. Quebec, five English-speaking Canadian provinces, and the Yukon territory voted against the Charlottetown Accord.

The failure of these Accords moved Quebec towards separation from Canada. In 1994, just as NAFTA supplanted CUSFTA, the Parti Quebecois came to power. It held a provincial referendum on separation in 1995. By the narrowest of margins, the people of Quebec rejected separation from Canada. Just exactly what "separation" would have meant was never entirely clear during the debate, perhaps deliberately so.

In 1998, Canada's Supreme Court ruled that Quebec could not "under the Constitution" withdraw unilaterally. To secede, Quebec would need to negotiate a constitutional amendment with the rest of Canada. See Reference re. Secession of Quebec, File No. 25506, Can. Supreme Ct. (Aug. 20, 1998). The rest of Canada would, likewise, be obliged to enter into such negotiations if a "clear majority" of Quebec's voters approved a "clear question" on secession in a referendum. Subsequently, the Canadian Parliament legislated rules which will make it difficult for Quebec to separate, should it ever wish to do so. That prospect now seems more remote, particularly because the Parti Quebecois lost power in 2003, though it has periodically resurged since then.

If Quebec ever separates from Canada, this will raise fundamental issues about Quebec and USMCA 2018. Would Quebec be forced to negotiate for USMCA membership? If so, would English-speaking Canada veto its application? If Quebec's relationship to Canada continues in some limited manner, such as for defense and international trade purposes, is the USMCA a non-issue? Might Quebec automatically "succeed" to USMCA, becoming a member without application? See Article 34(1) of The Vienna Convention of Succession of States in Respect of Treaties (1978) (not in force), 17 Int'l Legal Mats. 1488.

Customary international practice maintains existing treaties when nations sub-divide. This practice was applied to the Czech Republic, Slovakia, and various states of the former Yugoslavia. Custom thus suggests that fears in Quebec about losing NAFTA or USMCA benefits are exaggerated.

CHAPTER 3

NAFTA 1994: THE AGREEMENT

Mexico, like Canada, was and remains dependent on market access to the United States. In 1993, just prior to NAFTA 1994, approximately 75% of its exports went to the United States. The Canada-United States Free Trade Agreement (CUSFTA 1989, covered in Chapter 2) and European reluctance to enhance Mexican trade prompted President Carlos Salinas to request free trade relations with the USA. President George H. W. Bush was quick to support this bilateral goal. In time the Canadians correctly calculated that they could not afford to ignore negotiations that might dilute or adversely affect the benefits they enjoyed under CUSFTA. The Canadians soon realized they too had much to gain from trilateral NAFTA negotiations.

In an era when free trade and investment was still a positive political issue in the United States, Congress authorized "fast track" negotiations in 1991. Under such negotiations, Congress must vote up or down on agreements without amending them. Congress was willing to authorize fast track negotiations because the President promised to keep it heavily involved during the NAFTA negotiations.

Negotiations to create a North American Free Trade Area for Canada, Mexico and the United States commenced in July of 1991. These negotiations moved along smoothly. About a year later, the NAFTA 1994 agreement was in final form. President Bush, running for reelection in November of 1992, notified Congress of his intent to sign the NAFTA agreement. This notice ensured a vivid political debate on the merits of free trade and investment during the election.

Multi-millionaire Ross Perot, running as an independent, virulently attacked NAFTA. He asserted NAFTA would produce a "giant sucking sound" as U.S. jobs headed south of the border. Governor Bill Clinton of Arkansas generally supported NAFTA, but promised to negotiate better protection for workers and the environment. After Clinton defeated Bush in the November 1992 elections, lame-duck President George H.W. Bush signed the NAFTA 1994 agreement on behalf of the United States.

This agreement, as did CUSFTA 1989, allows any member to withdraw after six months' advance notice. Whether such notice requires Congressional approval, presumably by way of repeal of the NAFTA Implementation Act of 1993 (below), is unclear and is an issue associated with threats of withdrawal by President Trump.

RATIFYING NAFTA

Ratification of the NAFTA 1994 agreement became hostage to Governor Clinton's campaign promises. Negotiations were re-opened in the Spring of 1993 after Clinton became President. Two "side or supplemental agreements" emerged from these negotiations. The first concerned labor rights and working conditions while the second focused on the environment. See Chapter 4. In addition, an "understanding" on protective relief from import surges was concluded. The original NAFTA agreement negotiated by President Bush was sent to Congress under fast track procedures in the Fall of 1993. The side agreements on labor and the environment were treated as solely executive agreements not requiring Congressional approval, although provisions in the Implementation Act funded the U.S. share of expenses related to them.

In a remarkable display of hostility, the NAFTA 1994 agreement was vigorously opposed in Congress. Ross Perot, Ralph Nader, unions, environmental groups, the religious and political right, the Congressional Black Caucus, and many others blasted NAFTA. But for the success of Vice President Al Gore in debating Ross Perot on national television, NAFTA might have failed in Congress. The final vote in the House of Representatives was 234 to 200, followed by a 61 to 38 affirmation in the Senate of the NAFTA Implementation Act of 1993.

This Act, Public Law No. 103–182 (107 Stat. 2057), was accompanied by President Clinton's Statement of Administrative Action which provides a useful summary of required changes in United States law. The Implementation Act expressly provides that the NAFTA agreement does not modify U.S. law except as provided for by the Act.

Prime Minister Mulroney of Canada presciently secured approval of NAFTA prior to the Canadian elections in the Fall of 1993. Mulroney's Conservative Party was subsequently drummed out of office on a tide of anti-NAFTA sentiment. In Mexico, on the other hand, President Salinas had little difficulty in obtaining ratification of NAFTA from his PRI-controlled legislature.

INTERPRETING NAFTA

NAFTA's statement of objectives is important because Canada, Mexico and the United States agreed to "interpret and apply" NAFTA 1994 in light of those objectives. The objectives of NAFTA were listed in Article 102 and include:

- The elimination of barriers to trade in and facilitation of cross-border movement of goods and services;

- Promotion of conditions of fair competition;

- The increase "substantially" of investment opportunities;

- The provision of adequate and effective protection and enforcement of intellectual property rights;

- The creation of effective procedures for the implementation and application of the Agreement, for its joint administration, and for the resolution of disputes; and

- The establishment of a framework for further trilateral, regional and multilateral cooperation to expand and enhance the benefits of NAFTA.

The NAFTA partners also agreed to interpret the agreement in accordance with "applicable rules of international law." The reference to international law as an interpretive guide is somewhat ambiguous. International law on interpreting and applying treaties, conventions and international agreements is notably embodied in the Vienna Convention on the Law of Treaties. 8 *Int'l Legal Mat.* 769. The United States has not joined in this agreement, but generally follows its principles. More broadly, the reference to international law as an interpretive guide may embrace general principles of international law widely accepted in the world community.

Official interpretations of the NAFTA agreement could be issued by governmental consensus through the NAFTA Free Trade Commission. One such official interpretation was promulgated in response to investor-state arbitration awards (below) that exceeded "customary" international law rules on treatment of foreign investors.

NAFTA 1994, WTO 1995 AND OTHER INTERNATIONAL AGREEMENTS

The NAFTA agreement affirmed each nation's rights and obligations under GATT 1947 and other international agreements, but a general rule of NAFTA supremacy was created in Article 103. In some instances, provisions of the GATT 1947 agreement were incorporated by specific reference into NAFTA. This was notably the case with GATT Articles III (National Treatment), XI (Quotas) and XX (Exceptions).

If conflicts emerged with other trade agreements, NAFTA prevailed unless the NAFTA agreement provided otherwise. In some cases, the agreement did exactly that. Provisions of the CUSFTA 1989 agreement (Chapter 2), for example, were frequently retained to govern Canada-U.S. and sometimes even Canada-Mexico trade relations. Annex 608.2 provided that NAFTA was not supreme over the Agreement on An International Energy Program. Article 2103 provided similarly for international tax conventions.

Article 104 made it clear that NAFTA would *not* prevail over the following environmental and conservation agreements:

- The Washington Convention on International Trade in Endangered Species (1973, 1979);

- The Montreal Protocol on Substances that Deplete the Ozone Layer (1987, 1990);

- The Basel Convention on Control of Transboundary Movements of Hazardous Wastes and Their Disposal (1989);

- The Canada-U.S. Agreement Concerning Transboundary Movements of Hazardous Waste (1986); and

- The Mexico-U.S. Agreement on Cooperation for the Protection and Improvement of the Environment in the Border Area (1983).

NAFTA was implemented prior to final completion of the Uruguay Round of GATT negotiations and the creation of the World Trade Organization in 1995. NAFTA's relationship to the WTO Uruguay Round agreements was complex and less than clear, especially on the issue of which prevails in the event of conflict. Negotiated largely in parallel time frames, each influenced the other, but significant differences exist. For example, NAFTA covers business visas, state trading, competition policy, and has an entire chapter dedicated to energy, all of which are absent from the WTO Agreements. The WTO package covers customs valuation and pre-shipment inspection, which NAFTA did not. Nothing in the WTO agreements touches on labor or the environment, NAFTA's two side agreements. See Chapter 4.

On market access, procurement, investment and most services, NAFTA went further and faster than the Uruguay Round WTO agreements. There is significant overlap on intellectual property where NAFTA's leading edge was particularly influential. The WTO Agreement on Agriculture, on the other hand, exceeded by a good measure NAFTA's trade opening initiatives. The WTO package of agreements also addressed basic telecommunications, which was mostly omitted from NAFTA.

The jurisdictional scope of NAFTA 1994 and WTO 1995 revealed in the table below is important to dispute settlement. If both agreements apply, NAFTA permits the complaining country to ordinarily elect as between WTO versus NAFTA dispute settlement procedures.

NAFTA CHAPTERS AND
WTO AGREEMENTS

The NAFTA Chapters charted below indicate the closest parallel WTO agreements.

NAFTA 1994	**WTO 1995 AGREEMENTS**
Chapter 3, Trade in Goods	General Agreement on Tariffs and Trade 1994, Agreement on Textiles and Clothing
Chapter 4, Rules of Origin	Agreement on Rules of Origin
Chapter 5, Customs Procedures	No parallel
Chapter 6, Energy and Basic Petrochemicals	No parallel
Chapter 7, Agriculture and SPS Measures	Agreement on Agriculture, Agreement on SPS Measures
Chapter 8, Emergency Action	Agreement on Safeguards
Chapter 9, Product and Service Standards	Agreement on Technical Barriers to Trade
Chapter 10, Procurement	Agreement on Government Procurement (optional)
Chapter 11, Investment	Agreement on Trade-Related Investment Measures (TRIMs)
Chapter 12, Cross-Border Trade in Services	General Agreement on Trade in Services (GATS)

NAFTA 1994	**WTO 1995 AGREEMENTS**
Chapter 13, Enhanced Telecommunications	See GATS, Basic Telecommunications Covered
Chapter 14, Financial Services	See GATS
Chapter 15, Competition Policy, Monopolies and State Enterprises	No parallel, but see Understanding on Interpretation of GATT Article XVII
Chapter 16, Temporary Entry for Business Persons	No parallel
Chapter 17, Intellectual Property	Agreement on Trade-Related Aspects of Intellectual Property Rights (TRIPs)
Chapter 18, Administrative Provisions	Not applicable
Chapter 19, Antidumping and Countervailing Duty Dispute Settlement	No parallel, but see DSU and Agreement on Implementation of GATT Article VI
Chapter 20, Dispute Settlement	Understanding on Rules and Procedures Governing the Settlement of Disputes (DSU)

NAFTA 1994	**WTO 1995 AGREEMENTS**
Chapter 21, Exceptions	See GATT Articles XX, XXI and Understanding on GATT Balance of Payments Provisions
Agreement on Environmental Cooperation	No parallel
Agreement on Labor Cooperation	No parallel

THE PESO CRASH

Less than a year after NAFTA's launch, in December 1994, the Zedillo government suddenly announced a decision to discontinue its crawling-peg devaluation of the peso and let the peso float against other currencies. The peso quickly lost 35 percent of its value against the U.S. dollar and plunged nearly 100% before the crisis was over. Currency devaluations were not new to Mexico, and are a not-forgotten lesson in international finance. The 1994 crisis was in many ways a repeat of financial problems faced in much of Latin America since the late 19th century.

Governments have frequently relied upon foreign capital to make up for insufficient domestic savings. Additionally, in the case of Mexico, the inflation rate was greater than the rate of devaluation resulting in an overvalued peso. Over-valuation stimulated added private sector spending which in turn further decreased the domestic savings rate. At the same time, rising interest rates in the United States and improved investment conditions elsewhere in Latin America (particularly Brazil) reduced the flow of capital to Mexico. The country's problems were magnified by a new risk factor. Much of the foreign capital that Mexico had recently come to rely upon came from short-term investments by U.S. mutual fund managers. Quite a lot of this money took flight when the peso crisis arrived and was not likely to return.

In response to the peso crisis, the Zedillo government announced plans to increase the budget surplus (yes, Mexico actually had a budget surplus), expand privatization, tighten monetary policy and to continue to allow the peso to float. The goal was to cut the nation's current account deficit and thereby the amount of foreign (particularly short-term) capital needed. The program was painful for many, especially workers and the hitherto growing middle class in Mexico, whose incomes did not keep up with the increase in inflation. Increased interest rates from a tight money policy slowed the Mexican economy and pushed it into a recession. This made it harder for Mexico and Mexican corporations to repay their debts to foreigners.

A plan announced on January 31, 1995 by President Clinton helped Mexico work out its financial crisis. This $50 billion plan was a coordinated effort by the United States, the IMF, the Bank for International Settlements (BIS), Canada and several Latin American nations. The United States and the IMF provided about $28 billion in medium-term credits to Mexico. These were used primarily to replace Mexico's short-term debt as it matured.

Loan and loan guarantee conditions were attached, including restraints on the growth of Mexico's money supply, domestic credit, public sector borrowing and current account deficit. Mexico's central bank was made more independent and transparent. Privatization was accelerated and, in a notable commitment, Mexico pledged future revenues from its oil sales to the Federal Reserve Bank of New York as collateral. Mexico subsequently repaid the United States, thus freeing up its oil revenues.

Border areas saw a reversal in commerce as the devalued peso decreased Mexicans' purchasing power and correspondingly increased the purchasing power of U.S. consumers. Foreign businesses in Mexico wrote down the value of inventory, while manufacturers in Mexico who primarily exported their output realized cost-savings. However, much like the 1982 devaluation of the peso which sparked the maquiladora boom, the 1994 crisis in the longer term actually increased the attractiveness of Mexico as a place to invest in order to obtain inexpensive labor and supplies. Price, wage, financial and currency stability returned to Mexico.

In the process of dealing with this debacle, Mexico confirmed its commitment through to an outward-looking economic policy. Many poor nations caught in Mexico's bind would have blocked imports and restricted access to foreign currency. But the crisis raised fundamental questions about whether a common currency for NAFTA might not be desirable. Despite Mexican ideas about inventing a new currency (the "Amero"), the most likely scenario is "U.S. dollarization." Some Canadians have gradually come to believe that adopting the U.S. dollar as their national currency might be in their self-interest. Mexicans, despite their history of peso crashes, are less enthused. In either case, it is worth noting that permission from the United States to "dollarize" is not required, as Ecuador and El Salvador have demonstrated.

NAFTA: FREE TRADE IN GOODS

With the implementation of NAFTA 1994, the United States enjoyed free trade with two large purchasers of U.S. goods. Canada was always the largest buyer of U.S. goods. Mexico quickly surpassed Japan to become number two in the first year of NAFTA's operation. China later replaced Japan as the second largest buyer of U.S. goods, and at this writing Mexico is the third largest U.S. trade partner.

NAFTA created a North American free trade area for goods. Phased tariff removals were the means to this end. Article 302 of NAFTA prohibited all parties from increasing tariffs or establishing new tariffs on North American goods. This provision had the practical effect of ensuring that many Mexican goods could continue to enter the United States on a duty-free basis. This most often occurred prior to NAFTA

1994 under the U.S. program of generalized tariff preferences (GSP). The GSP program, with many exceptions and controls, grants duty free entry to goods from over 100 developing nations. Mexico had ranked number one in GSP duty free imports. The United States GSP program no longer applies to Mexico or other U.S. free trade partners. See R. Folsom, *International Trade Law including Trump and Trade* in a Nutshell.

TARIFFS AND CUSTOMS

Prior to NAFTA, Mexico's average applied tariff on U.S. goods was 10 percent, while the comparable U.S. tariff on Mexican goods was 4 percent. NAFTA preserved the 1998 deadline for the elimination of tariffs on goods traded between Canada and the United States. This gave Canadian exporters short-term market access advantages compared to their Mexican competitors who did not get full duty-free access to the U.S. until 2003. NAFTA phased out most tariffs on North American goods by 2003. By 2008, essentially all North American trade in goods became duty free.

Health and safety inspection fees could be collected, and the U.S. began new agricultural inspection fees along the Canadian border in 2007. The U.S. customs user fee was eliminated on Mexican-United States trade in North American goods on July 1, 1999. As under CUSFTA, *export* taxes or tariffs were generally prohibited. However, Mexico could employ them to keep essential foodstuffs like corn, flour and milk in the country.

Since these products have traditionally been subsidized in Mexico, United States or Canadian buyers might otherwise deplete them. Mexico could also apply export charges temporarily to foodstuffs in short supply.

Canada, Mexico and the United States retained their national tariffs for purposes of third-party trade. Customs tariff refunds (drawback) and tariff waivers were addressed under NAFTA. Essentially, NAFTA provided that drawbacks were not authorized on goods originating in North America which pass duty free across borders. Drawbacks were permitted on non-originating goods. They could also be used with originating goods not yet subject to duty free treatment up to the lesser of the amount of tariff due upon crossing a NAFTA border or the amount of duties originally paid upon importation. The net result was that since 2003, when most originating goods circulated duty free within NAFTA, drawbacks were basically prohibited.

NAFTA also banned new tariff waivers which were tied to performance requirements. The types of performance requirements that were prohibited included: 1) Export minimums; 2) local content; 3) local substitution or purchase minimums; 4) trade balancing export to import ratios; and 5) mandatory foreign exchange inflows.

IMPACT ON MAQUILADORAS

The NAFTA regime on drawbacks and tariff waivers was important to Mexico's export-driven maquiladora assembly plants (discussed in Chapter

2). Many maquiladoras have historically relied on tariff refunds and waivers on inputs. Under NAFTA, starting in 2001, Mexico stopped the beneficial application of tariff refunds and waivers to assembly plants. Full Mexican tariffs applied to imported components, which made it more difficult for goods assembled with components from outside NAFTA to qualify for free trade. However, Mexico subsequently reduced tariffs on some components, notably electronics, as an incentive to continued maquiladora production.

Many Asian manufacturers using Mexican assembly plants were impacted. As the drafters of NAFTA intended, no preferentially tariffed "export platforms" into Canada or the United States, were encouraged. Some such manufacturers switched to North American suppliers for their assembly plant inputs. Others, notably from Japan and Korea, arranged for their home country suppliers to join them in production in Mexico. Components from these loyal affiliates generally avoided the origin problems created under NAFTA after Mexican customs refunds and waivers were eliminated in 2001. They also added to the North American content of the assembled goods, the key to accessing duty free NAFTA (see *"Regional Value Content"* below).

Some 40% of the content of U.S. imports from Mexico (and 25% of U.S. imports from Canada) originates in the United States. As the North American content of U.S., Asian and other maquiladora operations rose to meet NAFTA's rules of origin governing free trade, greater access to the

Mexican market became available. Traditionally, sales of maquiladora products in Mexico had been limited. Starting in 1994, amendments to Mexico's Maquiladora Decree permitted such sales to increase based upon percentages of prior year individual maquiladora exports from Mexico. Since 2001, maquiladoras may sell their entire production in Mexico if they choose. This schedule was coordinated with Mexico's phase-out of customs duty drawback and waivers on imported components.

REGULATORY AND TAX TREATMENT, QUOTAS

NAFTA, like CUSFTA, incorporated by reference the national treatment duties of Article III of the GATT 1947 agreement. Each federal government had to generally treat North American goods in the same manner as its own goods. Article 301 further required states, provinces and local governments to treat goods from other partners as favorably as they treat goods from anywhere, including their own jurisdiction. These treatment duties affected taxes, fees, sale or distribution requirements, usage regulations and a range of other laws. Specific exceptions, many of which are derived from GATT grandfather rights, were listed in Annex 301.3.

Incorporation of GATT Article III made it a part of NAFTA 1994. This meant that the countries could pursue NAFTA or World Trade Organization (WTO) dispute settlement (below). WTO and NAFTA panel reports on Article III issues remained generally consistent. Article III arbitration decisions under

CUSFTA Chapter 18 also reflected a close adherence to GATT principles. See Chapter 2.

The restrictive rules on use of trade quotas and price controls embodied in Article XI of the GATT 1947 agreement were also incorporated by reference into NAFTA. Under CUSFTA, they were simply affirmed. As with Article III, NAFTA dispute settlement was an option on trade quota or price control issues. Mexico had 10 years from 1994 to eliminate its import licensing regime. Import and export quotas or restraints applied to goods from other nations were honored by the NAFTA partners.

NAFTA provided for quota relief on a variety of specific goods. Textile quotas on originating goods were generally removed. On non-originating textile goods, quotas were gradually phased out. Agricultural and food product quotas were reduced in number, and energy quotas were discouraged. Quotas on motor vehicles and their parts phased out. Most other traditional North American trade quotas were retained.

Export restraints justified under Articles XI or XX of the GATT were subjected to special additional rules applicable to CUSFTA (but not NAFTA) trade. These special rules required maintaining historically proportionate supplies, not pricing exports above domestic levels, and not disrupting normal channels of supply. These rules did not apply to Mexico. Mexico could therefore apply trade quotas and other export restraints subject only to GATT 1947 rules. Canada and the United States could restrain exports to Mexico under those same rules.

RULES OF ORIGIN

Mexico had the highest average tariffs on imported goods, the U.S. had the lowest, and Canada fell in the middle, all as negotiated per the GATT/WTO. Since free trade in goods only applied to goods that originated in North America, non-originating goods were subject to the normal tariffs of Canada, Mexico and the United States. Origin determinations were thus critical to NAFTA traders. There were Uniform NAFTA Regulations governing rules of origin and customs procedures, including a common Certificate of Origin.

Article 401 of the NAFTA agreement started with the primary rule that all goods wholly obtained or produced entirely inside NAFTA originated there. Canadian lumber, U.S. apples and Mexican oil provide examples. Such goods fell under NAFTA Preference Criterion A. Article 415 authorized free trade in goods made from materials that "originate" exclusively within NAFTA, Preference Criterion C. Agricultural, timber and mining products almost always qualified as such. A laptop computer whose components all come from Mexico, Canada or the United States would qualify under Criterion C.

Article 401 adopts the change of tariff classification rule of origin approach initiated in CUSFTA 1989. See Chapter 2. Subject to various exceptions, goods produced in one or more of the three countries with non-originating materials could be freely traded when all such materials (excepting a *de minimis* amount) underwent a change in tariff classification based upon the Harmonized Tariff

System (HTS). Ordinarily this required a change at the HTS product classification level and is known as Preference Criterion B. See *Cummins Inc. v. United States,* 454 F.3d 1361 (Fed. Cir. 2006) (crankshafts from Brazil reworked in Mexico fail change of HTS classification test). This Criterion was the most commonly used of all NAFTA's rules of origin for goods. See Example 1 below.

Meeting the change in tariff classification rule of origin was sometimes insufficient to allow free trading. Some goods *also* had to contain a minimum "regional value content" (discussed below) to qualify under Preference Criterion B. For example, footwear, chemicals and automobiles fell in this category. There were fewer such content requirements under NAFTA than under CUSFTA. Electronics and machinery were generally exempt. See Example 2 below.

Article 401 also permitted certain assembly goods that do not undergo a change in tariff classification to be freely traded if their regional value content was sufficient. This was NAFTA Preference Criterion D. For goods with very small non-originating content, NAFTA created a "*de minimis*" rule of origin. Article 405 generally permitted free trade in goods whose non-originating value is 7 percent or less. Such goods, in other words, were treated as originating in North America and freely traded.

Here are two U.S. Customs Service examples of goods that qualified for free trade under NAFTA Criterion B:

EXAMPLE 1

Frozen pork meat (HTS heading 0203) is imported into the U.S. from Hungary and combined with spices imported from the Caribbean (HTS subheadings 0907–0910). Then, the spiced meat is mixed with cereals grown and produced in the U.S. to make fresh pork sausage (HTS heading 1601).

The Annex 401 rule of origin for HTS heading 1601 states:

> "A change to heading 1601 through 1605 from any other chapter."

Since the frozen meat is classified in Chapter 2 and the spices are classified in Chapter 9, these non-NAFTA-originating materials meet the tariff shift requirement. Note that one does not need to consider whether the cereal meets the applicable tariff shift requirement, as the cereal is itself NAFTA-originating.

In conclusion, the fresh pork sausage is originating under NAFTA.

EXAMPLE 2

A manufacturer purchases inexpensive textile watch straps made in Taiwan (HTS heading 9113), to be assembled with originating mechanical watch movements (HTS heading 9108) and originating cases (HTS heading 9112). The value of the straps is less than seven percent (7%) of the total cost of the final watch (HTS heading 9102).

The rule of origin under Annex 402 for HTS heading 9102 states:

> "A change to heading 9101 through 9107 from any other chapter; A change to heading 9101 through

9107 from 9114, whether or not there is also a change from any other chapter, provided there is a regional value content of not less than:

a) 60 percent where the transaction value method is used, or

b) 50 percent where the net cost method is used."

Remember that only non-originating materials need to meet the required tariff shift requirement, and, in this case, the textile straps are the only non-originating component. As the value of the straps is less than seven percent (7%) of the total cost of the finished watch, the *de minimis* rule applies, and the finished watch is originating under NAFTA.

REGIONAL VALUE CONTENT

Article 402 established NAFTA 1994's "top down" regional content valuation methods. These methods represented a change from CUSFTA's "bottom up" measurement of value for purposes of determining the origin of goods. There were two NAFTA regional content valuation methods: transaction value and net cost value.

In most instances, the importer seeking to qualify goods for duty free treatment under NAFTA could elect between the transaction value or net cost methods. The net cost method was generally thought to be the more difficult rule of origin. For most transactions among related parties, the net cost method had to be used. Manipulation of prices in transfers among corporate affiliates might otherwise have taken advantage of NAFTA's transaction value method. The net cost method had also to be followed if Customs ruled the transaction value method "unacceptable."

The NAFTA transaction value method followed the GATT Customs Valuation Code of 1979 to which Canada, Mexico and the United States adhere. This method starts with an analysis of the F.O.B. price paid, including generally commissions, transport costs to the point of direct shipment, royalties on the goods, and manufacturing proceeds upon resale. Profits are included in the transaction value method of establishing the origin of goods as part of the price paid. The value of non-originating materials is then subtracted to arrive at the regional value content of the goods expressed in percentage terms. Normally, this percentage had to be at least 60 percent in order to free trade the goods under NAFTA.

The NAFTA net cost method started with a product's net cost to determine its regional value content. The value of non-originating materials was then subtracted. For NAFTA purposes, net cost was defined as total cost less expenses of sales promotion, marketing, after-sales service, royalties, shipping and packing, non-allowable interest charges and other "excluded costs." There were three authorized methods of allocating costs in calculating net cost (Article 402.8). The producer got to elect among these methods (provided the allocation of all costs was consistent with the Uniform NAFTA Regulations on Rules of Origin and Customs Procedures).

A regional content of 50 percent or more calculated on a net cost basis qualified most goods for free trade under NAFTA 1994. For light duty motor vehicles and their parts, a regional value content rising to 62.5 percent after 2002 was required. Other automotive goods had to possess 60 percent regional content after 2002. Automotive goods had to be valued on a net cost basis.

The value of non-originating materials (VNM) was excluded under both methods when determining the NAFTA origin of goods. This value was usually based on transaction values. If necessary, alternative values as determined under the GATT Customs Valuation Code of 1979 could be used. "Intermediate materials" fabricated by producers were generally treated as originating, a rule which benefited vertically integrated producers.

NAFTA embraced an "all or nothing" roll up approach to non-originating materials that resolved some of the disputes that emerged under CUSFTA 1989. In sum, the value of non-originating materials in components used to produce a good that was North American in origin was excluded from the VNM calculation in assessing regional content. This means that for both the transaction value and net cost methods, these materials were excluded in the determination of non-originating value. However, a tracing requirement for automobiles was added. This requirement was a prodigy of the CUSFTA *Honda* case discussed in Chapter 2. The value of non-originating automotive materials had to be traced back through suppliers. In the United States, cumulation provisions allow free trade partners to use inputs from other countries with which the U.S.

free trades and still qualify for preferential treatment.

Components that did not originate in NAFTA but possessed some originating materials, on the other hand, were rolled down on the same all or nothing basis. In other words, these originating materials were included in the determination of non-originating value. However, a nonintegrated producer could "accumulate" such originating material when calculating the regional value content of finished goods.

A diagram of the transaction (TV) and net cost (NC) methods of calculating regional value content percentages was provided in Article 402 of the agreement. For these purposes VMC equals the value of non-originating material.

$$\text{Regional Value Content} \quad = \quad \frac{\text{TV} - \text{VNM}}{\text{TV}} \quad \times \quad 100$$

$$\text{Regional Value Content} \quad = \quad \frac{\text{NC} - \text{VNM}}{\text{NC}} \quad \times \quad 100$$

TEXTILES AND APPAREL

Like automobiles, textiles and apparel had unique NAFTA rules of origin. Special production requirements were created that protect North American manufacturers. There was a "yarn forward" rule. This required: (1) Use of North American spun yarns; (2) to make North American fabrics; (3) that are cut and sewn into clothing in North America. Similarly, cotton and man-made fiber yarns had to be "fiber forwarded" for North American free trade.

These "triple transformation" rules of origin had a substantial impact. Initially, Mexican imports (heavily comprised of U.S. content) displaced East Asian apparel, though less so after 2001 when China joined the World Trade Organization. Furthermore, Mexico raised its tariffs on non-NAFTA textiles in the wake of its 1995 financial crisis, while continuing NAFTA tariff reductions. The margin of preferential access to Mexico for Canadian and United States textiles was thus magnified. Exports of U.S. textile components to Mexico were also been enhanced by greater allowance under NAFTA of maquiladora apparel sales inside Mexico. However, after 2005 when international textile and apparel quotas were eliminated by WTO agreement, Mexico lost substantial market share to China and East Asia.

Silk, linen and other fabrics that are scarce in North America were exceptions from NAFTA's triple transformation rules, but had still to be cut and sewn in North America. Textile products with less than 7 percent non-originating material measured by weight could also be freely traded. This amount was treated as *de minimis*. Some non-qualifying textiles and clothing could be preferentially traded under quotas within NAFTA.

ELECTRONICS

NAFTA created some unique rules of origin for consumer electronics products. These rules were based on changes in tariff classifications that contained particular components. For example, in order to qualify for free trade, traditional tube-type color television sets with screens over fourteen inches had to contain a North American-made picture tube. After 1999, color television sets had also to contain, among other things, North American amplifiers, tuners and power suppliers.

For a microwave oven, all the major parts, except the magnetron, had to be made in the North American countries. Computers needed to contain a North American motherboard. Traditional computer monitors, needed to contain a North American color picture tube to be considered NAFTA originating.

The initial impact of NAFTA on the electronics and computer industries was significant. United States, Japanese and Korean investment in electronics production facilities in Mexico grew, especially in the manufacture of those components that conveyed NAFTA origin. Mexican purchases of U.S. electronic components and finished goods produced in maquiladoras went up substantially. However, after 2001, as with textiles, there was some disinvestment from Mexico as firms moved their electronics plants to China and other low-cost Asian manufacturing centers.

More significantly, most production of flat screen panels is done in Asia, not Mexico. The NAFTA free trade incentive just simply did not overcome Asia's lower production costs and supply chain advantages. About 30 million of those panels and related parts were annually imported duty free into Tijuana via Long Beach CA, and turned into TVs for the NAFTA market. Roughly 15,000 Mexicans were employed to achieve this result.

EXPORTING FROM MEXICO UNDER ITS FREE TRADE AGREEMENTS

Mexico has dozens of free trade agreements. Most are centered in Latin America, including Chile, Colombia, Venezuela (dormant), Costa Rica, Bolivia, Nicaragua, Guatemala, Honduras, El Salvador, Peru, and Uruguay. Mexico trades freely with Japan, Israel and the European Union. In 2013, Mexico, Colombia, Peru and Chile formed the Pacific Alliance, a free trade deal that serves as a counterweight to Brazil-led MERCOSUR.

The EU-Mexican FTA was significantly revised and expanded in 2018. Mexico also signed in 2018 the Comprehensive and Progressive Trans Pacific Partnership (TPP-11) agreement, joined by 10 other nations, but not the USA. See R. Folsom, *International Trade Law including Trump and Trade* in a Nutshell. Mexican FTAs create an opportunity for producers of goods in Mexico, especially in maquiladoras, to enjoy duty free status in Latin American, European and Japanese markets.

The key to seizing this opportunity are the rules of origin under Mexico's free trade agreements. These rules are complex and not entirely uniform. They roughly track the NAFTA rules of origin with most transaction value regional content requirements ranging between 45 and 55 percent.

PROOF OF ORIGIN

NAFTA exporters were legally obligated to provide importers with a certificate of origin. A common customs form was created for these purposes. In the United States, this was Customs Service Form CF–434. Its Canadian and Mexican counterparts were essentially identical. Exporters could sign the certificate in reliance upon written representations from producers of goods.

Practically speaking, producers most often bore the bulk of the burden of keeping the records necessary to prove NAFTA origin. Five years was the normal retention period. Record keeping was especially difficult when regional value contents were involved. Tracing automotive suppliers was perhaps the most onerous burden. For some traders, especially of technology goods, proof of NAFTA origin was a burden that could outweigh the benefits of compliance. They sometimes elected to just simply pay most-favored-nation (MFN) tariffs, which average about 3 percent for the United States. Canada's MFN rates average about 4 percent, while Mexico currently averages about 8 percent (subject to the right to raise its MFN tariffs significantly). Naturally, the lower the relevant MFN tariff, the more likely traders were to pay that tariff instead of documenting NAFTA status.

Importers relied on certificates of NAFTA origin when they declared goods eligible for regional tariff benefits. The importing country could question the exporter or producer, or review their records in their presence, in any instance where NAFTA tariff preferences were sought. Customs service notice of an intent to conduct a verification of NAFTA origin proceeding was required. The consent of the exporter or producer was also needed, but if withheld NAFTA 1994 tariff benefits could be denied. The producer was entitled to have two observers at any on-site customs inspection.

NAFTA importers and exporters could obtain advance rulings from customs services before shipping goods across borders. All customs service determinations on NAFTA origin, whether by advance ruling or not, could be reviewed and appealed. Such appeals included at least one level of administrative review above the customs office making the initial determination. Thereafter judicial or quasi-judicial review of the final administrative decision was required. In the United States, judicial review of NAFTA origin decisions was taken to the Court of International Trade.

Country of origin marking requirements, such as those of the United States (19 U.S.C. § 1304), were permitted on NAFTA-originating goods. Marking in English, French or Spanish had to be generally be allowed. The origin of goods for marking purposes was not always governed by the same law as origin for purposes of NAFTA tariff benefits. This reality was well illustrated in the *CPC International* decision of the U.S. Court of International Trade (933 F.Supp.1093 (1996)). The CIT ruled that the NAFTA Implementation Act required meeting both the NAFTA Marking Rules and the traditional "substantial transformation" test of origin. On appeal, the Federal Circuit reversed, affirming that the tariff-shift NAFTA approach exclusively governed U.S. country of origin marking requirements. *Bestfoods v. United States,* 165 F.3d 1371 (Fed. Cir. 1999).

PROCUREMENT

Chapter 10 of NAFTA governed procurement of services and goods by state enterprises and governments. Since Mexico, unlike Canada and the United States, had not signed the GATT/WTO Procurement Code, the provisions of Chapter 10 gave Canadian and United States suppliers of goods and services priority status in Mexican procurement. NAFTA's procurement rules applied if three criteria were met: (1) The purchasing entity was covered; (2) the goods or services also were covered; and (3) the value of the contract met designated thresholds. If these criteria were met, then Canadian, Mexican and United States suppliers were free to compete on procurement.

NAFTA's special access rules on procurement did not apply universally. Generally speaking, for example, military and national security procurement was excluded. And not all civil government procurement was covered; only those purchasing entities listed in the Annexes to Chapter 10 were included. These Annexes hoped to list state and provincial entities, another expansion upon the CUSFTA rules, but their participation was "voluntary" and left to further negotiations. United States and Canadian minority and small business set-aside programs were also excluded.

NAFTA's procurement rules applied to some government enterprises (e.g., parastatal Mexican enterprises, Canadian Crown Corporations, the Tennessee Valley Authority). For example, PEMEX and the Mexican Federal Electricity Commission (CFE) procure billions of dollars of goods and services annually. In 1994, 50 percent of their purchases were opened to competitive NAFTA bidding and thereafter U.S. firms won PEMEX and CFE contracts. The balance was brought under NAFTA by 2003.

Goods and construction services listed in the Annexes to Chapter 10 were subject to competitive NAFTA bidding. For example, pre-erection site work, civil engineering and construction equipment rentals were listed in Annex 1001.16–3 and therefore included. Notably, transport, data processing, basic telecommunications, research and development, ship repair, management and other services were expressly excluded. But, apart from construction services, unless specifically excluded, services were subject to competitive NAFTA procurement.

Canada and the United States had agreed in CUSFTA to a threshold of $25,000 U.S. for federal goods procurement. NAFTA extended this agreement. The threshold for civil procurement between Mexico and the United States was $50,000

U.S. for goods and services. The threshold for construction services was $6.5 million U.S. The $50,000 and $6.5 million thresholds for covered services and construction services also applied between Canada and the United States. The contract thresholds for government enterprises were higher: $250,000 U.S. for goods and services, and $8 million U.S. for construction services. These contract thresholds applied, for example, to PEMEX and CFE.

Bid procedures were detailed at great length in the NAFTA agreement. NAFTA rules mandated notice of bid information, product specifications, qualifications for bidders, etc. Government and state enterprise agencies accorded national and most-favored treatment to NAFTA bidders. Discrimination on grounds of national origin, or foreign affiliation or ownership of the supplier, was prohibited. Notably, procurement of local content or purchase "offsets," used frequently in Canada and Mexico, were also prohibited. So were technical specifications that create unnecessary obstacles to trade. And the normal rules of product origin had to be employed.

NAFTA bidders were given an opportunity to challenge the results or any feature of the procurement process in an impartial forum. However, bids by service suppliers owned or controlled by non-NAFTA nationals that lacked substantial business activity in a NAFTA nation could be rejected.

In 2010, the United States agreed to provide temporary relief for Canadian exporters from Buy American restraints, long-term access to state and local U.S. procurement and a fast-track process for procurement disputes. Canada, in turn, opened up its procurement significantly to U.S. exporters. But, in 2018, New York and Texas "Buy Local" iron and steel laws blocked procurement purchases from Canadian sources. This caused Ontario to respond in kind regarding steel and iron ore from those two U.S. states.

MOTOR VEHICLES

Canada and the United States had a long tradition of free automotive trade and investment under their 1965 Auto Pact. CUSFTA 1989 and NAFTA 1994 made only a few changes to this relationship. The more demanding NAFTA rules of origin were substituted, notably the 62.5 percent regional value content requirement for passenger autos and light trucks (60 percent for other vehicles and parts). These content rules took full effect in 2002 and were calculated on a net cost basis traced back through suppliers.

NAFTA continued the preferential trade terms of the Canada-U.S. Auto Pact, but only for Auto Pact beneficiaries. Toyota and Honda Canada were not such beneficiaries, but had been receiving duty drawback and production-based customs duty remissions on auto parts which effectively matched Auto Pact benefits. When NAFTA required the elimination of these duty drawback and remission programs at the end of 1995, Honda and Toyota faced a 2.5 percent tariff on auto parts imported for assembly in Canada. The Canadian government, shortly after Honda and Toyota announced plans for expanded assembly plants, removed the 2.5 percent tariff in an effort at maintaining the costs of assembly in Canada.

Automotive investment and trade had been controlled by the Mexican federal government for many years. Prior to NAFTA, Mexico imposed tariffs as high as 20% on automobile imports, and required up to 80% local content for producers based in Mexico. Not a lot of cars or car parts entered Mexico under these restrictive rules, which also discouraged foreign investment to produce automobiles in Mexico. The 1989 presidential Decree for Development and Modernization of the Automotive Industry and related 1990 implementing regulations were in place as NAFTA was negotiated. Mexico kept this Decree in force until 2003. Mexico's refusal to allow importation of used vehicles remained effective until 2009. Thereafter, used auto imports were phased in over ten years based on the age of the vehicle.

Pre-NAFTA auto manufacturers in Mexico included Ford, General Motors, Chrysler, Volkswagen and Nissan. These producers were gradually relieved of "trade balancing" export obligations as a precondition to importing, but retained their exclusive import rights until 2003. Mexico also gradually reduced the percentage of Mexican value that auto manufacturers must add to vehicles. Since 2003, there has been no Mexican value-added requirement. As a result, fewer auto parts needed to be purchased from Mexican "national suppliers." In addition, auto components manufactured in Mexican maquiladoras were treated as Mexican in origin and United States and Canadian investors could wholly own Mexican auto parts suppliers. All limits on the importation of autos tied to sales volumes in Mexico were removed.

Other Mexican automotive trade and investment restraints were altered by NAFTA. The Auto Transportation Decree of 1989 regulating the production and importation of buses and trucks has been repealed. Since 1999 Mexico no longer requires its manufacturers to limit imports to 50 percent of Mexican production. Non-manufacturers have been able to import more buses and trucks under quotas auctioned by the Mexican government. These quotas corresponded to progressively higher percentages of Mexican production. Since 1999 they too disappeared.

Mexico and the United States had different auto tariff obligations. Mexico reduced its passenger automobile tariffs by 50 percent in 1994, and phased out the remainder by 2003. On light trucks, it cut tariffs immediately by 50 percent, phasing out the remainder by 1998. For all other vehicles, Mexico phased out its tariffs by 2003. In contrast, the United States immediately removed all tariffs on Mexican passenger automobiles. The United States also phased out tariffs on Mexican light trucks. All other United States tariffs on motor vehicles from Mexico were phased out after 2003. On auto parts, Mexico and the U.S. removed certain tariffs in 1994. They phased out most others over five years, and eliminated all tariffs on auto parts after 2003.

The United States minimum corporate fuel average economy rules (CAFE rules) provide a good example of United States regulations with trade restraining potential. No alteration in these standards was required by NAFTA. However, the United States agreed to permit inclusion of Mexican auto parts and vehicles under its CAFE regulations. Canadian parts and autos with at least 75 percent of their value added in Canada were classified as domestic and included under CAFE. Mexican goods have been equally treated since 2004.

Motor vehicles and their components were by far the most significant trade sector under NAFTA. This significance helps explain the level of detail in the NAFTA agreement concerning motor vehicles, especially their rules of origin (*supra*). Despite Mexico's financial crisis and ensuing recession, U.S. and Canadian exports of motor vehicles exploded. Shipments of completed vehicles to Mexico increased over 500 percent in the first three years of NAFTA.

New investment in auto production facilities after 1994 has significantly increased south of the border. Toyota, Audi, Daimler-Benz, Hyundai, Kia, BMW and Honda commenced production in Mexico, and pre-NAFTA auto plants (above) expanded. Investment in auto parts production in Mexico skyrocketed. A large share of the production of auto parts is being done by Mexican industrial conglomerates. Supply chains for auto production were greatly integrated, with parts often moving back and forth repeatedly. Auto exports from Mexico to destinations other than Canada and the United

States also rose notably, so much so that in 2012 Mexico agreed to voluntarily limit auto exports to Brazil.

Overall, the integration of the auto parts and production markets under NAFTA has enhanced the ability of North America to compete with Asian and European producers. For example, BMW in South Carolina and Mercedes-Benz in Alabama have risen to the top of the U.S. list of auto exporters. Both firms are also producing in China for its massive and growing internal market. Despite shipping costs to North America, rising Chinese labor costs and Trump tariffs, Ford, BMW and others expect to join GM (Buick) in exporting cars made in China to the USA. See R. Folsom, *International Trade Law including Trump and Trade* in a Nutshell.

ENERGY GOODS

Like cultural industries for Canada in the CUSFTA negotiations, energy was non-negotiable for Mexico in the NAFTA negotiations. Chapter 6 of NAFTA dealt with trade in energy and basic petrochemical goods. It opened with a most unusual sentence: "The Parties confirm their full respect for their Constitutions."

This is an oblique reference to the revolutionary Mexican Constitution of 1917 that reserved ownership and development of natural resources to the state. Today this constitutional clause is most evident in PEMEX, the state oil, gas and basic petrochemical monopoly. CFE, the state electricity monopoly, also embodies revolutionary state ownership principles.

NAFTA Annex 602.3 demonstrated what "full respect" for the Mexican Constitution means. In it, Mexico reserved to its state a lengthy list of strategic activities: Exploration, exploitation, and refining of crude oil and natural gas; production of artificial gas and basic petrochemicals; pipelines; foreign trade in and transport, storage and distribution of the same; virtually the entire supply of electricity to the public in Mexico; and nuclear energy. Cross-border trade in energy services was possible only by permit of the Mexican government. Cross-border trade in natural gas and basic petrochemicals was similarly allowed with PEMEX through regulated supply contracts.

No private Canadian, Mexican or United States investment was permitted in these areas. NAFTA investors could participate in all secondary and non-reserved basic petrochemicals, but there was a slowdown in privatization of such opportunities. Transportation, distribution and storage of natural gas were opened to private investors (including foreigners) in 1995 and several U.S. companies successfully bid on such opportunities.

Under NAFTA, Mexico allowed 100 percent foreign ownership of new coal mines. Existing joint ventures could become wholly-owned by NAFTA investors. Mexican tariffs on coal were completely removed at the outset. NAFTA nationals could own or operate electricity companies when the production was for the owner's use. Excess electricity had to be sold to CFE at rates agreed upon by contract. Co-generation was another possibility when electricity was generated by industrial production. Excess supplies went to CFE at agreed rates. Independent power production plants located in Mexico could be owned and operated by NAFTA nationals, but CFE got the electricity. This was done by leasing foreign-owned plants to CFE. In the border region, CFE can contract to sell electricity to United States utilities.

NAFTA incorporated by reference the GATT 1947 provisions relating to quotas and other restraints on trade in energy and petrochemical goods. Presumably, this applies to GATT Articles XI, XX and XXI. As in other areas, this incorporation permitted utilization of NAFTA dispute settlement in the energy field. Energy export licensing was permissible under NAFTA. Export taxes and other charges could be used only if they apply to energy goods consumed domestically. The regulation of energy was subject to NAFTA's general national and most-favored treatment duties. The more specific rules of NAFTA Chapter 6 on trade restraints and export taxes also applied. NAFTA nations agreed to "seek" to ensure that energy regulation did not disrupt contractual relationships "to the maximum extent practicable." They had to provide for "orderly and equitable" implementation of regulatory measures.

In addition, other rights and obligations relating to energy goods were established by NAFTA. There was an express prohibition of import or export price controls that applied to all parties. Following the controversial CUSFTA rules, in times of energy crises, Canadian (but not Mexican) restraints had to be proportionate to past export/domestic utilization ratios. Crisis restraints could not push export prices higher than those charged domestically. And the normal channels of supply had to be maintained. Mexico was also exempted from the NAFTA rules on restraining trade in energy goods for reasons of national security, but required to adhere to the general NAFTA rules on national security trade restraints.

Canada and Mexico remain important sources of United States energy imports. With oil embargoes in mind, energy security was a major goal for the United States in negotiating NAFTA. Nevertheless, the United States was unable to obtain the same degree of energy security from Mexico that it arguably secured from Canada under CUSFTA. See Chapter 2. However, Canada unilaterally issued in 1993 a declaration interpreting NAFTA as *not* requiring Canadian energy crisis exports at any given level or proportion.

Faced with steadily declining production and revenue levels, and a need for deep-water and shale technology, *unilateral* Mexican constitutional reforms in 2013, followed by 2014 legislative and regulatory initiatives, dramatically altered the PEMEX monopoly. Henceforth, private firms could under profit-sharing contracts explore and drill for oil. The powerful oil workers' union lost seats on the PEMEX board. Transparency reforms sought to deal with corruption issues, with tax and oil royalty law changes intended to loosen the link between PEMEX and the federal government's budget. The CFE monopoly was also altered to allow private power-generators to supply the national grid.

By 2017, the Mexican energy reforms were making an impact. Major foreign oil companies, including CNOOC from China, Total, BP, Shell, ExxonMobil, and Chevron, had obtained deep sea drilling rights in the Mexican Caribbean basin. Early wells produced some gushers. A longstanding U.S. trade deficit in oil, natural gas and refined petroleum products with Mexico flipped to a sizeable surplus. ExxonMobil has opened a chain of petrol stations in Mexico.

A substantial increase in Mexican oil and gas production has broad implications. It will reduce traditional U.S. dependency on Middle East oil and gas resources, already in substantial decline as a result of the use of fracking and horizontal drilling techniques in many U.S. states. Experts suggest that the United States, Mexico and Canada are on track to achieve North American energy independence by 2020.

STATE MONOPOLIES AND ENTERPRISES

Article 1502 of NAFTA dealt with federal (but not state or provincial) monopolies, such as PEMEX and CFE. Designating or maintaining federal monopoly providers or purchasers of goods or services in any economic sector was authorized under NAFTA. Such monopolies could or could not be state-owned enterprises. But all federal government monopolies, and all privately-owned monopolies designated after January 1, 1994, had to act consistently with NAFTA

1994 when exercising "governmental authority." This meant that when they issued trade licenses, approve contracts, imposed quotas, or levied fees or charges, monopoly enterprises fell within NAFTA's reach.

Furthermore, state monopolies had to act solely in accordance with commercial considerations. Hence, for example, PEMEX decisions about pricing, quality, availability, marketability, transport and other terms and conditions of purchase or sale had to be commercially justifiable. Federal monopolies had to give the better of national or most-favored-nation treatment to NAFTA investors, service-providers and sellers of goods. Monopoly positions were not to be used to engage in anticompetitive practices in non-monopolized markets to the disadvantage of NAFTA investors. For example, discrimination in the provision of monopoly goods or services, cross-subsidization, and predatory conduct were prohibited.

All of these rules attempted to get federal monopolies to behave as if they were subject to market forces and competition law. Acting "in accordance with commercial considerations" was even defined as acting consistent with practices of privately-held enterprises. The only exception was procurement for governmental purposes. More generally, NAFTA committed each nation to enforcement of business competition law (referred to as antitrust law in the United States) against private sector trade restraints. For Mexico, this commitment resulted in the adoption of the Federal Law of Economic Competition (June, 1993). This law prohibits monopolies, monopolistic practices (price fixing, market division) and anticompetitive concentrations (mergers and acquisitions).

All state enterprises owned or controlled by a NAFTA government were subject to Article 1503. Unlike monopolies, Article 1503 embraced state or provincial government enterprises, e.g., Hydro-Quebec. All governments had to ensure that state enterprises acted consistently with Chapters 11 (Investment) and 14 (Financial Services) of NAFTA 1994 when exercising governmental authority. Expropriation, for example, fell within this rule. Like monopolies, state enterprises had to sell to NAFTA investors by giving them the better of national or most-favored-nation treatment, but were generally not subjected to the same level of scrutiny as federal monopolies.

AGRICULTURAL GOODS

Trade in agricultural and food products is always sensitive. Mexico's large *ejido* communal land program is oriented towards subsistence farming and constitutionally protected. This makes change in agriculture hyper-sensitive. Nevertheless, agricultural free trade between the United States and Mexico was substantially advanced by NAFTA, and its impact on small Mexican farmers was harsh. Approximately 4.8 million Mexicans exited subsistent family farms, some into paid farmworker jobs, while others headed north to the USA to escape poverty. Critics of obesity generated by cheap, high calorie imported U.S. processed foods and soft drinks, note that Wal-Mart is now the largest Mexican food retailer.

Mexico and the United States undertook more diffuse agricultural trade reform. Approximately half of all Mexico-U.S. agricultural trade immediately became duty-free. The United States and Mexico also converted agricultural quotas, import licenses and other nontariff trade barriers into tariffs ("tariffication"). Equivalent restrictive tariffs or tariff-rate quotas (TRQs) replaced these restraints. Tariff rate quotas adjusted the level of applicable tariffs according to the volume of imports, generally rising with import volume.

Duty free entry at lower import volumes often accompanies TRQs. The amount of duty-free agricultural goods entering Mexico and the United States increased by 3 percent annually. Nearly all tariffs on Mexican-U.S. agricultural goods were eliminated by 2004. By 2008 tariffs for even the most sensitive agricultural items, such as corn and dry beans entering Mexico, became duty free. This contrasts remarkably with high pre-NAFTA Mexican agricultural tariffs, ranging from 15% on soybeans and processed vegetables to 215% on corn. Under NAFTA, Mexico has become the largest foreign market for U.S. corn, dairy products, poultry and wheat.

In 2008, settlement of a longstanding WTO dispute between Mexico and the United States officially brought free trade to sugar and sweeteners, but subsequent trade remedy disputes (below) now regulate the flow of these products across the U.S.-Mexico border.

Canada and the U.S. undertook only token changes in CUSFTA, not the least because each has powerful farm lobbies. These rules did reduce quota, import license and other agricultural nontariff trade barriers in a limited way, notably allowing Canada to retain high tariffs and other trade restraints on U.S. poultry, eggs, wine and dairy products. Agricultural export subsidies were generally restrained under NAFTA 1994. However, this restraint did not apply to Mexican-United States agricultural trade.

Notice and consultation had to precede any subsidization and a Working Group on Agricultural Subsidies monitored this volatile area. It was deemed "inappropriate" for one NAFTA partner to subsidize agricultural goods unless there were subsidized imports entering that market from a non-member country. The NAFTA partners promised to collaborate on retaliatory measures against the offending third-party. It was significant that NAFTA reserved for all partners the right to apply countervailing tariffs against subsidized agricultural imports. Canada, for example, assessed countervailing tariffs on United States corn.

Under the WTO Agricultural Agreement, Canada and the United States were obligated to "tariffy" many of their agricultural quotas. When Canada tariffied (using TRQs) a number of agricultural quotas at levels measured in hundreds of percent, the United States filed a complaint under NAFTA. This complaint was the first under Chapter 20 (below) to go to arbitration. A panel of five arbitrators unanimously ruled that Canada's tariffication and tariff levels were consistent with its NAFTA treaty obligations (CDA–95–2008–01).

FOOD STANDARDS (SPS)

Section B of Chapter 7 of NAFTA 1994 concerns food regulations, so-called "Sanitary and Phytosanitary Measures" (SPS). SPS regulations govern the protection of human, animal or plant life or health. They are focused on risks associated with animal or plant pests or diseases, food additives, and food contaminants (such as toxins). There is a WTO agreement on SPS Measures which tracks NAFTA quite closely. All SPS measures that directly or indirectly affect NAFTA trade were covered, including SPS acts of nongovernmental entities. Each NAFTA member had to secure compliance by state or provincial governments with the NAFTA SPS regime. Canada, Mexico and the United States retained their inspection and approval procedures for food products. Agricultural and food products that failed national SPS requirements could be banned from those markets.

Since each nation could adopt, maintain or apply any necessary SPS regulation, trade in food products continued to be a heavily controlled field. NAFTA authorized "appropriate" levels of protection. In other words, each nation established its own SPS risk management tolerance. The appropriateness of SPS protection included an assessment of lost production, lost sales and other economic injury. The cost-effectiveness of alternative approaches to limited risks had to be reviewed. The agreement's broad objective of minimizing negative trade impact was also considered.

SPS rules could reflect variable conditions, such as allowing imports from disease-free regions. Arbitrary or unjustifiable SPS discrimination was prohibited by NAFTA agreement. Each country promised to only adopt necessary levels of SPS protection, and no SPS regulation could be applied with the intent or effect of creating a disguised restraint on trade.

Chapter 7 of NAFTA attempted to minimize the potential for SPS regulations to block NAFTA trade in a variety of ways. All SPS regulations had to be based on scientific principles derived from a "risk assessment". They were to be eliminated when there was no longer any scientific basis for continuance. Risk assessments focused on the adverse potential of a pest or disease or the presence of additives or contaminants in foodstuffs. They had to take into account relevant risk assessment techniques and methodologies developed by international or North American standardizing organizations, relevant scientific evidence, and relevant processes and production methods. Risk assessments also needed to consider relevant inspection, sampling and testing methods, the prevalence of relevant diseases or pests (including the existence of pest-free or disease-free areas or areas of low pest or disease prevalence), relevant ecological and other environmental conditions, and relevant treatments, such as quarantines.

NAFTA mandated use of international SPS standards so long as there was no reduction in protection levels. SPS protection that surpassed international standards was expressly permitted. The SPS rules of the Codex Alimentarius Commission, the International Office of Epizootics, the International Plant Protection Convention and the North American Plant Protection Convention were specifically supported. Harmonized SPS regulations were negotiated through the NAFTA Committee on Sanitary and Phytosanitary Measures.

Canadian and United States SPS regulations are broadly compatible. National SPS regulations were treated as equivalent if the exporting country could objectively demonstrate that its regulations achieved the importing country's chosen level of protection. Scientific evidence evaluated under NAFTA's risk assessment methods were used to resolve issues of equivalency resulting in a written report.

SPS inspection and control procedures applicable to NAFTA trade had to be administered as done domestically. Such procedures had to be transparent and available for review by NAFTA traders. New or modified SPS regulations affecting NAFTA were preceded by public notice and often a statement of objectives and reasons. Such notice must highlight variances from international standards. An opportunity for written comment had to be available and, upon request, discussion. All of these procedural requirements were reinforced by official NAFTA "inquiry points" in each country. These centers responded to questions and provided information regarding SPS regulations, inspection and approval procedures, risk assessments and related subjects.

PRODUCT AND SERVICE STANDARDS-RELATED MEASURES (SRM)

Chapter 9 of the NAFTA agreement is titled "Standards-Related Measures (SRM)." SRM embrace standards, technical regulations and conformity assessment procedures. All of these terms were defined. Standards were voluntary, but technical regulations were mandatory, and conformity assessment procedures were used to determine if standards or technical regulations had been fulfilled.

Chapter 9 of NAFTA concerned service and product standards and technical regulations and certifications of compliance. Adherence to the GATT Agreement on Technical Barriers to Trade of 1979 (the GATT Standards Code) was affirmed (but not incorporated by reference) in Chapter 9. This Code was superseded by the WTO Agreement on Technical Barriers to Trade (1995) upon which Chapter 9 was largely modeled.

All other international agreements of Canada, Mexico and the United States affecting the regulation of goods were also affirmed. By specific provision in NAFTA Chapter 9, these included the Washington Convention on International Trade in Endangered Species of Wild Fauna and Flora (1973, 1979), the Montreal Protocol on Substances that Deplete the Ozone Layer (1987, 1990), the Canada-U.S. Agreement on Movement of Transboundary

Hazardous Waste (1986) and the Mexico-U.S. Agreement on Cooperation for the Protection and Improvement of the Environment in the Border Area (1983).

With relatively few qualifications (notably a duty not to discriminate), NAFTA permitted use of product and service standards and regulations as a nontariff trade barrier. Article 904 recognized the right of each country to adopt, maintain or apply SRMs based on "legitimate objectives." Protection of domestic industries was specifically excluded as a legitimate objective. "Legitimate objectives" was defined in Article 915 as including "sustainable development" as well as safety, health, environmental and consumer protection.

"Sustainable development" was not defined in the NAFTA agreement. At a minimum, it referred to Mexico's economic development goals. More generally, the term is often used to connote development that is *environmentally* sustainable. Thus, all the NAFTA partners could enact SRM that promote sustainable development. The level of protection of all of these interests was left to each NAFTA member-state and preserved for all levels of government. The power to prohibit the importation of nonconforming goods or services from a NAFTA partner was expressly reserved.

All legitimate objectives for product or service SRM needed to be reviewed in light of: (1) Fundamental climatic or geographical factors; (2) technological or infrastructural factors; or (3) scientific justification. "Assessments of risk" could be employed (but were not required) when evaluating legitimate trade regulatory objectives. NAFTA's SRM rules, unlike its SPS rules, were not firmly linked to science. When utilized, assessments of risk could take into account available scientific evidence or technical information, intended end uses, methodology, or environmental conditions.

Such assessments were strongly encouraged in establishing appropriate levels of national standards protection. In determining these levels, arbitrary or unjustifiable distinctions between similar goods or services could not be made if disguised restrictions on NAFTA trade, or discriminations between goods or services posing the same level of risk and providing similar benefits, resulted.

NAFTA 1994 required SRM to be administered without discrimination under national and most-favored-nation treatment rules. But each member needed only "seek" to ensure observance of these rules by state or provincial (not local) governments. Likewise, they needed only to seek compliance by nongovernmental standards organizations. Adoption of international SRM (such as the numerous International Standards Organization rules) was required except when inappropriate or ineffective to meet a nation's legitimate regulatory objectives. In a provision dear to environmentalists, NAFTA specifically provided that levels of protection that are higher than internationally mandated could be chosen.

No SRM creating unnecessary obstacles to NAFTA trade were permissible. No unnecessary obstacle to trade existed for these purposes if the demonstrable purpose of the SRM was to achieve a legitimate objective and goods meeting that objective were not excluded. The NAFTA partners promised to work jointly towards enhanced and compatible SRM. They agreed to treat each other's technical regulations and certification tests as equivalent when they adequately fulfilled the importing partner's legitimate objectives, a commitment not found in the WTO Technical Barriers Agreement. The 1993 CUSFTA dispute settlement arbitration on Puerto Rican regulations governing the importation of long-life milk from Quebec stands for the principle that each partner must give the others the chance to prove equivalency. See Chapter 2.

Testing and approval procedures (conformity assessments) were subject to minimum procedural requirements. The licensing of product testing in the other countries had to be on terms no less favorable than applied domestically. Lastly, there were extensive notification, publication, information-sharing, information center and technical cooperation duties intended to keep standards issues transparent. Further review, discussion and consultation were anticipated in a special NAFTA "Committee on Standards-Related Measures."

We know from decades of experience in the European Union that as tariffs decline, nontariff trade barriers take on major importance. In NAFTA 1994, unlike Europe or even portions of CUSFTA 1989, there was no commitment to uniform harmonization or mutual recognition of standards and certifications. Indeed, NAFTA's express reservation of the right to block trade in goods or services that did not meet diverse national SPS or SRM moved in exactly the opposite direction. That said, NAFTA's numerous cooperative Committees reached a wide range of SPS and SRM agreements.

There were comparatively few SPS or SRM disputes of major consequence. Mexico was supposed to have issued its standard for terminal attachment telephone equipment by January 1, 1995. Negotiations within the NAFTA Telecommunications Standards Subcommittee (TSSC) were prolonged by divisions of interest in market opening versus market protection. More than 2 years later, under U.S. pressure, the telecom standard was finally promulgated. Known in Mexico as a "norma," the standard contains 13 mandatory parameters and applies to telephones, fax machines, modems and other end-user devices.

EXCEPTIONS TO FREE TRADE

Every chapter of NAFTA had specific exceptions that accompanied it. Chapter 21, labeled "Exceptions," was of wider application. For example, information flows adverse to law enforcement could be restrained under NAFTA as could flows that affected personal privacy or financial information rights. Perhaps the best-known exception was for Canadian cultural industries, which was extended to Canadian-Mexican trade, and retained under the USMCA. See Chapter 2. This exception does not apply to Mexico-United States trade.

In addition, Chapter 21 incorporated by reference into NAFTA Article XX of the GATT 1947 (and its interpretative notes). Article XX, previously discussed in Chapter 2, authorizes restraint on international trade in goods (not services) in the name of public morality, public health, protection of intellectual property, conservation of natural resources and so forth. Article 2101 of NAFTA sought to clarify Article XX of the GATT. It declared environmental protection a legitimate reason to restrain NAFTA trade. So was conservation of living and non-living exhaustible natural resources.

The health protection exception contained in Article XX of the GATT was specifically replaced by NAFTA's provisions on sanitary and phytosanitary (SPS) regulations (above). It was also agreed that all health, safety and consumer protection laws had to be consistent with NAFTA. They could not be administered in arbitrary or unjustifiably discriminatory ways. Nor could they amount to a disguised restriction on NAFTA trade.

The NAFTA national security exceptions to free trade followed those created in CUSFTA 1989. See Chapter 2. As a general rule, NAFTA did not impact national tax laws. However, Article 301 (national treatment) applied to tax regulations "to the same extent as does Article III of the GATT." Article III bans discriminatory taxation of imported goods and frequently applies to sales, excise and value-added taxes. Income, capital gains taxation, and corporate capital taxation, if applied to a particular service, had also be given national treatment.

Articles 2103.2 through 2103.6 indicated that international tax conventions would prevail over NAFTA. The most recent relevant conventions are the 1980 Canada-United States Tax Convention, the 1992 Canada-Mexico Tax Convention, and the 1994 Mexico-United States Tax Convention.

NAFTA, with an eye towards Mexico, governed the extent to which balance of payments problems justify restraints of trade. Article 2104 legitimized use of quotas, surcharges and the like only if authorized by the International Monetary Fund. This made it unlikely that NAFTA nations could restrain payments on current transactions, dividends, royalties and the like. Capital transfers, on the other hand, are not subject to IMF controls. Mexico could therefore restrain major capital outflows.

TEMPORARY IMPORT RESTRAINTS (SAFEGUARDS)

Canada and the United States severely limited their ability to bilaterally protect their markets when imports surge and cause or threaten serious injury to a domestic industry. See Chapter 2. These limitations continued in force under NAFTA. Chapter 8 of NAFTA, governing Mexico and the United States, substantially reproduced the CUSFTA provisions on emergency import protection.

Article 802 of NAFTA applied to all three countries when global safeguard proceedings were pursued. To start, there was a rebuttable presumption that NAFTA goods would be excluded from global actions. Rebuttal was possible if the NAFTA imports were a "substantial share" of total imports, and those NAFTA imports "contribute[d] importantly" to serious domestic industry injury or its threat. "Substantial share" was defined as "normally" including only the five largest supplier-nations. In other words, imports from Canada, Mexico or the United States had to be in the top five for any global safeguard relief to apply. Furthermore, NAFTA imports with growth rates that were appreciably lower than the growth rate from all sources were "normally" not be considered to "contribute importantly" to injury. NAFTA imports could later be included should a surge in NAFTA trade occur.

Any global escape clause remedies could not reduce the flow of goods across NAFTA borders below levels corresponding to a recent representative time period plus reasonable growth. The exporting NAFTA partner could in turn pursue substantially equivalent compensatory action. Lastly, NAFTA detailed in Article 803 and Annex 803.3 procedures that must be followed in bilateral or global emergency protective proceedings. These procedures did not differ substantially from those already used in United States law as administered by the U.S. International Trade Commission.

The legality under the WTO Safeguards Agreement of excluding or favoring Mexico or Canada from global U.S. escape clause measures has been repeatedly denied by the WTO Appellate Body. See *U.S.-Lamb Meat from New Zealand*, WT/DS 177/ AB/R (May 16, 2001).

THE CORN BROOM CASE

In its first application of Section 302 of the NAFTA Implementation Act, the U.S. International Trade Commission found in 1996 that the elimination of tariffs on Mexican corn brooms resulted in a surge of imports that were the substantial cause of serious injury or its threat to the U.S. broom industry (USA–97–2008–01). The ITC subsequently recommended tariff increases starting at 12 percent above the MFN level declining to 3 percent above that level in the fourth year of relief. This recommendation concerned brooms from Mexico and other nations excepting only Canada and Israel. No. TA–201–65, ITC Pub. 3984. Aug. 1996.

President Clinton decided against tariff increases, but instructed the USTR to attempt to negotiate solutions with Mexico and other countries while the Labor, Commerce and Agriculture Departments developed an adjustment plan for the U.S. corn broom industry. Mexico, meanwhile, requested consultations under NAFTA Chapter 20 dispute resolution (below). Late in 1996, President Clinton deemed the negotiations a failure and imposed substantial tariffs and tariff-rate-quotas (TRQs) on broom imports from Mexico and other countries for 3 years. Mexico, in turn, raised tariffs on U.S. wine, brandy, bourbon, whiskey, wood office and bedroom furniture, flat glass, telephone agendas and chemically-pure sugar, fructose and syrup products. This retaliation was deemed by Mexico "substantially equivalent" to the U.S. broom tariff surcharges valued at roughly $1 million.

Early in 1998, the NAFTA Chapter 20 arbitration panel ruled in Mexico's favor (USA–97–2008–01). Specifically, the panel ruled that the ITC had failed to explain why plastic brooms were not directly competitive with corn brooms, and therefore part of the U.S. domestic industry. U.S. officials indicated they would comply, but then took nine months to terminate the safeguards in a decision that did not cite the NAFTA arbitration as a reason for termination. Mexico subsequently removed its retaliatory tariffs.

SPECIAL SAFEGUARD CLAUSES

Textile and apparel goods, some agricultural goods, frozen concentrated orange juice and major household appliances benefited from special escapes from import competition under NAFTA 1994. Many of these provisions were created to secure passage of NAFTA through the United States Congress. For example, textile and apparel goods were subject to a unique import protection scheme found in Annex 300–B. Standard safeguard relief on originating goods was possible under less demanding conditions until 2003. For non-originating goods, until 2003, quotas could be used as remedies by the United States or Mexico. The most important alteration concerned decision-making. The Interagency Committee for the Implementation of Textile Agreements (CITA), thought to be more pro-industry than the ITC, was the body that determined safeguard relief for textiles and apparel under NAFTA.

A special provision located in Article 703 benefitted U.S.-grown chili peppers, eggplants, watermelons, tomatoes, onions and other agricultural goods. These could be protected using tariff-rate-quotas. The United States NAFTA Implementation Act, in Section 309, protected against imports of frozen concentrated orange juice from Mexico until 2007. Additional tariffs applied if the futures price for OJ fell below historic levels for five consecutive days. Tariffs on Mexican OJ imports were "snap-backed" to the lower of the present or July 1, 1991 most-favored-nation GATT rates. These tariffs were eliminated when the average historic price level was exceeded for five days. This statistically driven protective mechanism, a monument to Florida politicians, was frequently triggered.

The President's Statement of Administrative Action (SAA) accompanying the NAFTA Implementation Act contained yet another special escape from import competition. This time the beneficiaries were United States producers of major household appliances. It is thought that this statement, and its arcane rules of operation under Chapter 8 escape clause relief, secured critical votes in the House of Representatives for the passage of NAFTA.

NAFTA: FREE TRADE IN SERVICES

The United States is the world's largest exporter of services. Needless to say, it was keenly interested in advancing North American free trade and investment in services, and did so in a manner that clearly exceeds the WTO General Agreement on Services (GATS) (1995). See R. Folsom, *International Trade Law including Trump and Trade* in a Nutshell.

A major shift in approach to trade in services was made by NAFTA. Instead of following CUSFTA's "positive list" for coverage of services, NAFTA employed a "negative list." Under CUSFTA only services listed in the agreement were included. Under NAFTA all services were covered unless specifically excluded. In other words, there was a presumption of coverage and services unknown at the time qualified for NAFTA treatment.

NAFTA negatively lists sectors that cannot be freely traded. These include most legal, procurement, maritime, general aviation, basic telecommunications, cultural industry, and government-produced (health, social security and law enforcement) services. All of the services covered in the CUSFTA agreement were subject to NAFTA free trade, including financial services. NAFTA's approach extended free trade to aircraft repair, specialty air, land transport, intermodal terminal, warehouse, maritime port and enhanced telecommunication services.

However, some services were restricted by NAFTA quotas (even zero quotas). The United States, for example, imposed quotas on provision of radio communication, cable TV, natural gas transport, postal and national park concession services. Overall, NAFTA's impact on services trade was mixed, and perhaps a bit disappointing to the United States.

SERVICE PROVIDER RIGHTS

The right to "provide" covered services across borders was guaranteed by NAFTA. This right included the production, sale, purchase, payment, transport and delivery of services. Furthermore, no beneficiary was obliged to maintain an office or other local presence in a second or third NAFTA country. The beneficiaries of this right included nationals of NAFTA countries and incorporated enterprises that principally carried on their business within NAFTA.

This meant that most service companies owned by third party investors (e.g., Europeans, Asians and Latin Americans) principally doing business in NAFTA were beneficiaries under its services provisions. The only general exceptions were third parties from countries with whom there are no diplomatic relations or trade embargoes (e.g., Cuba). In addition, regarding financial services, Canada reserved the right to exclude all third-party providers regardless of their business operations inside NAFTA.

Chapter 12 created two standards for dealing with NAFTA service providers. NAFTA beneficiaries were entitled to the better of the two standards. First, under Article 1202, federal governments had to grant national treatment to NAFTA service providers. Secondly, under Article 1203, federal governments had to accord most-favored-nation treatment to NAFTA beneficiaries. State or provincial governments also had to give NAFTA beneficiaries the most favorable treatment they granted any service provider from their country.

The rights and treatment standards granted service providers under NAFTA were qualified by various quotas and "reservations." These reservations permitted each nation to continue to apply certain pre-NAFTA restraints or discriminations. However, such "non-conforming" laws could not be amended so as to further conflict with NAFTA.

LICENSING AND CERTIFICATION

Article 1210 of NAFTA governed licensing and certification of service providers, notably professionals. It provided for use of objective and transparent criteria under the least burdensome regulations necessary to maintain quality services. Disguised restrictions on cross-border trade in services were prohibited.

Mutual recognition of national professional licenses was not mandatory. However, professional service providers had to be allowed to prove that their education, experience, licenses or certifications justify licensure. "Professional services" were defined in NAFTA as services provided by persons whose right to practice necessitates specialized post-secondary education or equivalent training or experience. This definition excluded, for example, most trades-persons and vessel or aircraft crew. Since 1996, there were no citizenship or permanent residency obligations for professional service providers. Retaliatory equivalent requirements were authorized in the same professional services sector should a NAFTA nation fail to honor this rule.

Annex 1210.5 created a general duty to process applications for professional licenses and certification in a reasonable time. The applicant had to be informed of the final determination, but there was no right to challenge or appeal the outcome. Canada, Mexico and the United States agreed to develop mutually acceptable licensing and certification criteria based upon recommendations from professional bodies. Education standards, examinations, experience or training requirements, rules of professional conduct or ethics, professional development and recertification, practice scopes, local knowledge needs, and consumer protection all fell within the ambit of such recommendations. While long-term permanent licensing and certification of NAFTA professionals was the goal, temporary short-term licensing could also occur.

The first professional group under NAFTA to enjoy mutual recognition of educational, experience and exam backgrounds was engineers. In June of 1995, mutual recognition was achieved through negotiations of the Canadian Council of Professional Engineers, the Mexican Comite Mexicano para la Practica Internacional de la Ingeniera and the U.S. Council for International Engineering Practice. Both temporary and permanent licensing of engineers were subject to mutual recognition. Canada and Mexico have formally ratified the agreement. In the United States, however, licensing is subject to state law and only Texas ratified the mutual recognition pact. Mutual recognition for accountants was agreed in 2003, and for architects in 2007.

FOREIGN LEGAL CONSULTANTS

Mexico has a unified national licensing system for attorneys (Abogados). Canada licenses its attorneys (Barristers and Solicitors) on a provincial basis. The 50 states of the United States and the District of Columbia do likewise. While the traditional perception that business lawyers are not fungible is open to challenge in a regional economy, it is reasonable to conclude that the services of Canadian, Mexican and United States lawyers cannot generally be substituted.

Professor James Smith has argued that United States and Mexican legal traditions, constitutions and political systems are so "markedly different" that legal training and law practice in one country is more likely to "hinder rather than aid" in understanding each other's legal systems. See 1 U.S.-Mexico L.J. 85 (1993). Certainly, the different Civil and Common Law legal traditions and ethical rules found in Quebec, the rest of Canada (ROC), Mexico, and among the states of the United States support this conclusion. On balance the broad exclusion of legal services from NAFTA seems justified, though less so for international business attorneys.

Against this background, NAFTA sought an alternative to mutual licensing of lawyers based on their national certifications. This alternative, the licensing of "foreign legal consultants," proved agreeable. A number of U.S. states had already authorized licensing foreign legal consultants primarily in order to retain opportunities for U.S. lawyers practicing abroad, especially in France. New

York, California, Florida, Texas, Alaska, Connecticut, the District of Columbia, Georgia, Hawaii, Illinois, Michigan, New Jersey, Ohio, Oregon and Washington had done so prior to NAFTA. British Columbia, Ontario and Saskatchewan also licensed foreign legal consultants. Mexico had no experience with such licensure, but promised to do so under NAFTA for jurisdictions granting reciprocal rights to Mexican attorneys.

In Section B of Annex 1210.5, the NAFTA partners agreed to promote the licensing of foreign legal consultants. This, of course, is ultimately a decision for the states and provinces of the U.S. and Canada. It was also agreed that such consultants would be permitted to practice or give advice on the laws of their home jurisdiction. It was unclear whether this includes the right to practice "international law" as a foreign legal consultant. One could argue that since the law of NAFTA is by ratification or implementation part of the law of Canada, Mexico and the United States that foreign legal consultants should at a minimum be able to counsel on it.

The issue of just what law a foreign legal consultant can practice has split U.S. states. Alaska, California, Connecticut, Florida, Georgia and Texas only permit foreign legal consultants to advise on the law of their home jurisdictions. Nearly all the other participating states follow the Model Rule of the American Bar Association which permits practice of law except that of the licensing state and the United States.

LAND TRANSPORTATION

CUSFTA omitted land transportation from its scope. NAFTA Annex 1212 brought most cross-border bus, trucking and railroad services into the North American free trade and investment regime. Vehicles and equipment used in NAFTA cross-border transport could enter and exit on any route. Such routes had to be reasonably related to economic and prompt departure by the transport company. If different points of entry and departure were used, bonds or after ties could not be imposed. Specifically, no release from obligations or bonds imposed upon entry could be denied due to exit from another point. Furthermore, shipping containers did not need to return on the same carrier or vehicle used for entry. The bulk of all transport used in North American trade was covered in detail, but implementation of the agreement in this area proved hard to achieve.

In 1997, contrary to the NAFTA agreement, Mexico and the United States failed to establish border-free commercial trucking in contiguous states. Mexican and U.S. trucks serviced only narrow border bands in each country. This failure centered on United States perceptions of inadequate Mexican safety regulations for trucks and their personnel, and inadequate U.S. border-state enforcement capacity. Moreover, the powerful reality of Teamsters Union hostility to Mexican trucking in the United States cannot be ignored. Indeed, the Teamsters actually announced the U.S. refusal to implement the agreement in 1997 prior to the Department of Transportation.

Mexico's initial response was to exclude U.S. trailer trucks. Complete cross-border point-to-point trucking was supposed to begin in 2000. Mexico allowed minority NAFTA ownership of its cross-border trucking companies. By 2003, complete ownership in Mexican trucking companies should have been permitted.

Bus transportation also proved to be a difficult area to implement under NAFTA. Tour and charter bus operators were free to provide cross-border services after 1994. But scheduled bus services, which were due for similar treatment in 1997, fell victim to the Mexico-U.S. safety disputes. Ownership of Canadian, Mexican or United States bus companies by investors from NAFTA was expected from 2003.

By 1998, Mexico's patience and cooperative efforts were exhausted. It invoked its right to a Chapter 20 arbitration of the dispute. In 2001, the trucking dispute Chapter 20 arbitration panel ruled unanimously in Mexico's favor (USA–98–2008–01). President George W. Bush indicated that the U.S. would comply, which after regulatory and litigation delays finally did happen as a "pilot program" in 2007. Congress and the Teamsters continued with challenges in the courts and appropriations bills, which bore fruit in the Obama economic stimulus bill (H.R.1105). A provision that withdrew funding for the pilot program was buried in that 2009 law.

Mexico, its patience exhausted, retaliated (as the NAFTA agreement anticipated) by imposing tariffs on a wide range of U.S. exports and it rotated these tariffs among different goods ("carousel retaliation"). Mexican truckers also filed a $6 billion damages claim under NAFTA Chapter 11.

Late in 2010, Mexico and the U.S. reached accord on settling the trucking dispute. Mexico's compensatory tariffs on U.S. goods were removed. In 2011, the U.S. commenced a three-year pilot program allowing Mexican trucking firms that comply all U.S. regulations (safety, customs, immigration, vehicle registration and taxation) to operate anywhere in the United States. The Teamsters Union, asserting concerns with Mexican driver training and truck maintenance, attempted but failed in the courts to block this program. See *Int'l Brotherhood of Teamsters v. Dept. of Transportation*, 714 F.3d 580 (Fed. Cir. April 19, 2013).

Cross-border railway services were mostly unrestrained even prior to NAFTA. The NAFTA agreement specifically guaranteed the right to market rail services in the region. The right to operate trains inside NAFTA with the owner's locomotives was also guaranteed, as was the right to construct and own rail terminals as well as finance railroad infrastructure. The big news in the railway sector was the privatization sale of major Mexican lines to the United States investors and their partners. Nothing in NAFTA required privatization of Mexico's railways. Indeed, there was every indication that Mexico intended to preserve state ownership. Then the peso collapsed late in 1994. Railway privatization suddenly seemed a prudent way to fill state coffers in a time of need. It did not hurt that railway unions were not closely allied with Mexico's dominant political party, the PRI.

The first privatization in December 1996 was of the Northeast Railway, the most significant carrier of goods between Mexico and the United States. It went to a consortium of Kansas City Southern Industries and the shipping company Transportacion Maritima Mexicana for a remarkable $1.4 billion. The second came in mid-1997 when Union Pacific Corp. joined Empresas Ingenieros Civiles Asocidos and Grupo Industrial Minera Mexico (the majority owner) in purchasing the Pacific North Railway for $396 million. The Mexican government retained 20 percent ownership in the Pacific North Railway. Late in 1997, Mexico privatized three short lines, including a 44-mile link between Tijuana and Tecate just below the California border.

ENHANCED AND BASIC TELECOMMUNICATIONS

Chapter 13 of NAFTA created North American rules for much of the "enhanced" telecommunications industry. Enhanced or value-added telecommunications services were defined in the agreement as those employing computer processing applications that act on customer-transmitted information, provide customers with information or involve customer interaction with stored information. Such services included, for example, voice mail, cellular phone, fax, paging systems and electronic mail services. It is noteworthy that the enhanced telecommunications provisions of NAFTA were supreme if inconsistencies with any other part of the agreement arose.

The NAFTA rules on enhanced telecommunications can be summarized as follows. Domestic and international public telecommunications networks and services had to be made available on reasonable, nondiscriminatory terms and conditions. Providers of enhanced or value-added telecommunications services, information services, and internal corporate communication systems specifically benefitted from this provision. Access terms had to generally be reasonable and allow leasing private lines, attachment of equipment to public networks, switching, signaling and processing functions, and selection of operating protocols. All national licensing rules and procedures governing NAFTA telecommunications providers had to be transparent, expeditiously applied and nondiscriminatory. A review of the financial solvency and ability of providers to meet technical regulations was anticipated. Furthermore, unlike many utilities, enhanced telecommunications providers did not need to cost-justify their rates, make mandatory interconnections, nor provide services to the public. Investment by North Americans in enhanced telecommunications companies has been essentially free of restrictions since 1995.

NAFTA also set some general rules for public telecommunications networks. Transport rates, for example, were based on actual economic costs, but cross-subsidization between services was permissible. A flat-rate basis was used to price privately leased circuits. Standards for equipment attached to public networks were authorized only to prevent technical damage or interference, to prevent billing problems, or to guarantee safety. Mutual reciprocity for equipment test results undertaken in each NAFTA country was the rule and there was agreement on promoting international standards for compatibility. In this regard, the delayed arrival of Mexico's telecom standards was discussed below. Mexico's acceptance of U.S. telecommunications test data was also delayed until 1997.

Public telecommunications monopolies were not prohibited by NAFTA provided they did not engage in anticompetitive conduct regarding enhanced services. The agreement specifically prohibited cross-subsidization, predatory behavior and discriminatory access terms in the enhanced telecommunications sector. Each NAFTA government had to provide effective access to the information necessary for companies and users to benefit from NAFTA's enhanced telecommunications regime. Specifically, information on public network tariffs and contract terms, interface requirements, standards organizations, attachment conditions and licensing controls was mandatory.

Cross-border services and investment in *basic* telecommunications and public networks were *not* authorized by NAFTA. Nevertheless, the privatization of TELMEX (with a 10 percent U.S. partner) and Mexico's participation in the WTO agreement on basic telecommunications have made a difference. Mexico now allows 49 percent foreign ownership in wire services, and 100 percent ownership in cellular and private leased-line services. AT & T, MCI, SPRINT and other long-distance U.S. carriers have invested in the Mexican market, but success has proved elusive.

One key issue is what local network connection rates TELMEX can charge these carriers. This issue was first subject to intense private negotiations which failed. In 1996, the Mexican Ministry of Communications and Transport (SCT) set rates following "international norms." These rates were viewed by U.S. companies as providing TELMEX with a subsidy for its inexpensive local phone services. Likewise, they increased the incentive to invest in new telecommunications infrastructure so as to be able to avoid connecting through TELMEX entirely. The rates were reduced significantly in 1998, but not before TELMEX had turned the competitive tables by establishing very effective long-distance services in the United States targeted at Mexicans and Mexican-Americans calling "home."

In 2000, the U.S. commenced WTO dispute settlement procedures that in 2004 led to a favorable outcome. WT/DS 204/R (June 1, 2004). A WTO panel ruled that TELMEX's interconnection rates were not "cost-oriented," and exceeded the cost rate for connecting U.S. cross-border telecoms suppliers. In addition, the panel found that Mexico had failed to prevent anticompetitive practices by TELMEX, in particular market sharing. Further, Mexico had failed to provide U.S. firms access on "reasonable terms" to public telecoms transport networks and services. In 2005, the two countries settled this dispute when Mexico published new regulations allowing the commercial resale of long distance and international services in Mexico. Internal Mexican constitutional reforms adopted in 2013 targeted the TELMEX (now America Movil) monopolistic positions in landline and wireless communications.

GENERAL EXCEPTIONS

For the most part, the general exceptions to NAFTA free trade in goods also applied to trade in services. For example, all of the national security, balance of payments and cultural industries exceptions applied to services. However, the Article XX GATT exceptions did *not* apply to services.

More specifically, Chapter 21 of the NAFTA agreement reaffirmed each nation's right to restrain trade in services in order to secure compliance with health, safety and consumer protection regulations. As with goods, such regulations had to be NAFTA consistent, and could not constitute a means of arbitrary or unjustifiable discrimination, or a disguised restraint on NAFTA trade.

On taxation, the national and most-favored-nation and most-favored state or provincial treatment standards that govern services, financial services and investment applied to the purchase or consumption of services except as otherwise specified. For both goods and services, the use of performance requirements in conjunction with taxation was limited. NAFTA's rules concerning expropriation also governed services taxation.

FINANCIAL SERVICES

The NAFTA provisions on financial services differed from services generally. Cross-border provision of financial services was not fully ensured. Indeed, each partner retained existing cross-border restraints absent a specific commitment to do otherwise. Greater freedoms were allowed, however, to invest in the financial services sectors of each country, especially Mexico.

Investment and trade in financial services (including insurance and securities) were governed by Chapter 14 of NAFTA. The prior commitments made by Canada and the United States to each other under CUSFTA were retained. See Chapter 2. While the Canadians extended to Mexico the financial services commitments made to the United States under CUSFTA, the United States CUSFTA commitments were not fully extended to Mexico. For example, United States banks may not underwrite Mexican debt.

Mexico nationalized its banks in the early 1980s and then proceeded to privatize them to Mexicans (only) in the early 1990s. Foreign competition was relatively unknown in Mexico's financial services sector prior to NAFTA. Citibank, for example, stood alone in offering banking services in Mexico. Since 1994, and subsequent to capital and market share limits that have passed, Canadian and United States investors have been able to establish or purchase Mexican-chartered

A bank or securities company established in Mexico by NAFTA investors could create a holding company in order to offer most financial services. In this respect, NAFTA investors enjoy equal treatment with Mexican-owned financial firms. The range of possible services is quite wide since Mexico permits financial group holding companies to engage in banking, foreign exchange, securities, leasing, insurance, mutual fund management, factoring, bonding, warehousing and other services.

Certain limitations that apply to Mexican-owned financial institutions also apply to NAFTA investors. For example, the investor must already offer the type of financial services it seeks to establish or acquire in Mexico. All investments in Mexican financial services must be wholly-owned, except for insurance joint ventures with Mexican partners. Banks and securities firms may not be affiliated with Mexican industrial or commercial companies, although affiliations with firms operating outside Mexico are possible.

Canadian banks have been expanding south under CUSFTA and NAFTA. In the United States they operate primarily through branches, although the several do business through a U.S. banking subsidiary. Canadian banks have also moved significantly into Mexico using representative offices. United States banking, insurance and securities presence in Mexico has also been growing. Most major U.S. money center banks and securities firms, for example, have established subsidiaries in Mexico. Mergers and acquisitions have transformed Mexico's banking industry to the point where it is now largely owned by foreign firms, notably from Spain and the United States.

TREATMENT OF FINANCIAL SERVICES PROVIDERS

The NAFTA provisions on treatment of financial services providers covered a wide gamut. The leading provisions were the following: (1) Article 1403 (establishment of financial institutions); (2) Article 1404 (cross-border trade); (3) Article 1405 (national treatment); (4) Article 1406 (most-favored-nation treatment); (5) Article 1407 (new financial services and data processing); and (6) Article 1408 (senior management and boards of directors). All of these provisions were subject to various reservations and specific commitments found in Article 1409. For example, Article 1409 grandfathered certain pre-existing national financial services regulations ("non-conforming measures").

First-time NAFTA financial services investors ordinarily had to be given entry. They could, however, be obliged to incorporate and be regulated locally. Purchasers of financial services could obtain services when they crossed borders as visitors, and providers could solicit their business without a license to do business locally.

A general rule of national treatment governed the provision of financial services. This rule extended to existing and new investors as well as cross-border

NAFTA providers. Establishing, acquiring, expanding, managing, conducting, operating, selling or otherwise disposing of financial institutions and investments were embraced within the scope of the general rule of national treatment. State and provincial governments had to grant home state treatment, in like circumstances, to NAFTA investors in financial institutions.

NAFTA governments were required to provide "equal competitive opportunities" for financial services providers. (Article 1405.5) Specifically, NAFTA financial institutions could not be disadvantaged in their ability to provide services in competition under like circumstances with local financial institutions. For these purposes, differences in market share, profitability or size did not alone establish a denial of equal competitive opportunities. However, such differences could represent evidence of such a denial.

Article 1406 of NAFTA established a general most-favored-nation treatment obligation. However, if a NAFTA partner recognized the "prudential" (public interest licensing and control) regulations of a non-NAFTA country, most-favored-nation treatment was not automatic. An opportunity to demonstrate equivalent prudential regulations or to negotiate a comparable arrangement was all that NAFTA required. The NAFTA nations did promise to work towards uniform prudential regulations for financial institutions.

Since uniformity is often absent and mutual recognition was not agreeable, each NAFTA nation could adopt its own set of "reasonable" prudential regulations governing protection of investors, depositors, market participants, policy holders, fiduciary beneficiaries and the like. Maintaining the soundness and integrity of financial institutions and each country's financial system was also an authorized basis for prudential regulation, as was control of monetary transfers between parties related or affiliated to financial institutions or service providers. Nondiscriminatory public regulation in pursuit of monetary, credit or exchange rate policies was also allowed.

NAFTA financial institutions had to be permitted to offer, in like circumstances, any *new* financial services or products similar to those of domestic institutions. Prior authorization of such new services could be required. Electronic transfer of data required by NAFTA financial institutions operating across borders was protected. Member states could not mandate senior managers and other essential personnel of a particular nationality, but could stipulate that a simple majority (but not more) of the board of directors of NAFTA financial institutions be composed of its nationals or residents. This latter stipulation could be imposed even if it impaired the NAFTA investor's ability to control its investment.

Securing the benefits of NAFTA on financial services typically involved applying for national authorizations. Such applicants received procedural protections under Article 1411. NAFTA governments had to clarify their application requirements and keep applicants informed regarding the status of their applications. Perhaps most significantly, the authorities were required "whenever possible" to reach a decision on "completed" applications within 120 days. Applications were not complete until all relevant hearings were held and all necessary information received.

Some cross-border provision of financial services was rather ambiguously subject to rights "in principle." These ambiguities reflected fundamental differences found in Canadian, Mexican and United States regulation of financial services that were unresolved when NAFTA came into force. For example, financial service-providers establishing a commercial presence in any NAFTA nation should "in principle" have been allowed to choose the form of their investment. In banking, however, Canada and Mexico required foreign banks to establish local subsidiaries not branches (which are thought to be harder to regulate than subsidiaries). The United States generally permits either.

Providing a full range of financial services through separate institutions, expanding geographically, and nondiscriminatory ownership of local financial institutions were also NAFTA "principles." The first of these principles clearly reflected prior U.S. banking law restraints on dealing in securities under the Glass-Steagall Act of 1933. Mexico and Canada generally follow the "universal banking" model which permits financial institutions to engage in banking, trust and loan, insurance and securities services. The second principle was aimed at United States interstate banking restraints that were largely removed under the Interstate Banking and Branching Efficiency Act of 1994. The third principle demonstrated disappointment with historical Mexican restraints on foreign ownership of banks and Canadian requirements for foreign bank subsidiaries.

FINANCIAL SERVICES DISPUTE SETTLEMENT

The NAFTA Financial Services Committee was in charge of Chapter 14. This Committee included representatives from the Canadian Department of Finance, the Mexican Secretaria de Hacienda y Credito Publico and the U.S. Treasury Department. On insurance matters, however, the Department of Commerce represented the United States.

The NAFTA Financial Services Committee reviewed any issue referred to it by a NAFTA government. Such intergovernmental disputes were preceded by member state consultations. If a dispute was not resolved by consultation or Committee review, Chapter 20 NAFTA dispute settlement procedures (below) could be invoked. The only variations were that the Chapter 20 panelists be experts in financial services, and the normal Chapter 20 remedies could be limited.

The Financial Services Committee could also review certain private investment disputes concerning financial services, so-called investor-state disputes (below). This occurs when a member state claims exclusion from arbitration of the dispute on the basis of Article 1410 (prudential regulation, national monetary policy). In such a case, the arbitration tribunal set up under NAFTA Chapter 11 referred the exclusion issue for resolution by the Financial Services Committee.

The Committee then decided whether Article 1410 provided a valid defense to the investor's claim and its decision was final and binding. If for any reason the Committee failed to render its decision within 60 days, the arbitration tribunal generally could rule on the exclusion issue. However, if a member state requested a dispute settlement panel under Chapter 20, then this panel decided the issue.

No particularly prominent financial services disputes emerged under NAFTA.

NAFTA BUSINESS VISAS

Preferential visa treatment for business visitors, traders, investors, intra-company transferees, and certain professionals was established by NAFTA. Only Canadian, Mexican and United States citizens could benefit from these nonimmigrant entry rights. Spouses who accompanied NAFTA visa entrants could not work without individual permission. Many of the beneficiaries were service providers or investors, however, NAFTA's temporary entry rules were not limited to services.

NAFTA permitted temporary duty-free entry of certain goods accompanying business persons crossing borders on NAFTA visas. Such persons could bring with them professional equipment, press or television broadcasting and film equipment, sports goods, commercial samples, advertising films, and display or demonstration goods. These "tools of trade" were temporarily admitted on a duty-free basis. Their origin and the existence or nonexistence of domestically produced competitive or substitutable items were irrelevant to exercise of this right.

However, customs duty bonds for non-originating goods, return responsibilities, and prohibitions against soliciting, selling or leasing such goods or equipment could apply. Failure to adhere to any of these conditions resulted in payment of the relevant tariff. Commercial solicitation samples of negligible value and printed packets of advertising materials entered duty free regardless of their origin and could remain in the country of entry.

NAFTA dispute settlement under Chapter 20 (below) regarding entry rules could be triggered only when a pattern of practice was found and all available national administrative remedies exhausted. There was a tumultuous dispute over the legality under NAFTA of the 1996 Helms-Burton LIBERTAD Act (110 Stat. 785) restraints on entry into the United States of persons who traffic in Cuban confiscated goods.

The United States maintained that such restraints were exempt as national security measures. Canada and Mexico argued that they directly contravene the temporary entry rights enshrined in Chapter 16 of NAFTA 1994. They lodged a complaint under Chapter 20, which has not gone to arbitration only because Presidents Clinton, George W. Bush, Obama and Trump repeatedly suspended application of Helms-Burton.

BUSINESS VISITORS

NAFTA increased the number of Canadian, Mexican and United States citizens able to obtain temporary entry visas. NAFTA also increased the types of permissible activities of business visitors. For example, temporary entry visas were available for purposes of research and design, purchasing, production, marketing, sales, distribution and after-sales service. Such visas could also be had by persons providing general services, including credentialed professionals, managers, supervisors, financial services personnel, public relations officers, advertising staff, tourist leaders, tour bus operator and translators. One of the requirements for temporary business visitor visas was non-remuneration in the country of entry. For this reason, there were no pre-entry employment validation or labor certification screening procedures in connection with NAFTA business visitor visas (B–1 visas in the United States).

Numerical limits on the number of NAFTA business visitors were banned. However, entry could be barred for reasons of public safety or national security. Normally, business visitors needed only prove citizenship, document their scheduled NAFTA business activities, and offer evidence that they are not seeking to enter the local labor market. Oral declaration at the border as to source of remuneration, principal place of business, and predominant outside accrual of profits were usually sufficient to meet these criteria.

The administration of business visitor visas differed among the member states. Canadian business visitors could cross United States borders without advance visas. United States business visitors to Canada could do likewise. Mexicans, however, must obtain advance business visitor visa approvals to enter Canada and the United States. Similarly, Canadian and United States business visitors must get visas in advance of going to Mexico.

TRADERS AND INVESTORS

NAFTA traders and investors also enjoyed preferential temporary entry visas. "Traders" were defined as persons employed to carry on substantial trade in goods or services principally between NAFTA countries. "Investors" were defined person employed to establish, develop, administer or provide advice or key technical services to the operation of an investment to which a substantial amount of capital has been or is in the process of being committed. For both categories, preferential NAFTA treatment was available only if the person concerned acted in a capacity that was supervisory, executive or involved essential skills. In practice, these provisions chiefly benefited Canadians and Mexicans entering the United States. NAFTA gave treaty trader and investor status to Mexicans for the first time.

Standard public safety and national security exceptions applied to NAFTA traders and investors. Pre-entry labor certification screening was not necessary, and there were no numerical limits to these temporary entry visas (E–1 and E–2 visas in the United States). However, by special provision, such visas could be denied if settlement of a current labor dispute or employment of persons involved in the dispute would be adversely affected.

INTRA-COMPANY TRANSFEREES

NAFTA further benefitted executives, managers or employees with specialized knowledge rendering services to their employer, its subsidiary or affiliate in another NAFTA country. Such persons could obtain special "intra-company transferee" temporary entry visas. Public safety, national security and labor dispute reviews applied. There were no pre-entry labor certification screens, nor any numerical limits to intra-company transferee visas. In the United States these are known as L–1 visas. The United States, but not Canada and Mexico, required proof of employment for the same or a related employer during one of the three prior years.

PROFESSIONALS

Credentialed professional employees (not self-employed professionals), including economists, management consultants and lawyers, were also beneficiaries of NAFTA's preferential visa regime. Temporary entry was available only to members of professions listed in Appendix 1603.D.1 to Annex 1603. Standard public safety, national security and labor dispute reviews applied. As between Canada and the United States, no pre-entry labor screens were used. But such screens did apply to Mexican professionals entering the United States.

There are no United States limits for Canadians on temporary entry professional employee visas (so-called TN visas). The United States initially restricted to 5,500 annually the number of such visas available to Mexican professionals. In no year was the Mexican quota filled. The United States eliminated this quota in 2003. Canada and Mexico had the option of imposing comparable limits on U.S. professional employee entrants, but elected not to do so.

Proof by Canadians at time of entry into the United States of citizenship, educational credentials (and licensing if necessary), and a professional job offer sufficed to obtain a TN visa. United States professionals seeking entry to Canada could just as easily do the same. Hundreds of thousands of Canadian professionals entered and remain (by renewal of their TN visas) in the United States in this manner. Mexicans had to apply in advance for TN visa status. Because TN visas are harder to use as a springboard for permanent resident alien status (a "Green Card"), which in turn can lead to naturalization as a U.S. citizen, Mexican professionals have demonstrably preferred H–1B visas (a traditional category not related to NAFTA) which can relatively easily lead to green cards and ultimately citizenship.

With limited exceptions in the U.S.-Chile, U.S.-Australia, and U.S.-Singapore FTAs, post-NAFTA U.S. free trade agreements do *not* create business visas. The USMCA largely replicates the NAFTA business visitor visas.

NAFTA: FOREIGN INVESTMENT

The cross-border investment rules established in 1989 by Canada and the United States were reviewed in Chapter 2. NAFTA expanded upon these rules with special emphasis on relaxation of Mexico's foreign investment controls. These controls find their roots in the revolutionary 1917 Mexican Constitution, the Mexican nationalization of foreign oil and gas interests in 1937, and the widespread adoption of foreign investment control commissions throughout Latin America during the 1970s.

In 1973, Mexico promulgated an Investment Law that allowed use of joint ventures if approved by the National Foreign Investment Commission. This Law was the most restrictive of its kind in Mexican history. By the 1980s, after years of mismanagement and corruption while awash in petro dollars, Mexico had a massive national debt problem. Foreign investment regulations issued by Presidential decree in 1989 shifted significantly towards allowance of wholly-owned subsidiaries. However, these regulations conflicted with the 1973 Investment Law. These uncertainties were finally resolved in 1993 as a direct consequence of NAFTA when Mexico adopted a new Law on Foreign Investment.

The 1993 Law is much more permissive of foreign investment without prior approval of by the Mexican Investment Commission. Although adopted on the eve of NAFTA, the 1993 Law opens many of the same doors to all investors, not just those from North America. Investment opportunities based upon the NAFTA 1994 agreement that are not generally available include the suspension of many performance requirements, the phased removal of market share caps on financial services, and reduced thresholds triggering Investment Commission review.

Acquisitions or sales of existing Mexican companies were initially subject to Commission review if they exceeded $25 million U.S. This threshold increased to $150 million U.S. for NAFTA investors in 2003. For NAFTA investors, no permission from the National Commission was required to invest on a wholly-owned basis or acquire or sell Mexican companies whose values fell below this threshold.

NAFTA INVESTOR RIGHTS

In an unusual provision, Article 1112 subordinated all of Chapter 11 on investment to the rest of the NAFTA agreement. In other words, if there were inconsistencies between Chapter 11 and other parts of the NAFTA, those other parts were supreme. That said, NAFTA provided investors and their investments with a number of important rights.

Canadian, Mexican and United States citizens, permanently resident aliens, and other designated persons were eligible to benefit from NAFTA's investment rules. In addition, most private and public, profit and nonprofit businesses "constituted or organized" under Canadian, Mexican or United States law also qualified. This coverage specifically included businesses operating as corporations, partnerships, trusts, sole proprietorships, joint ventures and business associations.

Furthermore, in a notable change from CUSFTA, it was not necessary for such businesses to be owned or controlled by Canadian, Mexican or U.S. nationals or enterprises. **As with services, this meant that businesses owned by anyone which were "constituted or organized" inside NAFTA benefitted from the agreement *provided* they carried on substantial business activities in North America.** Thus Asians, Europeans and Latin Americans (for example) could invest in North America and benefit from NAFTA investment law. Exceptions were made for NAFTA businesses owned or controlled by third parties from countries lacking diplomatic relations with, or economically embargoed by Canada, Mexico or the United States.

Beneficiaries of NAFTA rights enjoyed a broad definition of "investment." This definition included most stocks, bonds, loans, and income, profit or asset interests. Real estate, tangible or intangible (intellectual) business property, turnkey or construction contracts, concessions, and licensing and franchising contracts were also generally included (Article 1139). However, under Annex III, each member state reserved certain economic activities to its state or domestic investors. Mexico did so under its 1993 Foreign Investment Law. For purposes of Chapter 11, investment was defined so as to exclude claims to money arising solely from commercial contracts for the sale of goods or services, or trade financing, and claims for money that did not involve the interests noted above.

TREATMENT OF FOREIGN INVESTORS AND INVESTMENTS

NAFTA established a so-called "minimum standard of treatment" for NAFTA investors and investments: "treatment in accordance with international law," including "fair and equitable treatment and full protection and security" (Article 1105). For example, if losses resulted due to armed conflict or civil strife, NAFTA investors and investments had to be accorded nondiscriminatory treatment in response. An official NAFTA interpretative ruling indicates that Article 1105 embraces treatment in accordance with "customary" international law, a ruling intended to limit the scope of protection afforded to foreign investors. Customary international law is said to result from "a general and consistent practice of States that they follow from a sense of legal obligation". In addition, limiting definitions of "fair and equitable treatment" and "full protection and security" were established.

Beyond this minimum, NAFTA investors and their investments were entitled to the better of national or most-favored-nation treatment from federal governments. Such treatment rights extended to establishing, acquiring, expanding, managing, conducting, operating, and selling or disposing of investments. From state or provincial governments, NAFTA investors and their investments were entitled to receive the most-favored treatment those governments granted their own investors and investments. Along these lines, United Parcel Service found Mexico lacking when it was initially limited to using smaller vans than Mexican competitors. UPS persuaded the United States to lodge a complaint under Chapter 20 (below), which led to intergovernmental consultations followed by NAFTA Commission mediation. These efforts lasted many months but eventually UPS got permission to use smaller vans.

Article 1102 of NAFTA prohibited requiring minimum levels of equity holdings by nationals of the host government. Hence the historic bias in Mexican law towards mandatory joint ventures was overcome. No NAFTA investor could be forced on grounds of nationality to sell or dispose of a qualified investment. Mandatory appointment of senior managers on the basis of nationality was prohibited. However, it was permissible to require boards of directors and corporate committees with majorities from one nationality or residence, provided this did not materially impair the investor's ability to exercise control. Canadian law often made such stipulations. Residency requirements were generally authorized if there was no impairment of the treaty rights of NAFTA investors.

Article 1106 of NAFTA bars various investment performance obligations, including tax-related measures, in a scope that surpasses the WTO Agreement on Trade-Related Investment Measures (TRIMs) (1995). Requirements relating to exports, domestic content, domestic purchases, trade balancing of foreign exchange inflows or earnings, import/export ratios, technology transfers, and regional or global sales exclusivity ("product mandates") were broadly prohibited. All other types of investment-related performance requirements, such as employment and research and development obligations, were not prohibited and therefore presumably lawful.

Article 1106.3 of NAFTA further prohibits conditioning the receipt or continued receipt of "an advantage" (e.g., a government subsidy or tax benefit) on compliance with requirements relating to domestic content, domestic purchases, domestic sales restraints or trade balancing. But "advantages" could be given when the requirements concerned production location, provision of services, training or employing workers, constructing or expanding facilities, or carrying out research and development locally. By way of exception, domestic content or purchase requirements *and* advantages could be linked to investor compliance with: (1) Laws and regulations that were consistent with NAFTA; (2) laws necessary to protect human, animal or plant life or health; or (3) laws needed to conserve living or non-living exhaustible natural resources. However, such requirements could be applied arbitrarily or unjustifiably, and could not constitute a disguised restraint on trade or investment.

All monetary transfers relating to NAFTA investments were to be allowed "freely and without delay." (Article 1109) Such transfers had to be possible in a "freely usable currency" at the market rate of exchange prevailing in spot transactions on the transfer date. For these purposes, monetary transfers specifically included profits, dividends, interest, capital gains, royalties, management, technical assistance and other fees, returns in kind, and funds derived from the investment. Sale or liquidation proceeds, contract payments, compensatory payments for expropriation and NAFTA dispute settlement payments were also encompassed.

Requiring investment-related monetary transfers or penalizing them was prohibited. However, such transfers could be controlled in an equitable, nondiscriminatory and good faith application of bankruptcy, insolvency, creditors' rights, securities, criminal, currency reporting and satisfaction of judgment laws. Whereas tax withholding was a justifiable basis for restricting monetary transfers under CUSFTA, this was not the case under NAFTA. Special restraints could arise in connection with balance of payments problems and taxation laws.

EXPROPRIATION

Article 1110 of NAFTA generally prohibited direct or indirect nationalization or expropriation of NAFTA investments. Measures "tantamount to" nationalization or expropriation, such as creeping expropriation or confiscatory taxation, were also prohibited. Expropriation, nationalization or tantamount measures could occur for public purposes on a nondiscriminatory basis in accordance with due process of law and NAFTA's "minimum level of treatment" (above).

Any authorized expropriation had to result in payment of compensation without delay. The amount of payment had to be equivalent to the fair market value of the investment immediately prior to expropriation. In valuing the investment, going concern value, asset value (including declared tax values of tangible property) and other appropriate factors were considered. Payment was required to be made in a manner that was fully realizable, such as in a "G7" currency (U.S. dollars, Canadian dollars, EUROS, British pounds sterling, Japanese yen). Interest at a commercially reasonable rate had also to be included. If payment was made in Mexican pesos, this amount was calculated as of the expropriation date in a G7 currency, plus interest.

Certain governmental acts were not treated as expropriations. For example, NAFTA specified that nondiscriminatory measures of general application that imposed costs on defaulting debtors were not tantamount to expropriation of a bond or loan *solely* for that reason. Compulsory licensing of intellectual property rights was not an expropriation. Revocation, limitation or creation of such rights as allowed by Chapter 17 of NAFTA was also deemed not an expropriation.

These provisions embodied an historic change in Mexico's position on expropriation law. Without explicitly saying so, Mexico essentially embraced the U.S. position that under "international law" expropriation of foreign investments requires "prompt, adequate and effective" compensation. Mexico had specifically rejected this standard in negotiating a settlement of its oil and gas (and land) expropriations in the 1930s. Down through the years Mexico adamantly clung to its view that compensation would only be paid according to Mexican law. For investors protected under NAFTA (which are not just Canadian and U.S. investors), Chapter 11 represented the dawn of a new era.

FOREIGN INVESTMENT LAW EXCEPTIONS AND RESERVATIONS

Annexes I–IV of NAFTA reveal a host of investment-related reservations and exceptions. Many pre-existing, non-conforming regulations were grandfathered though most (not including basic telecommunications, social services and maritime services) were subject to a standstill agreement intended to avoid relapses into greater protection. In contrast, regulations promoting investment "sensitive to environmental concerns" were expressly authorized. Mexico's tradition of assessing the environmental impact of foreign investments therefore continued. There was also a formal recognition that creating exceptions to environmental laws to encourage NAFTA investors to establish, acquire, expand or retain their investments was inappropriate. However, NAFTA's Chapter 20 dispute settlement mechanism could not be invoked concerning this "commitment." Only intergovernmental consultations were mandatory.

Other investment-related exceptions concerned government procurement, subsidies, export promotion, foreign aid and preferential trade arrangements. These exceptions applied mostly to the rules on nondiscriminatory treatment and performance requirements. Most general exceptions to NAFTA, such as for Canadian cultural industries (see Chapter 2), also applied to its investment rules. The general national security exception, for example, allowed the United States to block the acquisition of U.S. companies by foreigners (including Canadians and Mexicans) under "Exon-Florio" regulations (50 U.S.C. App. § 2170).

ARBITRATION OF FOREIGN INVESTOR-STATE DISPUTES

NAFTA created an innovative and controversial investment dispute settlement system, one that was notably revised under the USMCA. See Chapter 6. This system provided a way for foreign investors to challenge governmental and state enterprise acts and recover damages for violation of rights established in Chapter 11. Remarkably, investors could not only assert claims as individuals, but also on behalf of NAFTA enterprises they own or control directly or indirectly (Article 1117).

"Investor-state disputes" were subject to binding arbitration for damages. This amounted to another major concession on the part of Mexico, which had always adhered to the "Calvo Doctrine." That doctrine (widely followed in Latin America) requires foreign investors to forego protection by their home governments, be treated as Mexican nationals, and pursue legal remedies exclusively in Mexico. See Article 27 of the Mexican Constitution.

Individual investors claiming that a government breached NAFTA investment or state enterprise obligations, or that one of its monopolies did so, commenced the dispute resolution process. All claims were filed against the federal government even when it was state, provincial or local government action that was being challenged. This placed Canada, Mexico and the United States in the awkward position of defending sub-central governmental acts. See *Metalclad* and *Loewen* below.

The investor had to allege that the breach of NAFTA caused loss or damage. Such claims needed to be asserted no later than three years after the date when knowledge of the alleged breach and knowledge of the loss or damage was first acquired or should have been first acquired. However, decisions by the Canadian or Mexican foreign investment control commissions, national security actions, and Canadian cultural industry reservations could not be the basis for such a claim. Moreover, a host of reservations and exceptions contained in Chapter 11B denied access to NAFTA's investor-state arbitration remedy. Even so, as outlined below, the number of claims filed was significant, some claims produced unexpected results, and the process itself fell under dispute.

Before submitting a claim to arbitration, individual investors had to give 90 days' advance notice to the host country. Such notice had to include an explanation of the issues, their factual basis and remedies sought. Claimants also consented in writing to arbitrate under the procedures established in the NAFTA agreement. They had to *waive* in writing their rights to initiate or continue any other damages proceedings. See *Commerce Group Corp. v. El Salvador* (ICSID, 2011) (CAFTA-DR tribunal dismisses complaint due to pending litigation). Individual investors did not need, however, to waive their rights to injunctive, declaratory or other extraordinary relief not involving damages. These remedies could not be awarded through NAFTA arbitration of investor-state disputes.

ARBITRATION PROCEDURES, APPEALS AND REMEDIES

The NAFTA nations consented unconditionally in advance to the submission of investor claims to arbitration under NAFTA procedures. Furthermore, they agreed not to assert insurance payments or other investor indemnification rights as a defense, counterclaim, right of setoff or otherwise.

The investor submitting a claim to arbitration against a NAFTA state ordinarily could elect between the following arbitration rules:

- The ICSID Convention* if both member states adhered. (Canada and the United States have ratified ICSID);

---

* The Convention on the Settlement of Investment Disputes between States and Nationals of Other States (1966). The

- The Additional Facility Rules of ICSID, provided one member-state (i.e., the United States or Canada) adhered to the ICSID Convention; or

- The U.N.-derived UNCITRAL Arbitration Rules.

NAFTA investor-state tribunals had three panelists. The investor and the state each chose one arbitrator. If possible, the third presiding panelist was chosen by agreement. The ICSID Secretary-General selected the presiding arbitrator if agreement was not reached within 90 days. That person was chosen from a consensus roster of acceptable names, but could not be a national from either side of the dispute.

Investor-state tribunals decided the dispute in accordance with the NAFTA agreement and "applicable rules of international law." The responding state could raise defenses based upon reservations or exceptions contained in Annexes I–IV to NAFTA. In such instances, the NAFTA Commission (not the arbitration panel) generally issued a binding ruling on the validity of such a defense. Defenses based upon permissible regulation of monetary transfers by financial institutions were normally decided by the NAFTA Financial Services Committee.

By agreement of the parties, the investor-state arbitration tribunal could obtain expert reports on

---

Convention is administered through the World Bank in Washington, D.C. and has been ratified by over 150 nations.

factual issues concerning environmental, health, safety or other scientific matters. The tribunal could also order temporary relief measures to preserve rights or the full effectiveness of its jurisdiction. It could, for example, order the preservation of evidence. The tribunal could not, however, order attachment or enjoin governmental regulations being challenged.

NAFTA investor-state tribunals were authorized to award investors or NAFTA enterprises actual *damages* and interest, or restitution of property, or both. Damages were awarded against and paid by Canada and Mexico, but *not* the United States. If the award was to an enterprise, any person could *also* pursue relief under "applicable domestic law." If restitution was ordered, the responsible member state could provide monetary damages and interest instead. NAFTA tribunals could apportion legal fees between the parties at their discretion. Such fees routinely ran into hundreds of thousands, if not millions, of dollars. The costs of administering Chapter 11 tribunals, including generous fees for the arbitrators, often exceeded $500,000. The losing party is typically required to pay these costs.

The award of the Chapter 11 tribunal was binding on the parties, but subject to revision or annulment in the courts of the arbitration's situs. Absent agreement, the arbitrators determined situs. Chapter 11 awards were specifically not "precedent" in future NAFTA arbitrations (Article 1136), yet routinely cited and argued in Chapter 11 proceedings and decisions. NAFTA investor-state arbitration awards were supposed to be honored. If this did not occur, the investor could seek enforcement of the award. NAFTA nations agreed to provide the means for such enforcement.

The NAFTA investor-state dispute settlement system met the various requirements of the ICSID Convention, its Additional Facility Rules, the New York Convention on Recognition and Enforcement of Foreign Arbitral Awards (1958), and the Inter-American Convention on International Commercial Arbitration (1975). Should it become necessary to judicially enforce an investor-state arbitration award, the New York Convention provided a likely recourse as all three nations adhere to it. See *In re Arbitration between Thunderbird Gaming Corp. v. United Mexican States*, 473 F.Supp.2d 80 (D.C. 2007) *aff'd* 255 Fed. Appx 531 (Fed. Cir. 2008).

If there was no compliance with the award and enforcement proceedings failed, the investor's government could as a last recourse commence intergovernmental dispute settlement under Chapter 20 of NAFTA (below). This panel ruled on whether noncompliance inconsistent with the NAFTA agreement had occurred and could recommend compliance. If compliance still was not made, benefits granted under NAFTA to the noncomplying nation could be suspended.

FOREIGN INVESTOR CLAIMS AGAINST STATES UNDER NAFTA

Investors did not hesitate to invoke the innovative investor-state arbitration procedures authorized under Section B of Chapter 11 of NAFTA. In an official Interpretation, Chapter 11 was construed as not imposing a general duty of confidentiality. The NAFTA governments have therefore released documents submitted to or issued by Chapter 11 arbitration tribunals. A particularly good collection of these materials can be found at www.naftaclaims. com. Moreover, after late 2003 open Chapter 11 hearings became the rule, as did permissive procedures for non-party submissions (amicus curiae).

Many investors alleged state action that is "tantamount to expropriation." This is a claim that Article 1110 authorized and one which could be construed to fit many fact patterns. National treatment and the NAFTA minimum standard of treatment (see above) were also commonly disputed. Some examples of these disputes follow.

Metalclad v. Mexico. A prominent dispute involved Metalclad Corp. of California, which had acquired a hazardous waste site operated by a Mexican company in Guadalcazar, San Luis Potosi subject to various federal approvals, all of which were obtained. State and local opposition to opening the site after an expensive clean-up resulted in the denial of a building permit in a newly created "ecological zone." Metalclad claimed these acts were tantamount to expropriation, and denial of national and the NAFTA minimum standards of treatment. It sought $90 million in damages from the Mexican federal government, which despite having supported the Metalclad contract was obliged to defend the hostile local and state actions. Metalclad received an award of $16 million under NAFTA Chapter 11 in 2000. The arbitration was conducted under the ICSID Additional Facility rules.

Mexico instituted judicial proceedings to set aside the award in British Columbia, the arbitration's legal *situs*. Canada intervened in support of Mexico. The arbitrators had found the Mexican regulatory action a breach of NAFTA's minimum standard based on a lack of "transparency," and tantamount to expropriation without adequate compensation. The British Columbia Supreme Court, ruling under the B.C. International Arbitration Act, agreed that the expropriation decision fell within the scope of the dispute submitted and was therefore valid. It rejected, however, the transparency decision as beyond the scope of the submission. The court found no transparency obligations in Chapter 11, and none as a matter of *customary* international law (which traditionally bars only "egregious," "outrageous" or "shocking" conduct).

Mexico subsequently paid Metalclad approximately $16 million U.S., the first payment by a state to an investor under Chapter 11.

Ethyl v. Canada and *Methanex v. United States.* A second prominent dispute involved Ethyl Corp. of the USA, which claimed $250 million U.S. damages against the Canadian government as a consequence of 1997 federal legislation banning importation or interprovincial trade of the gasoline additive, MMT. Canada was the first country to ban MMT as a pollution and health hazard, although California has also done so. MMT is a manganese-based octane enhancer alleged to interfere with the proper functioning of catalytic converters. Ethyl Corp. is the sole producer of MMT in North America. Ethyl claimed that the new law was tantamount to expropriation, violated NAFTA's national treatment standards and constituted an unlawful Canadian-content performance requirement (because the ban would favor Canadian ethanol as a substitute for MMT).

A dispute resolution panel under Canada's Agreement on Internal Trade struck down the interprovincial trade ban. In 1998, Canada withdrew its ban on MMT and paid $13 million to Ethyl Corp. Ethyl then withdrew its $250 million arbitration claim. Canada noted the current lack of scientific evidence documenting MMT harm, an apparent abandonment of the "precautionary principle." Environmentalists decried evidence of NAFTA's negative impact, and Europeans cited *Ethyl* as good reason to reject multilateral investment guarantee agreements in the OECD (Organization for Economic Cooperation and Development). Both groups believed Chapter 11 created a privileged class of "super-citizens" who are a threat to state sovereignty.

Methanex Corp. of Canada submitted a claim that was in some ways the reverse of *Ethyl*. Methanex claimed that California's ban of the MTBE gasoline additive (for which it makes feedstock) amounted to an expropriation of its business interests and violated its minimum treatment rights. It sought $970 million in damages and simultaneously filed a petition under the North American Environmental Cooperation Agreement asserting that California failed to enforce its gasoline storage regulations, which Methanex saw as the source of MTBE water pollution.

In 2002, the *Methenex* panel working under the UNCITRAL Rules largely rejected the complaint on jurisdictional grounds, allowing a limited re-filing on the question of intentional injury. The *Methanex* panel notably ruled that it would accept NGO amicus briefs, in this instance from the International Institute for Sustainable Development. This position was subsequently ratified for all Chapter 11 arbitrations by the NAFTA Free Trade Commission in 2003.

Loewen v. United States. The Loewen Group of Canada was held liable by a jury in 1995 to $500 million in a Mississippi breach of a funeral home contract suit. The case was settled for $150 million after the Mississippi Supreme Court required posting a $625 million bond prior to appealing the jury's verdict, a sum in excess of Loewen's net worth. In 1998, Loewen filed a claim under NAFTA alleging discrimination, denial of the minimum NAFTA standard of treatment, and uncompensated expropriation. This claim, like that of Ethyl Corp., was destined for controversy. Among other things, it challenged the discretion of American juries in awarding punitive damages. Note that it did so in a forum that did not give the American Trial Lawyers Association an opportunity to respond.

In 2003, the *Loewen* panel, calling the Mississippi decision "a disgrace," nevertheless ruled heavily against the bankrupt funeral home giant because its status as a Canadian (versus U.S.) company entitled to NAFTA investor rights was in doubt.

Pope & Talbot v. Canada. Pope and Talbot, Inc. of Portland, Oregon claimed that the 1996 Softwood Lumber Agreement (see Chapter 2) violated the national treatment, most-favored-nation treatment, minimum treatment and performance requirements rules of NAFTA. The claim asserted that the company's British Columbia subsidiary was the victim of discrimination in that the Canadian export restraints required under that Agreement applied only to four Canadian provinces. Pope & Talbot sought $20 million in compensation from the Canadian government. Rejecting most of the claims, the *Pope & Talbot* panel found Canada did violate the NAFTA minimum standard of treatment in denying export authorization to the company's B.C. subsidiary.

Although the award was only about $460,000 U.S., the panel's reasoning set off fireworks. In its view, Article 1105 demanded something more than the level of treatment commanded by customary international law. "Fair and equitable treatment" and "full protection and security" were seen as "additive;" new and expansive norms created by NAFTA's novel investor protection regime.

The additive reading of *Pope & Talbot* was subsequently rejected by the British Columbia Supreme Court in *Metalclad* (above), and collectively negated by a binding interpretation of Article 1105 issued by the three NAFTA parties in 2001. This controversial, defensive interpretation "clarifies" that Article 1105 corresponds to and thus does not expand the *customary* international law standard of minimum treatment (see *Metalclad* above), and that a breach of a NAFTA obligation does not ipso facto constitute a breach of that Article.

S.D. Myers v. Canada. S.D. Myers is an Ohio company specializing in hazardous waste management of PCBs. Its Canadian affiliate imported PCBs from Ontario, to the consternation of the only Canadian PCB remediation company, Chem-Security of Alberta. In 1995, Canada banned PCB exports, intentionally giving Chem-Security a monopoly. S.D. Myers asserted this export ban violated the national treatment, performance requirements, expropriation and fair and equitable treatment provisions of Chapter 11.

The arbitrators found in favor of S.D. Myers on the national treatment and fair and equitable treatment claims, awarding over $6,000,000 CDN in damages. Canada appealed to the courts of Ontario, the situs of the arbitration, and lost. In Ontario, at least, considerable deference is given to arbitral decisions. Compare British Columbia in *Metalclad* (above). Subsequently, S. D. Myers and Canada settled the dispute.

Mondev v. United States. Mondev is a Canadian company engaged in commercial real estate development. It pursued various claims against the City of Boston and the Boston Redevelopment

Authority in the Massachusetts courts, which were denied on sovereign immunity grounds. Mondev then filed a Chapter 11 claim arguing primarily unfair and inequitable treatment in the Massachusetts courts. In its complaint, Mondev directly challenged the 2001 Interpretation of Article 1105, arguing it was de facto an amendment of the NAFTA agreement. Mondev also argued that customary international law should be construed in light of conclusions reached under hundreds of bilateral investment treaties and modern judgments.

The tribunal recognized that fair and equitable treatment had evolved by 1994 (NAFTA's effective date) beyond what is "egregious" or "outrageous," and that bad faith on the part of states need not be shown. It then ruled against Mondev's denial of justice claims.

Glamis v. United States. Glamis, a Canadian mining company, alleged that government regulations limiting the impact of open-pit mining and protecting indigenous peoples' religious sites made its *proposed* California gold mine unprofitable. Under Chapter 11, it asserted violations of the NAFTA rules against government acts tantamount to expropriation, and denial of fair and equitable treatment. In June of 2009, a Chapter 11 tribunal accepted, in principle, that "regulatory taking" measures could amount to "creeping expropriation."

That said, the tribunal undertook a detailed accounting of Glamis' alleged losses and found the mine project still had a net positive value of $20 million U.S. Hence it concluded Glamis was not impacted sufficiently to support a NAFTA expropriation claim. While the outcome once again allowed the United States to avoid paying Chapter 11 damages, the willingness of the tribunal to entertain a regulatory taking claim was controversial (to put it mildly) and once again raised concerns that foreign investors may have greater rights under NAFTA than U.S. investors possess under United States law.

Chemtura v. Canada. Crompton (Chemtura) Corp. of the USA filed a "tantamount to expropriation" Chapter 11 complaint against Canada after it banned lindane-based pesticides. The arbitral tribunal, in 2010, unanimously noted that this ban had been undertaken in a non-discriminatory manner motivated by human health and environmental concerns. As such, it was a valid exercise of Canada's police powers and did not constitute expropriation.

Corn Syrup Sweeteners v. Mexico. Late in 2009, a Chapter 11 tribunal ruled against Mexico concerning its 20% tax from 2002 to 2007 on the production and sale of soft drinks using High Fructose Corn Syrup (HFCS). This tax was imposed in the context of a trade dispute between the U.S. and Mexico over HFCS exports south of the border and Mexican sugar exports headed north. U.S. agribusiness giants Cargill, Corn Products International and Archer Daniels Midlands, along with British Tate and Lyle's U.S. subsidiary, successfully argued that the tax constituted a "performance requirement" in violation of NAFTA Article 1106. The Mexican government was ordered to pay a total of $170 million plus interest, which id paid.

AbitibiBowater v. Canada. In August 2010, the Canadian federal government agreed to pay $130 million CDN to settle a Chapter 11 claim by a U.S. pulp and paper multinational, AbitibiBowater (AB). In 2008, AB closed a longstanding mill in Newfoundland via bankruptcy, terminating 800 workers without severance. Newfoundland passed a law returning, without compensation, the company's water and timber rights to the crown, and expropriating with compensation AB lands, buildings and dams in the province. AB asserted NAFTA expropriation violations.

This settlement, along with the *Glamis* decision (above), raised concerns that resource-related NAFTA investor claims might increase. For example, a Brazilian company with a U.S. subsidiary received a $15 million settlement form Canada after alleging permit delays for rock quarrying.

Apotex v. United States. Apotex is a Canadian manufacturer of generic pharmaceuticals. It filed at least three Chapter 11 claims against the United States. These filings challenged U.S. federal court decisions denying its efforts to obtain "patent certainty" for drugs (in order to allow its generic versions to proceed), FDA denial of approval for another Apotex generic drug, and FDA import inspection practices for drugs.

All of these complaints were rejected by a Chapter 11 arbitration panel in 2014.

Exxon/Mobil v. Canada. Exxon/Mobil developed off shore oil fields in Canadian waters. It first challenged Canadian Petroleum Board rules mandating fees to support R & D in Newfoundland and Labrador in the Canadian courts and lost at trial and on appeal. Exxon subsequently filed a Chapter 11 claim which a panel affirmed in 2012, holding these fees amounted to NAFTA-prohibited "performance requirements." The damages awarded amounted to nearly $15 million.

Bilcon v. Canada. Bilcon of Delaware sought to develop a quarry and marine terminal in Nova Scotia, subject to environmental review. A joint federal/province review denied approval based upon "incompatibility with community core values". Bilcon alleged NAFTA Chapter 11 violations of the national and minimum treatment standards (the latter claim focused on fair and equitable treatment). By agreement, the UNCITRAL Rules controlled before the Permanent Court of Arbitration.

In a split 2015 decision, the arbitrators held in favor of Bilcon, noting particularly an absence of fair notice and treatment in the environmental review process, and a fundamental departure from the "likely significant adverse effects after mitigation" standard of evaluation required by Canadian law.

Eli Lilly v. Canada. Eli Lilly filed a claim for damages under Chapter 11 after Canadian courts invalidated patents on two of its blockbuster drugs on grounds that their utility was not shown. Eli Lilly argued unfair, inequitable and discriminatory treatment. A 2017 arbitration panel rejected these arguments, noting that the "promise of utility" doctrine developed by Canadian courts was well established, putting Eli Lilly on notice prior to its patent claims.

This dispute was unusual because it asserted violation of NAFTA Chapter 11 by Canadian *courts*, not by Canadian legislation or regulation. Subsequently, in June of 2017, the Canadian Supreme Court overturned the "promise doctrine" under its patent law.

Windstream Energy v. Canada and *Mesa Power Group v. Canada.* Windstream Energy of the USA sought to participate in Ontario's green energy program, and obtained a contract to build an offshore wind farm. Subsequently, Ontario imposed a moratorium on offshore wind projects pending further scientific study. This had the effect of suspending but not terminating the Windstream contract. Other participants in the program were offered alternative opportunities to join the green energy program, but Windstream was not.

Windstream filed a Chapter 11 complaint before the Permanent Court of Arbitration arguing discrimination, indirect expropriation and unfair and inequitable treatment. A 2017 arbitration panel rejected all but the unfair and inequitable treatment claim, recognizing that Ontario had not within a reasonable time clarified the relevant science or the status of the contract, leaving Windstream in legal limbo. It assessed 21 million Euros damages, minus certain adjustments, based upon the value of comparable transactions in Europe.

Mesa Power challenged Ontario's award of power purchase contracts under its green energy program as discriminatory and unfair under Chapter 11 before the Permanent Court of Arbitration in The Hague. In a split decision, the arbitrators rejected Mesa' claims of unfair bidding rules and procedures for power contracts.

Other Foreign Investor Claims of Note. Several U.S. companies commenced Chapter 11 proceedings against Canada asserting damages based on Quebec's moratorium on "fracking", the use of water and chemicals to release sub-surface oil and gas reserves.

After President Obama's rejection in 2015 of the Keystone Pipeline from Alberta's tar sands to Texas, Trans Canada has filed a Chapter 11 claim against the United States alleging discriminatory (non-national) treatment, breach of the duty of most-favored-nation treatment, U.S. governmental acts tantamount to expropriation, and unfair and inequitable treatment. Trans Canada sought in excess of $15 billion in damages, but withdrew its claim after President Trump approved the pipeline.

SUMMARY

These examples of investor-state claims under NAFTA represent only a partial summary of the impact of NAFTA Chapter 11. Lawyers learned that Chapter 11 could be used to challenge or threaten to challenge all sorts of existing or proposed government actions, particularly regulatory decisions. There is leverage in these broad investor rights, and in its mandatory arbitral procedures. Mutations on the law of investor-state claims appeared in the U.S.-Chile, U.S.-CAFTA and U.S.-Panama/Peru/Colombia free trade agreements. See R. Folsom, *International Trade Law including Trump and Trade* in a Nutshell.

These mutations were in part a response to Congressional concerns expressed in the Trade Promotion Authority (fast-track) Act of 2002 that Chapter 11 of NAFTA accorded "greater substantive rights" to foreigners with respect to investment protection than enjoyed by U.S. investors in the United States.

NAFTA: INTELLECTUAL PROPERTY

There was no coverage of intellectual property rights under CUSFTA. In contrast, Chapter 17 of the NAFTA agreement contained a comprehensive set of rules for North American intellectual property rights. NAFTA's provisions were closely related, but somewhat **more** extensive than those of the WTO Agreement on Trade-Related Intellectual Property Rights (TRIPs) (1995). See R. Folsom, *International Trade Law including Trump and Trade* in a Nutshell.

Both NAFTA and TRIPs stipulate that whichever agreement affords the broadest protection of intellectual property will prevail.

While its primary impact has been on Mexico, Canada and the United States also amended their intellectual property laws after NAFTA. U.S. free trade agreements in the Americas since NAFTA have notably expanded "TRIPs Plus" coverage of intellectual property rights. *Id.*

Prior to 1991, Mexico had a Technology Transfer Commission with a veto power over most intellectual property licensing and franchising agreements. The Commission also controlled the terms and conditions of technology transfer agreements. It even decided the level of acceptable royalties. Commissions of this kind are best understood by remembering that developing nations like Mexico are basically technology importers. While Mexico needed technology, it did not wish to pay excessively for technology that was not always at the cutting edge. So it, like most of Latin America, empowered the Commission to get better terms. What happened instead was that technology transfers to Mexico slowed to a trickle.

In 1991, well prior to NAFTA, Mexico abolished the Commission and most technology transfer controls. Most other Latin American jurisdictions have retained such controls, whereas in Mexico licensors and licensees are free to bargain over the terms and conditions of their agreements.

However, Mexico's patent, copyright, trademark and trade secret laws remained (by United States standards) less than fully protective of intellectual property rights. This was of concern because many Mexican patents and copyrights, for example, are owned by U.S. corporations and investors. NAFTA brought fundamental alterations to Mexican law in these areas. In 1994, Mexico joined the Patent

Cooperation Treaty. Obtaining Mexican patents is now as simple as checking a box designating Mexico as a country in which protection is desired.

INTELLECTUAL PROPERTY RIGHTS IN CONTROVERSY

Why are intellectual property rights so controversial? From the perspective of the industrial world (including Canada and the United States), patents, copyrights, trademarks and trade secrets are essential to their modern technology-driven economies. Such rights are used as incentives and rewards for innovative research, development and progress. Needless to say, this perspective corresponds with a very high degree of ownership of intellectual property rights around the world.

From the perspective of the developing world (including Mexico), patents, copyrights, etc. are often expensive barriers to economic improvement. Third world nations are basically technology importers, and done legally this means paying royalties to owners of intellectual property rights. The stream of royalty payments from the developing to the industrial world is huge, with much smaller sums headed the other way. Such payments add to the costs of development, and in some cases are quite simply unaffordable.

These competing perspectives on intellectual property rights have resulted in certain patterns of law and behavior. The industrial nations have pushed hard at every opportunity for recognition in the laws of developing nations of the right to obtain intellectual property protection. This push illustrates a fundamental point: No nation must grant patent, trademark, copyright or trade secret protection unless that is their wish. If a developing world nation decides to allow patents on pharmaceuticals, in reality it is opening its market to the multinational drug companies. They will end up owning the lion's share of the Mexican, Thai or Nigerian (for example) pharmaceutical patents.

Without effective patent protection, these companies will face local competitors who need not pay them royalties. Such "pirates" are found in some developing nations, but it is important to remember that under the laws of their nation they are not necessarily pirates. Indeed, they may even be encouraged in their efforts by their governments as part of a low-cost development strategy.

It is easy to understand why the United States and Canada (to a lesser extent) as technology exporters share the common goal of obtaining effective protection for intellectual property rights around the world. In NAFTA, Mexico promised to meet (if not exceed) their greatest expectations. For Mexico, building upon its 1991 Law for the Fostering and Protection of Industrial Property, NAFTA represented a coming of age on intellectual property rights.

GENERAL OBLIGATIONS

Specific commitments on patents, copyrights, trademarks, trade secrets and other intellectual property rights were made in NAFTA. These are discussed individually below. NAFTA 1994 also contained some general intellectual property rights obligations. Many of these obligations have counterparts under the TRIPs agreement. For example, except for secondary use of sound recordings, there was a general NAFTA rule of national treatment.

There was also a general NAFTA duty to protect intellectual property adequately and effectively, as long as barriers to legitimate trade were not created. At a minimum, this duty necessitated adherence to NAFTA Chapter 17. This general duty also embraced adherence to the substantive provisions of: The Geneva Convention of Phonograms (1971); the Berne Convention for the Protection of Literary and Artistic Works (1971); the Paris Convention for the Protection of Industrial Property (1967); and the 1978 or 1991 versions of the International Convention for the Protection of New Varieties of Plants. Protecting intellectual property rights more extensively than these Conventions was expressly authorized.

The process of intellectual property rights enforcement was covered in detail under NAFTA. Speaking generally, these provisions required fair, equitable, and not unnecessarily complicated, costly or time-consuming enforcement procedures. Written notice, independent legal counsel, the opportunity to substantiate claims and present evidence, and protection of confidential information were stipulated for civil enforcement proceedings. Overly burdensome mandatory personal appearances could not be imposed.

Remedies to enjoin infringement (new to Mexico), prevent importation of infringing goods, and order payment for damages and litigation costs had to exist. However, proof of knowing infringement or reasonable grounds for such knowledge was an acceptable criterion. Recovery of profits or liquidated damages had to be available when copyright or sound recording infringement is involved. Disposition of infringing or counterfeit goods outside the ordinary channels of commerce or even by destruction was anticipated by NAFTA. All administrative intellectual property rights decisions were reviewable by a court of law.

COUNTERFEITING

Criminal penalties were required under NAFTA for willful trademark counterfeiting or copyright piracy undertaken on a commercial scale. For United States law on point, see the Trademark Counterfeiting Act of 1984 (18 U.S.C. § 2320 et seq.). When the counterfeit or pirated goods came from outside the region, those affected had to be given the opportunity to bar importation and possibly obtain their destruction or other satisfactory disposal.

Despite strong provisions in NAFTA to fight counterfeiting and promote protection of intellectual property, Mexico is seen by some as still not measuring up. Annual submissions by the International Intellectual Property Alliance to the USTR under Special 301 procedures (19 U.S.C.

§ 2242) document the ineffectiveness of Mexico's anti-piracy law enforcement. Hundreds of millions of dollars of fake CDs, DVDs, software and the like can be found in Mexican marketplaces and the amount is increasing. Prosecutions to combat counterfeiting have been limited. For example, some 2500 Mexican government raids in 1998 netted just 35 convictions with no fines in excess of $1,000.

Mexico's Customs Law of 1996 placed border controls in the hands of the Mexican Institute of Industrial Property (IMPI) for the first time. This Institute was created in 1993 specifically for the task of enforcing Mexican intellectual property rights. Unlike the U.S. Patent and Trademark Office, IMPI has the power to enforce patent owners' rights against actual and potential infringers. It can prevent any commercialization of an infringing product, including removal from the stream of commerce. Mexico also has had, since 1993, a multi-departmental Anti-Piracy Commission.

In 1998, the U.S. and Mexico reached agreement on new measures to combat counterfeiting in Mexico. These include a national anti-piracy campaign, tax crimes against counterfeiters, expeditious search and seizure and arrest warrants, and increased administrative enforcement resources. These measures in a limited way have helped to stem counterfeit goods in Mexico.

GRAY MARKET TRADING

One important intellectual property rights issue to which NAFTA did not speak was gray market trading. Gray market goods consist of goods produced abroad with authorization which end up being imported into markets without authorization. Trade in gray market goods has exploded in recent years, often because of sharply fluctuating currency exchange rates. Such fluctuations create opportunities to import and sell the "real thing" at a discount from local price levels. K Mart, Wal-Mart and other retailers have devoted significant resources to gray market trading. Consumers, as a rule, are only too happy to benefit from this form of price competition.

Manufacturers and their authorized distributors, on the other hand, are frequently upset with gray marketeers. They often call such traders "free riders." That is to say, some manufacturers and authorized distributors believe that gray marketeers are benefiting from and not paying their fair share of advertising, promotional, service, warranty and other associated costs. In a general sense, manufacturers worry that gray market goods will dilute their brand names. Some manufacturers will not do warranty work on gray market goods (cameras and Mercedes Benz autos, for example). In response, some retailers of gray market goods provide their own warranties.

To stem the tide of gray market imports, manufacturers ordinarily turn to intellectual property rights that accompany the goods. Most goods, for example, are trademarked. United States law concerning the use of intellectual property rights as import barriers has a checkered history. The most important legislation in this complex area is the Genuine Goods Exclusion Act of 1922 (19 U.S.C. § 1526). This Act bars unauthorized importation of goods bearing trademarks owned by U.S. citizens. Such persons or companies may register their marks with the U.S. Customs Service which is empowered to seize the offending goods.

For a variety of reasons, including the legislative history of the Act, the U.S. Customs Service created two exceptions to the general rule against importing trademarked gray market goods. These are known as the "common control" and "authorized use" exceptions. Under these exceptions, gray market goods can enter the U.S. market if the trademark in question is under common ownership or control, or its use on the goods was authorized by the U.S. owner. Practically speaking, these exceptions allowed entry to most gray market goods until 1988. In that year, the U.S. Supreme Court ruled that only the common control (not the authorized use) exception was a reasonable administrative interpretation of the Act. *K Mart Corp. v. Cartier*, 486 U.S. 281 (1988). Even so, United States law remains relatively open to gray market trading. More so, for example, than Canadian law. For more on the law of gray market trading, see R. Folsom, *International Trade Law including Trump and Trade* in a Nutshell.

The question that gray market trading posed for NAFTA was the same as has been debated for decades in Europe. Should national intellectual property rights be allowed to function as trade barriers inside the region? Europe, especially the

European Court of Justice, has by and large said no. See R. Folsom, *European Union Law including BREXIT* in a Nutshell.

In the European Union, free trade interests usually trump national intellectual property rights. Under NAFTA, there is no clear answer. Chapter 17 takes pains to expand and protect national intellectual property rights, and specifically addresses the issue of counterfeiting, but not gray market trading. The relevant law of each NAFTA nation remains intact.

PATENTS

Article 1709 of NAFTA assured the availability of patents "in all fields of technology." New products and processes resulting from an inventive step that are capable of industrial application were patentable. Patents for pharmaceuticals, computer software, microorganisms and microbiological processes, plant varieties and agricultural chemicals were specifically included under NAFTA and caused changes in Mexican law. In addition, protection for layout designs of semiconductor integrated circuits was provided by Article 1710. All patent rights had to be granted without discrimination as to field of technology, country of origin, and importation or local production of the relevant products.

NAFTA specifically reserved the right to deny patents for diagnostic, therapeutic and surgical methods, transgenic plants and animals, and for essentially biological processes that produce plants or animals. But if commercial exploitation might endanger public morality or "ordre public" (state security) no patents needed be granted. Patent denials to protect human, animal or plant life or health, or to avoid serious injury to nature or the environment, were also justifiable under NAFTA.

It was agreed that patents in NAFTA nations would run either for 20 years from the date of the filing of the patent application, or 17 years from the grant of patent rights (the traditional U.S. approach). However, the subsequent TRIPs agreement stipulated a 20-year patent term from the date of filing. Canadian, Mexican and United States patent laws now follow this rule. For pharmaceutical patents, effectively speaking, additional protection from generic competition was often achieved because NAFTA required five years of exclusivity for product approval test data. Under NAFTA, patent owners generally possessed the right to prevent others from making, using or selling the invention without their consent. No mention was made of the right to block infringing or unauthorized imports. If the patent covered a process, this included the right to prevent others from using, selling or *importing* products obtained directly from that process. Assignment or transfer of patents, and licensing contracts for their use and exploitation, were also expressly protected.

On the touchy subject of compulsory licensing, not authorized under U.S. law, Canada and Mexico could allow limited nonexclusive usage without the owner's authorization if the invention has not been used or exploited locally through production or importation. This was generally permissible only after reasonable attempts at securing a license. However, under emergency, competition law or public noncommercial circumstances, no prior attempt at securing a license was required. In all cases of compulsory licensing, there was a duty to adequately remunerate the patent owner.

Apart from compulsory licensing, NAFTA authorized "limited exceptions" to exclusive patents rights. Such exceptions could not "unreasonably conflict" with the normal exploitation of the patent. Nor could they "unreasonably prejudice" the owner's "legitimate interests."

COPYRIGHTS

The NAFTA provisions on copyrights promoted uniformity in North America. Canada, Mexico and the United States promised extensive protection of copyrights, sound recordings, program-carrying satellite signals and industrial designs. Copyrights are available on all works of original expression. These include books, articles, choreography, photographs, paintings, sculpture, films, videos, records, tapes, CDs and other traditionally copyrighted materials. In most instances, copyrights had to be granted for at least 50 years. The United States grants 70-year copyrights.

Computer programs and data compilations which constitute intellectual creations were subject to copyrights. See *Feist Publications, Inc. v. Rural Telephone Service Co.*, 499 U.S. 340 (1991). Article 1707 of NAFTA requires criminal sanctions for makers and sellers of unauthorized decoding devices, and civil sanctions for unauthorized receivers of satellite signals.

Copyright holders also received the rights enumerated in the Berne Convention for the Protection of Literary and Artistic Works (1971). However, translation and reproduction licenses permitted by the Berne Convention were not allowed under NAFTA if these needs could be fulfilled voluntarily by the copyright holder but for national laws. In addition, Article 1704.2 specifically conveyed to copyright holders:

- Control over importation of unauthorized copies;

- First public distribution rights over the work (whether by sale, rental or otherwise);

- Control over communication of the work to the public; and

- Control over commercial rental of computer programs.

If the original or a copy of a computer program is put on the market, this did not exhaust rental rights. Despite the specific reference to control over unauthorized imports in Article 1704.2, it was doubtful whether NAFTA can be construed so as to block free trade in copyrighted goods after their first sale in the United States, Canada or Mexico. The "first sale doctrine" limits an owner's rights to control copyrighted goods to their first sale or transfer. Thereafter, the goods can be freely exchanged. See *Quality King Distributors, Inc. v. L'anza Research*

International, Inc., 523 U.S. 135 (1998); *Kirtsaeng v. John Wiley & Sons,* 568 U.S. 519 (2013).

Licensing and conveyance of copyrights, royalties and the like were freely transferable under NAFTA. Assignment of works of creation to employers by employees was also protected. However, Article 1705.5 somewhat vaguely allowed limits or exceptions in "special cases" that did not conflict with "normal exploitation" of the work. Presumably, "fair use" of copyrighted material fell within this provision. These exceptions could not unreasonably prejudice the owner's legitimate interests.

TRADEMARKS

Trademarks are found on most products, and service and other marks are commonly used. The pervasiveness of marks arguably makes them the most important of NAFTA's intellectual property provisions. Such marks help make markets work by signaling attributes, qualities, price levels and other relevant information. The NAFTA provisions on marks fostered uniform law.

Canada, Mexico and the United States agreed to register trademarks, service marks, collective organizational marks and certification marks. All of these marks had to be capable of distinguishing goods or services. Internationally "well-known" marks were given special protections against pirates. Whether a mark was "well-known" depends upon knowledge of it in the sector of the public normally dealing with the goods or services, including knowledge in a NAFTA country resulting from promotion of the mark there. A reasonable opportunity to petition to cancel trademark registrations had to be granted. In contrast, a reasonable opportunity to oppose registration applications was not mandatory under NAFTA. The nature of the goods or services *per se* could not justify a refusal to register.

To apply for trademark protection, there was no NAFTA requirement of prior usage on goods or services. However, if actual usage did not occur within 3 years, Chapter 17 provided that registration may be denied. Immoral, deceptive, scandalous and disparaging marks, and those that falsely suggest a connection with or contempt of persons, institutions, beliefs or national symbols could be denied registration. No registration of words in English, French or Spanish that generically designated goods or services was permitted. Registration of marks indicating geographic origin could be rejected if "deceptively mis-descriptive."

Under NAFTA, trademark registrations had to be valid for at least 10 years. They could be renewed indefinitely provided use was continuous. If circumstances beyond the owner's control justified non-use, registrations could be continued. For all these purposes, the NAFTA nations agreed that use was continued when undertaken by franchisees or licensees.

NAFTA trademark owners could prevent persons from using identical or "similar" signs on identical or similar goods or services if this would cause a "likelihood of confusion." However, the "fair use" of descriptive terms could be allowed. Mandatory use of a second "local" trademark (as Mexico once required) was banned. Mandatory use that reduced the function of trademarks as source indicators was also prohibited. Furthermore, compulsory licensing of trademarks was contrary to NAFTA, but contractual licensing and assignment of trademarks could be conditioned.

TRADE SECRETS

NAFTA was the first international agreement on trade secret protection. Its primary impact was on Mexican law. At a minimum, each nation had to ensure legal means to prevent trade secrets from being disclosed, acquired or used without consent "in a manner contrary to honest commercial practices" (Article 1711). Breach of contract, breach of confidence, and inducement to breach of contract were specifically listed as examples of dishonest commercial practices. Moreover, persons who acquired trade secrets knowing them to be the product of such practices, or who were grossly negligent in failing to know this, also engaged in dishonest commercial practices. This was true even if they do not use the secrets in question.

NAFTA did not mention, however, the practice of "reverse engineering". This practice is thought to be common and has been authoritatively endorsed by the U.S. Supreme Court. See *Kewanee Oil Co. v. Bicron Corp.*, 416 U.S. 470 (1974).

For NAFTA purposes, information was "secret" if it was not generally known or readily accessible to persons who normally dealt with it, had commercial value because of its secrecy, and reasonable steps were taken to keep it secret. This definition covered, for example, the secret formula for making Coca-Cola, perhaps the world's best kept trade secret. Nevertheless, trade secret holders could be required to produce evidence documenting the existence of the secret in order to secure protection. Release of such information to government authorities obviously involves risks that will need to be considered.

No NAFTA government could discourage or impede the voluntary licensing of trade secrets (often referred to as "knowhow licensing"). Imposing excessive or discriminatory conditions on knowhow licenses was prohibited. More specifically, in testing and licensing the sale of pharmaceutical and agricultural chemical products, there was under NAFTA a general duty to protect against disclosure of proprietary data.

NAFTA DISPUTE SETTLEMENT

NAFTA employed a range of dispute settlement procedures. Chapters 19 and 20 were the best known, most visible and most formal. Chapter 19 concerned antidumping and countervailing duty disputes. Chapter 20 created general dispute settlement procedures that applied unless there were more specific provisions in the agreement. For example, Section B of Chapter 11 (below) established investor-state arbitration procedures that operated outside Chapter 20. Environmental and labor cooperation disputes were governed by special procedures found in the two "side agreements" to NAFTA. These procedures are covered in Chapter 4.

Not all dispute settlement under NAFTA was formal in character. Disputes were often avoided or settled informally by intergovernmental and advisory NAFTA committees and working groups. To name just a few, such committees range in focus from trade in goods to trade in worn clothing, from automotive standards to labeling of apparel, from agricultural subsidies to trade and competition policy, and from small business to financial services.

All Chapter 19 and 20 decisions, the Code of Conduct, and procedural rules referred to in this section are reproduced at www.nafta-sec-alena.org.

CHAPTER 19—ANTIDUMPING AND COUNTERVAILING DUTIES, BINATIONAL PANELS

Chapter 19 of the NAFTA agreement is substantially similar to Chapter 19 of CUSFTA 1989. See Chapter 2. Binational panels acted as a substitute for national judicial review of final administrative determinations, subject only to extraordinary challenges taken to NAFTA "Committees" (ECC). Once again, the North Americans were unable to follow the European path and eliminate antidumping (AD) and countervailing (CVD) duties on internal trade. In contrast, national judicial review, not binational panels, govern final AD and CVD administrative determinations under post-NAFTA U.S. free trade agreements, e.g., CAFTA/DR. All that said, at vigorous Canadian insistence, the USMCA retains binational panel review of national AD and CVD decisions. See Chapter 6.

National antidumping and countervailing duty laws continue to govern all proceedings, including decisions by Chapter 19 panels. However, these laws have generally been harmonized by common adoption of GATT codes. For example, each NAFTA nation adheres to the WTO Antidumping and Subsidies Codes (1995). **Specific AD and CVD disputes could simultaneously be challenged under NAFTA 1994 by private parties and by governments under WTO dispute settlement procedures.** This could lead to different outcomes, as it did in one of the endless Softwood Lumber disputes between Canada and the United States when a NAFTA panel upheld but a WTO panel rejected a USITC finding of domestic injury. See below and Chapter 2.

NAFTA 1994 committed each nation to "effective and fair" AD and CVD rules. NAFTA also created the possibility of consultations and "special committee" review if "fundamental failures" occur in Chapter 19 dispute settlement. From 1994 to date, no "declaratory opinion" or "special committee" review took place. This should not be taken, however, as a sign that all was quiet on the antidumping and countervailing duty front.

United States administrative AD and CVD determinations (mostly annual reviews of prior proceedings) were reviewed by NAFTA Chapter 19 panels more often than Canadian or Mexican determinations. Goods from Mexico were involved in the U.S. determinations more than twice as frequently as Canadian goods. Leather apparel, porcelain-on-steel cookware, cement, oil country tubular goods and fresh cut flowers provide examples of U.S. imports from Mexico that were the subject of Chapter 19 panel decisions. Live swine, concrete, color picture tubes and carbon steel imports from Canada were also decided under Chapter 19. Nearly all of these decisions concerned the imposition of U.S. antidumping duties. U.S. exports of synthetic baler twine, steel sheet, malt beverages and refined sugar to Canada, and flat coated steel, steel plate and polystyrene to Mexico, provide examples of Chapter 19 panel decisions reviewing Canadian and Mexican AD and CVD determinations.

Only three U.S.-requested extraordinary challenges to NAFTA Chapter 19 panel decisions were raised. These challenges concerned Cement from Mexico (ECC–2000–1904–01), Magnesium from Canada (ECC–2003–1904–01) and Softwood Lumber from Canada (ECC–2004–1904–01). All of them were rejected by the Extraordinary Challenge Committees, and none were as provocative as the ECC under CUSFTA 1989. See Chapter 2.

SELECTING PANELS—CONFLICTS OF INTEREST

Under NAFTA, the use of binational panels and extraordinary challenge committees as a substitute for national judicial review of administrative determinations continued despite questions of constitutionality under U.S. law. See B. A. Ackerman and D. Golove, *Is NAFTA Constitutional?* (1995).

NAFTA did, however, seek to "professionalize" the process by adding judges and retired judges to the roster of acceptable Chapter 19 panelists. The panelists under CUSFTA were more often lawyers, economists or academicians. Each party to the dispute chose two panelists (invariably from their home country). Each party could peremptorily reject without cause four panelist selections. The fifth panelist was chosen by agreement if possible, or by lot if not. The panel then selected its chair (who had to be a lawyer) by majority vote or failing that by lot. This panel selection procedure differed significantly from the "reverse selection" process used in Chapter 20 disputes (below).

All Chapter 19 and 20 panelists were governed by a Code of Conduct. Panelists could be removed only by mutual agreement if the Code of Conduct was breached. The Code broadly stipulated disclosure of any circumstances that raised a conflict or an appearance of conflict, with no time limits or materiality requirements. Conflict issues repeatedly delayed the Chapter 19 dispute resolution process. Undisclosed conflicts of interest were alleged in the CUSFTA Chapter 19 *Softwood Lumber* dispute. ECC–94–1904–01 USA.

Judge Wilkey's dissent in the *Softwood Lumber* Extraordinary Challenge made it perfectly clear that he believed the Code had not been followed by two Canadian attorney-panelists:

This part of my opinion is much shorter than the first. Do not think that the issue addressed is one whit less important. Indeed, it may well be the more important of the two, the greater threat to the integrity of the whole process.

* * *

There is an obligation for a prospective panelist, at the time he is originally placed on a general list and at the time he is queried as to his willingness and his capacity to serve on a specific Panel, to disclose any and everything which might affect his impartial performance of his duties on the Panel, or affect the judgment of the contending parties as to whether to accept the particular panelist or reject him. The two governments do not send their investigative agencies to pry into the details of the prospective panelist's business and personal affiliations. There is no subpoena of the records of the panelist or his law firm, no review of his business contacts, public or private records to determine his sources of income for past years. The two governments rely exclusively on the honesty—and just as importantly, the diligence—of the prospective panelist to reveal any and everything which could seemingly have an impact on his being chosen to serve or not.

Attorney Homer E. Moyer, Jr. presented an alternative and perhaps more persuasive perspective:

An analysis of panel decisions suggests that the level of bias in Chapter 19 binational panel decisions is very low. For example, almost no cases have involved a split among panelists along national lines. The presence of actual conflicts of interest (as distinguished from possible appearances of conflicts) has been rare; lawyers who have served as panelists and have subsequently described their experiences, with only rare exceptions, have highly praised the objectivity and fairness of panelists. Where sharp disagreements among panelists have emerged, they have tended to be the result of a panelist's ideological view of the panel process itself, rather than any conflicts of interest related to clients or panelists' nationality.

The *Softwood Lumber* case, which is the most celebrated case involving an allegation of conflict of interest, suggests the importance of separating issues of conflicts of interest from disagreements over substantive issues or the merits of a case. To many observers and participants, the claims of conflict of interest in the *Lumber* case appeared disingenuous: they were raised for the first time more than two years after the litigation had begun and only after the complaining parties had lost the case on the merits. Moreover, many of the after-the-fact conflict allegations were far-fetched, relating to work done years before, in some cases by firms with which panelists had long since severed their relationships.

Therefore, the Chapter 19 experience suggests that we should carefully differentiate between questions of possible conflicts of interest and dissatisfaction with judgments on the merits. 3 *S.W.J. Law & Trade in the Americas* 423, 425–26 (1996).

STANDARDS OF REVIEW—JUDGE WILKEY DISSENTS

Some CUSFTA Chapter 19 panels were accused of ignoring or poorly implementing their duty to apply Canadian and U.S. standards of review for administrative determinations. This was especially true in the *Softwood Lumber* dispute, ECC–19–1904–01 USA. Judge Wilkey of the U.S. Federal Court of Appeals served on the Extraordinary Challenge Committee in that dispute. He concluded that the Panel had produced "egregiously erroneous results." Judge Wilkey did not mince his words:

> I submit that the well-intentioned system of Extraordinary Challenge Committees, as a substitute for the standard appellate review under United States law, has failed. It has failed both at the Panel and the Committee level to apply United States law, substantively, and most clearly in regard to the United States standard of review of administrative agency actions. The system runs the risk, not only of producing egregiously erroneous results as in the instant three to two Panel decision, but also of creating a body of law—even though formally without precedential value—which will be divergent from United States law applied to countries not members of NAFTA.

> I believe that I have demonstrated that this is so in this particular case, and I suggest that analysis demonstrates that this should be no surprise.

> Consider the position of the Binational Panels. The members are to be experts, distinguished practitioners in the esoteric field of trade law. Surely, a better mechanism for review of agency action than a single judge from the Court of International Trade or a three judge panel of a Circuit Court of Appeals? Not necessarily. The record shows that five (or in this case three) distinguished "experts" have shown no deference whatsoever to the "experts" in the ITA of the Commerce Department.

Psychologically, why should they be expected to show the deference to administrative agency action which is required as a fundamental tenet of U.S. judicial review of agency action? The panel members are experts; they know better than the lowly paid "experts" over the Commerce Department, and they have felt inclined to say so. Repeatedly, most vividly in this particular case, they seem to have substituted their judgment for that of the agency. They have not hesitated to say that the agency was wrong on its methodology, wrong in the choice of alternate economic analyses, wrong in its conclusions, and that the Panel of five experts knows far better how to do it. All of this of course is directly contrary to long-standing United States law concepts of review of agency action.

Why do these distinguished Panel experts make this type of error? The answer is, I suggest, that they are experts in trade law; they are not experts in the field of judicial review of agency action; they do not necessarily have any familiarity whatsoever with the standards of judicial review under United States law. This would particularly be true of the Canadian members. . . .

While not all agree with Judge Wilkey, his opinion certainly helped push Canada and the United States into a dialogue on standards of review. As a result of this dialogue, NAFTA 1994 created a specific example of a binational panel that manifestly exceeds its powers, authority or jurisdiction (one of the grounds for reversal before an Extraordinary Challenge Committee). Any failure "to apply the appropriate standard of review" was the example. (Article 1904.13(a)(iii)). "Standards of review" for each country were defined in Annex 1911 by reference to national statutes, which the parties were free to amend. For Canada and the United States these are the same standards stipulated by CUSFTA discussed in Chapter 2. See Subsection 181(4) of the Federal Court Act of Canada; Sections 516A(b)(1)(A) and (B) of the U.S. Tariff Act of 1930.

Thus, despite the heated rhetoric, there was no change in the U.S. or Canadian statutory standards of review or in the grounds for reversal by Extraordinary Challenge Committees. At a minimum, however, the United States hoped this example would drive home the obligation of binational panels to apply its standards in Chapter 19 disputes challenging U.S. administrative determinations, and the obligation of ECCs to consider such issues when panel decisions are challenged. This obligation was anticipated by extending the ECC review period from 30 to 90 days and by adding a requirement that the ECC examine the legal and factual analysis underlying the panel's findings and conclusions. See Annex 1904.13(3).

For Mexico, Article 238 of the Federal Fiscal Code was the source of the standard of review that NAFTA panels applied in Chapter 19 proceedings. Article 238, drafted specifically for NAFTA and amended several times after 1994, provided (in rough very simplified translation) that SECOFI* antidumping

---

* Secretaria de Comercio y Fomento Industrial (Ministry of Commerce and Industrial Development). SECOFI makes dumping and subsidy determinations as well as domestic industry injury determinations under Mexican law.

and countervailing duty "resolutions" will be declared illegal if there is official "incompetence" (lack of authority), omissions of formal legal requirements or procedural errors affecting individual defenses and the result of the resolution, mistaken facts underlying the resolution, issuance of resolutions in violation of law or incorrect application of law, and exercises of discretion not corresponding to the purposes behind discretionary powers.

The competence issue was central to several Panel reviews of SECOFI determinations. See MEX–94–1904–01, 02 and 03. In Case 02, for example, a U.S. attorney and a U.S. law professor joined with a Mexican attorney to conclude that SECOFI lacked competence to levy antidumping duties because it had not been established in strict accordance with Mexican procedural formalities. A Mexican and U.S. attorney dissented; they wanted to undertake a substantive examination of SECOFI's determinations.

MEXICO AND CHAPTER 19

In Mexico, antidumping and countervailing duty law is relatively new, as is judicial (Federal Fiscal Tribunal) and NAFTA panel review of trade agency actions. For all concerned, Chapter 19 was a learning process. Professor Robert Lutz analyzed some of the early issues and differences in approach that Chapter 19 panels must follow according to Mexican law. See 3 *S.W. J. Law & Trade in the Americas* 391 (1996). Professor Lutz emphasizes that Mexican *constitutional* law (specifically Articles 14 and 16 guaranteeing "legal security" and "legality") govern administrative action. NAFTA panels reviewing SECOFI determinations split on whether these provisions apply. One reason for this split is that the national "law" that Chapter 19 panels must apply is defined in the NAFTA agreement as consisting of "relevant statutes, legislative history, regulations, administrative practice and judicial precedents" (Article 1904). This definition does not reference constitutional law.

As Professor David Gantz noted, there are additional conflicts and uncertainties in Mexican law as applied in binational panel decisions. See 29 *Law & Policy Int'l Bus.* 297 (1998). These include counsel access to confidential information with or without powers of attorney and bonding, the direct applicability of the GATT/WTO Antidumping Code in panel proceedings, and the power of the panel to dismiss SECOFI proceedings.

Professor Lutz also notes that Mexican doctrine on precedent ("jurisprudencia") depends upon five consecutive appellate decisions agreeing on the same issue, and that "writ of amparo" proceedings may be used to challenge NAFTA panel decisions in the Mexican federal courts. Indeed, two U.S. companies successfully initiated amparo proceedings against the Panel in MEX–94–1904–1 notwithstanding the NAFTA provisions eliminating national judicial review of AD and CVD proceedings and the alternative of Extraordinary Challenge Committee review of panel decisions.

The writ of amparo is a uniquely Mexican lawsuit which is the source of great pride in the Mexican legal community. The writ asserts infringement of rights. It is constitutionally based (see Articles 103 and 107 of the Mexican Constitution). The writ of amparo allows individuals and legal entities to challenge virtually all state acts or omissions when ordinary remedies have been exhausted or are not available. Such challenges can be raised against federal, state or local authorities, including legislative, executive, administrative or judicial authorities. Writs of amparo, for example, are frequently used to challenge judicial decisions.

THE TOMATOES DISPUTE

There were a number of Chapter 19 antidumping and countervailing duty panels involving U.S.-Mexico trade. The most prominent dispute, however, never got that far. This dispute concerned Mexican exports of tomatoes at prices that were rapidly taking market share from U.S. growers.

After failing to persuade the U.S. International Trade Commission to pursue safeguards (escape clause) relief, Florida growers alleged dumping by Mexican tomato producers early in 1996. This politically high-profile petition eventually led to a "suspension agreement" between the U.S. Commerce Department and Mexican growers. The Department promised to suspend its antidumping probe (dumping at a 17.56 percent margin had been found) in return for a commitment by Mexican growers not to sell at less than a specified "reference price." This price was based on the lowest average import price in a recent period not involving dumping. It amounted in 1996 to 20.68 cents per pound. At that price, there was no limit on the volume of Mexican tomatoes that could be shipped to the U.S. market.

Critics from states like Arizona alleged "political blackmail" as the settlement came just days before the 1996 Presidential election vote. President Clinton carried Florida in 1996, something he had failed to do in 1992. In 2013, bowing to pressure from Florida growers, a revised, more restrictive suspension agreement was reached by the Obama administration shortly after his re-election to office. This suspension agreement, like its predecessor, raised prices and managed trade in a most remarkable manner. Challenged in court by Florida growers, it did not significantly slow Mexico's market penetration. Prior to NAFTA, Mexican tomatoes held about 25% of the U.S. market. At this point, Mexican tomatoes enjoy at least a disputed 30% percent U.S. market share.

In 2019, a new five-tear antidumping dispute suspension agreement was agreed. This agreement raises the per pound reference prices of Mexican tomatoes, notably so for organic tomatoes. Once again the power of Florida politics prevailed.

THE SWEETENER DISPUTES

Another example of a dumping/subsidy suspension agreement resulting in controlled trade between the U.S. and Mexico involves a longstanding dispute over Mexican sugar exports to the USA and U.S. corn syrup exports to Mexico, often called the "sweeteners disputes". Several intergovernmental suspension agreements have been in place, and the latest in 2017 under President Trump reduced the flow of refined sugar to the U.S. U.S. firms also successfully challenged Mexican taxes on corn syrup (below), collecting damages under Chapter 11 arbitration proceedings.

NAFTA CHAPTER 20
INTERGOVERNMENTAL DISPUTE
SETTLEMENT/THE WTO ALTERNATIVE

The intergovernmental dispute resolution procedures found in Chapter 20 of the NAFTA agreement applied absent more specific NAFTA provisions. As was the case with CUSFTA, these procedures were intended to be an alternative to GATT 1947 dispute settlement (since replaced by much more effective World Trade Organization (WTO) procedures). See R. Folsom, *International Trade Law including Trump and Trade* in a Nutshell.

Private parties did not participate in Chapter 20 dispute settlement. Moreover, NAFTA Article 2021 expressly prohibited rights of action asserting inconsistency with NAFTA against a member state. The United States Trade Representative (USTR), however, did afford interested persons the opportunity to comment on Chapter 20 proceedings. Private parties lodged complaints with the USTR about member state measures that adversely affected them. Whether to proceed to Chapter 20 dispute settlement is strictly a matter of USTR discretion.

**The right of each member state to elect
between NAFTA and WTO dispute settlement
was generally preserved under NAFTA.**
However, once made, the election was exclusive and
final. Use of Chapter 20 under NAFTA was denied if
the complainant took the issue to the WTO. That
said, as part of a broad evaluation of NAFTA/WTO
choice of forum opportunities and risks, Professor
David Gantz noted that nations sometimes
judiciously framed their disputes so as to gain access
to both NAFTA and WTO forums. See 14 *American
U. Law Rev.* 1025 (1999) (citing Mexico-U.S. sugar/
corn syrup trade complaints and the Canada-U.S.
farm products blockade dispute).

In Chapter 2 we noted that preserving the option
of WTO dispute settlement allows the U.S. to
challenge Canadian cultural industry trade
restraints that have been excluded from CUSFTA
and NAFTA. For any complaint that the remaining
NAFTA nation wishes to join, the two complainants
must resolve the choice of forum. Absent resolution,
the dispute "normally" was to be heard under
NAFTA.

The right to elect as between NAFTA or WTO
dispute settlement was qualified. If the dispute fell
in certain categories, the responding nation could
force the issue to be heard under Chapter 20. This
was the case when the dispute concerned topics
covered above:

- Specified environmental or conservation
  agreements;

- Sanitary and phytosanitary (SPS) health regulations; or

- Environmental, health, safety or conservation product or service standards (SRM).

Why were these categories the only disputes where the responding nation could insist on the NAFTA forum? One reason was the perception that these areas involve unusually sensitive trade matters. Another was the desire to ensure that national standards were absolutely respected (as NAFTA requires) and insulated from potentially global challenges at the WTO. A third was the "lessons" learned in the pre-NAFTA challenge by Mexico under GATT 1947 of the U.S. Marine Mammal Protection Act (dolphin-safe tuna). See BISD 39 Supp. 155 (1993). The United States certainly wanted no repetition of that adverse GATT Panel ruling, which it "blocked" by pressuring Mexico into a negotiated settlement under the 1995 Panama Declaration.

Congress authorized the importation of tuna from Panama Declaration adherents in 1997. Nevertheless, in 2008, Mexico initiated WTO dispute proceedings against U.S. "dolphin-safe" label rules and a Ninth Circuit decision requiring no usage of purse seine nets for tuna labeled dolphin-safe; *Earth Island Institute v. Hogarth*, 494 F.3d 757 (2007). In 2010, the U.S. instituted NAFTA Chapter 20 dispute proceedings seeking to force Mexico to withdraw its WTO complaint and re-file it under NAFTA, which Mexico declined to do. In 2011, a WTO panel ruled in favor of Mexico's complaint, which was upheld in 2016 by the Appellate Body, and in 2017 authorized

$163 million in Mexican retaliation against U.S. goods. However, a subsequent 2018 WTO ruling reversed this authorization and upheld the U.S. rules on dolphin-safe labeling.

Recourse to Chapter 20 dispute settlement could ordinarily be had if an actual or proposed act was or would have been inconsistent with NAFTA obligations. Canada and Mexico, for example, threatened to carry to arbitration their challenge of the 1996 U.S. "Helms-Burton" law (110 Stat. 785) against trafficking in U.S. property confiscated by Cuba. For some provisions of the agreement, Chapter 20 could also be used to challenge measures that were consistent with the NAFTA but caused "nullification or impairment" of expected benefits. But the provisions in NAFTA governing procurement, investment, telecommunications, financial services, competition law and monopolies, temporary entry of business persons, and automotive trading (Annex 300–A) typically could *not* be challenged in this way.

Any member state with a substantial interest in a Chapter 20 dispute could join as a complaining party and thereby participate in solutions to the dispute. However, in all cases, NAFTA's general dispute settlement procedures were *not* binding. Instead, consultations followed by mediation by the NAFTA Free Trade Commission followed by arbitration before a 5-member panel.

A "reverse selection" process was used to select the arbitration panel from a roster of acceptable panelists. It was possible to propose a panelist from off the roster, but such nominees could be vetoed without cause by the other side. First, the chair was selected by consensus or by lot. The chair could not be from the selecting country, but could come from outside NAFTA. For example, in the first Chapter 20 panel the chair came from Britain and in the second from Australia. Two panelists were chosen by both parties. Each side had to select persons who were citizens of the *other* country.

CHAPTER 20 ARBITRATIONS

A Chapter 20 report was completed 120 days after the request for arbitration. There was no appeal to a higher body such as the Extraordinary Challenge Committee under Chapter 19. If the dispute was not resolved, the prevailing party could pursue equivalent compensatory action within 30 days. Normally this should have been in the same economic sector, and could be challenged by panel review only if "manifestly excessive." Compensatory action could be undertaken by a member state that failed to join the dispute as a complaining party. The third NAFTA partner could not "normally" commence WTO or NAFTA proceedings on substantially equivalent grounds absent a significant change in economic or commercial circumstances.

Professor David Lopez provided a revealing portrait of early Chapter 20 dispute settlement, one which emphasizes just how few disputes were pushed to arbitration. See 32 *Texas Int'l Law J.* 163 (1997). Of the eight complaints he cites as lodged by the end of 1996, only three went to arbitration: Canadian agricultural tariffication (see Chapter 2), U.S. escape clause restraints on Mexican brooms (above), and U.S. refusal to admit Mexican trucks (above). To this date, these three disputes remain the only Chapter 20 arbitration decisions. Professor Lopez suggests that complaints lingered at the consultation/ mediation stages of Chapter 20 dispute settlement because there is no compulsion to move the dispute forward, the appointments of panelists could and sometimes were blocked, and because political realities temper that decision.

Some disputes are settled (e.g., tomatoes above) while others just keep on lingering (Helms-Burton). More often, NAFTA disputes were taken to the WTO, where dilatory dispute settlement tactics were much less available. In 2000, the United States refused to fill vacancies on the Chapter 20 roster of panelists. Thereafter, there were no state-to-state NAFTA dispute settlement proceedings.

PRIVATE COMMERCIAL DISPUTES

The NAFTA Advisory Committee on Private Commercial Disputes was very active. The Committee developed model mediation and arbitration clauses for international contracts. The promotion of mediation and arbitration as an alternative to litigation of NAFTA commercial disputes rests partly on the absence of an agreement on enforcement of judgments. This contrasts with adherence by all NAFTA member states to the New York Convention on Recognition and Enforcement of Arbitral Awards. It also rests, although not explicitly so, on a desire to avoid problems associated with Mexican linkages between penal and civil commercial dispute proceedings.

Mexican law permits civil litigants to file criminal charges, obtain judicial detention orders and dispute bail while the other party remains in jail. See Camp, 5 *U.S. Mexico L.J.* 85 (Symposium 1997). Needless to say, a negotiated settlement often arrives in short order. U.S. attorneys and clients doing business in Mexico have been on both sides of such a strategy. Back in the United States, settlements agreed to in Mexico in this manner may be void as the product of the crime of "compounding." The Texas Supreme Court has so ruled. *Lewkowicz v. El Paso Apparel Corp.,* 625 S.W.2d 301 (Tex. 1981).

CHAPTER 4

THE 1994 SIDE AGREEMENTS ON LABOR AND THE ENVIRONMENT

THE ENVIRONMENT

Environmental concerns appeared very selectively in the NAFTA 1994 agreement negotiated by President George H. W. Bush. No chapter of NAFTA was dedicated exclusively to the environment. This absence of focus and priority offended many environmentalists. Public Citizen even filed suit to enjoin NAFTA for lack of an accompanying environmental impact statement. See *Public Citizen v. USTR*, 5 F.3d 549 (D.C. Cir. 1993). If the environmentalists were upset, labor was outraged. There was absolutely no coverage of labor rights and protections in NAFTA. NAFTA's pro-business tilt activated organized labor in Canada and the United States.

Bill Clinton made NAFTA's inadequacies on labor and the environment an election campaign issue in his defeat of President Bush in 1992. Once in office President Clinton proceeded to negotiate several "side agreements" to NAFTA 1994: The North American Agreement on Environmental Cooperation (NAAEC), the Mexico-United States Border Environmental Cooperation Agreement (BECA), and the North American Agreement on Labor Cooperation (NAALC). These Agreements helped assure U.S. ratification of NAFTA. U.S. free trade agreements after NAFTA directly incorporated coverage of labor and the environment, as does the USMCA.

NAFTA PROVISIONS ON THE ENVIRONMENT

NAFTA 1994's supremacy was subordinated to the "specific trade obligations" of five pre-existing environmental and conservation agreements (Article 104). The least NAFTA-inconsistent manner of implementing these trade obligations had to be selected:

- The Convention on International Trade in Endangered Species of Wild Flora and Fauna (Washington, 1973, amended 1979);

- The Protocol on Substances That Deplete the Ozone Layer (Montreal, 1987, amended 1990);

- The Convention on the Control of Transboundary Movement of Hazardous Wastes and Their Disposal (Basel, 1989) (which the United States has not ratified);

- The Canada-U.S. Agreement Concerning Transboundary Movement of Hazardous Waste (Ottawa, 1986); and

- The Mexico-U.S. Agreement on Cooperation for the Protection and Improvement of the Environment of the Border Area (La Paz, 1983).

It is noteworthy that NAFTA supremacy was subordinated to no other types of international agreements.

Under NAFTA, each member state retains the right to establish its own levels of environmental protection. For example, "sustainable development" is specifically recognized as a legitimate objective for environmental regulation of trade goods. See Chapter 3. NAFTA also prioritizes the need for scientific evaluation of environmental risks in establishing environmental product and SPS (food) standards. *Id.* Furthermore, if environmentally-related trade disputes emerge, there is heavy emphasis on employment of scientific experts to resolve them. *Id.* Most significantly, NAFTA forced disputes about environmental standards or the pre-existing agreements listed above into NAFTA dispute settlement. Such issues, if taken to the WTO by the complainant, could be brought back to NAFTA Chapter 20 by the respondent. *Id.*

The NAFTA agreement also articulates a commitment not to lower environmental standards for purposes of attracting investment ("pollution havens"). See Chapter 3. However, since this promise is not subject to NAFTA dispute settlement and possible sanctions under Chapter 20, it was not exactly a ringing endorsement of environmental concerns.

THE NORTH AMERICAN AGREEMENT ON ENVIRONMENTAL COOPERATION (NAAEC)

A trilateral Commission for Environmental Cooperation (CEC) was established under the NAAEC side agreement. The Commission's Environmental Council of Ministers was comprised of cabinet-level officers from each member state. The Council could discuss, recommend and settle environmental disputes publicly by consensus. The Commission's Secretariat (located in Montreal) investigated, reviewed and reported with recommendations to the Council on environmental matters.

The Executive Director of the Secretariat rotated every three years among the NAAEC countries. He or she chose the staff of the Secretariat on the basis of "competence and integrity." However, "due regard" had to be given to recruiting "equitable proportions" from each country (Article 11). The CEC Council of Ministers and Secretariat were advised, especially on technical and scientific matters, by a 15-person Joint Public Advisory Committee.

Under the NAAEC, each member state agreed to maintain "high" levels of environmental protection, but this commitment was not enforceable through NAAEC dispute settlement. Rather, NAAEC focused on enforcement of the individual environmental protection standards of each nation. This focus, politically speaking, targeted Mexico. There was a widespread perception in the United States that Mexican enforcement of its environmental laws states was inadequate. It is perhaps ironic therefore that many of the complaints lodged under NAAEC challenged Canadian and U.S. environmental law enforcement.

ARTICLE 13 REPORTS

Article 13 authorized the CEC Secretariat to issue reports on virtually any environmental matter not involving law enforcement. Notice of intent to issue such a report had first to be given to the CEC Council of Ministers. If the Council objected by a two-thirds vote, no report could be undertaken. Nongovernmental organizations (NGOs) and others could and did petition for Article 13 reports by the Secretariat. For example, the two first Article 13 reports concerned long range transport of air pollutants and the death of 40,000 migratory birds at the Silva Reservoir in Guanajuato. The latter report determined that avian botulism was the cause of the deaths and fostered a clean-up and cooperative information exchanges.

A 2004 report on the effects of transgenic maize in Mexico was noticeably high profile. Other reports concerned continental pollutant pathways, electricity and the environment, green building in North America, and sustainable freight transport. An Article 13 report concerned water use in the Fort Huachuca, Arizona region. It was undertaken at the initiative of the CEC Secretariat after an Article 14 complaint (below) concerning riparian areas for migratory birds was dismissed. (The Secretariat determined that preparation of a factual record was not warranted.) Thus Article 13 reports could serve as an alternative to direct challenges raised under Article 14. They represented a "name and shame" technique.

ARTICLE 14 CITIZEN AND NGO SUBMISSIONS

The NAAEC, under Article 14, contained its own submission, response and dispute resolution process. "Whistleblower" complaints could be filed with the CEC Secretariat by any person or nongovernmental organization (NGO) concerning workplaces, enterprises or sectors that produce NAAEC—traded or NAAEC—competitive goods or services. For example, notable complaints were filed in 2017 by Canadian environmental advocacy groups against their government's alleged inadequate response to toxic leaks from tailing ponds in the oil sands of Alberta.

Article 14 submissions had to allege that a NAAEC nation was not "effectively enforcing" *its* environmental law. See SEM–97–005 (submission challenging Canada's ratification [but not implementation by statute] of Biodiversity Convention did not concern effective enforcement of *Canadian* law). SEM stands for Submissions on Enforcement Matters. Guidelines for such submissions were issued by the CEC Secretariat. They can be found at the Secretariat's excellent web site, www.cec.org.

The Secretariat could dismiss Article 14 submissions on a variety of grounds. For example, the NAAEC agreement stipulated that no ineffective enforcement of environmental law existed when the action or inaction reflected a reasonable exercise of official discretion in investigatory, prosecutorial, regulatory or compliance matters. Furthermore, since "environmental law" was defined in NAAEC as excluding occupational safety and health laws, and laws that primarily managed the harvest or exploitation of natural resources, such complaints could also be dismissed. See SEM–98–002 (submission concerning Mexican commercial forestry dispute dismissed). The submission had to "appear to be aimed at promoting enforcement rather than harassing industry." (Article 14(1)(d)). It also needed to be filed in a timely manner. See SEM–97–004 (submission filed three years after Canadian environmental decision not timely). And it had to provide "sufficient information" to allow the Secretariat to review the submission. See SEM–10–002 (Alberta Tailing Ponds) and SEM–04–005 (U.S. Coal-Fired Power Plants).

The CEC Secretariat determined if the submission merited a response from the nation whose environmental law enforcement practices were being challenged. Private remedies available under national law had to have been pursued and pending administrative or judicial proceedings kept the CEC from moving forward on the complaint. See *Canadian Wetlands* and *Canadian Fisheries Act* (CEC rejects citizen and NGO submissions) SEM–96–002 and 003. Since the NAAEC required extensive private access to environmental remedies, including the ability to file complaints with administrative authorities, access to administrative, quasi-judicial and judicial proceedings, and the right to sue for damages, mitigating relief and injunctions, exhausting national remedies first was a major prerequisite. In evaluating whether a submission merited a response, the Secretariat was also to be "guided" by whether the submission alleged "harm" to the complaining party. Proof of such harm was not mandatory, merely a relevant issue. Several of the Secretariat's early decisions suggested that it takes a liberal view of this "standing" question. See *Cozumel Pier*, SEM–96–001 (discussed below).

In addition, as the rejection by the Secretariat of the first two Article 14 submissions made clear, legislative actions that diminish environmental law enforcement could be challenged SEM–95–001 and 002. Complaints by various NGOs against the suspension of enforcement of the U.S. Endangered Species Act listing provisions and elimination of private remedies for U.S. timber salvage sales (both alleged to have been accomplished in appropriations bills) failed to proceed under Article 14.

FACTUAL RECORDS

With or without a response from the member state alleged to be inadequately enforcing its law, the Secretariat had to decide whether development of a factual record was warranted and inform the Council of its reasons. The Council had to approve development of a factual record by a two-thirds vote. If there were past, pending, or possible national administrative or judicial proceedings, the Secretariat or Council were unlikely to allow this to occur. NAAEC governments were obliged to submit relevant information throughout the factual record process, but the Secretariat could not enforce this obligation.

The third submission under Article 14 was made by Mexican NGOs alleging that the Mexican government had failed to conduct an environmental impact review before authorizing a cruise ship pier at Cozumel Island, SEM–96–001. The CEC Secretariat ruled that this complaint passed muster under Article 14 and compiled the first factual record under NAAEC, Factual Record No. 1 (1997). After summarizing the submission and Mexican response, the CEC "presented" facts with respect to the "matters raised in the submissions." In this record, the CEC adopted the role of a neutral finder of facts.

The second Factual Record concerned a submission that alleged that the Canadian government failed to enforce the Fisheries Act to ensure protection of fish and fish habitat in connection with hydroelectric dams in British Columbia, SEM–97–001. Subsequent Article 14 Factual Records concerned Canadian enforcement of the Fisheries Act in the Arctic (Oldman River, SEM–97–006), logging rules in British Columbia (SEM–00–004), and mining in British Columbia (SEM–98–004).

Other Factual Records covered U.S. law enforcement regarding migratory birds (SEM–99–002), Mexican enforcement of hazardous waste law in Tijuana (SEM–98–007), and Mexico City (SEM–03–004), shrimp farming regulations in Nayarit (SEM–98–006), wastewater river pollution in Sonora (SEM–97–002), pulp and paper mill pollution in Canada (SEM–02–003), Canadian migratory bird protection from logging (SEM–02–001), (SEM–04–006), access to environmental justice by Mexican Indigenous communities (Tarahumara, SEM–00–006), copper smelting pollution in Sonora, Mexico (Molymex II, SEM–00–005) pollution of Lake Chapala in Mexico (SEM–03–003), auto pollution in Quebec (SEM–04–007) and toxic pollutants in Montreal (SEM–03–005). All of these Records are available at www.cec.org.

ENVIRONMENTAL COUNCIL OF MINISTERS

The Secretariat's factual record went to the Environmental Council of Ministers. By a two-thirds vote, the Council could release it to the public, as was done in the *Cozumel Pier* dispute. Such releases were the only available "sanction" unless there had been a "persistent pattern of failure" (from January 1, 1994) to effectively enforce environmental law. For these purposes, persistent pattern was defined as a "sustained or recurring course of action or inaction" (Article 45). If (and only if) there was such a pattern did formal NAAEC dispute settlement commence. The *Cozumel Pier* dispute, for example, did not get beyond preparation by the CEC of a factual record.

Formal dispute settlement started with consultations which were followed by Council mediation and conciliation. Ultimately, the Council by a two-thirds vote could forward the dispute to arbitration, with monetary penalties against the offending nation conceivably possible. No such arbitrations were ever undertaken.

SUMMARY

In sum, the NAAEC established five environmental dispute settlement mechanisms.

First, the Secretariat could report on almost any environmental matter. *Second*, the Secretariat could develop a factual record in trade-related national law enforcement disputes. *Third*, the Council could release that record to the public. *Fourth*, if there was a persistent pattern of failure to enforce national environmental law, the Council was to mediate and conciliate. *Fifth*, if such efforts failed, the Council could send the matter to arbitration and awards could be enforced by monetary or tariff penalties.

In actual operation over 24 years, the NAEEC functioned primarily, and for the most part ineffectively, as a "name and shame" mechanism.

THE MEXICO-UNITED STATES BORDER ENVIRONMENTAL COOPERATION AGREEMENT

Long before NAFTA or NAAEC, Mexico and the United States had negotiated an Agreement on Cooperation for the Protection and Improvement of the Environment in the Border Area (the 1983 La Paz Agreement). This Agreement and its support system remains in place under the USMCA.

With rapid maquiladora growth along the border in the 1980s and 1990s, border environmental issues came to the forefront. In 1992, Mexico and the United States established and financed an integrated border environment cleanup program that prioritized drinking water, waste treatment, hazardous waste and law enforcement. A "Border 2020 Plan" continues these orientations, along with reductions in CO_2 emissions.

In 1993, as a NAFTA side agreement, the two countries ratified the Mexico-U.S. Border Environment Cooperation Agreement. Under this agreement, the Border Environment Cooperation Commission (BECC) was created with offices in El Paso, Texas and Ciudad Juarez, Mexico. The BECC is intended to provide expertise on border environmental protection. If the BECC certifies infrastructure proposals as meeting technical and environmental criteria, funding (and assistance in obtaining funding) by the North American Development Bank (NADBank) is possible.

The NADBank was inaugurated by the 1993 Agreement and is funded and governed jointly by Mexico and the United States. It is located in San Antonio, Texas. Priority is given to water and solid waste initiatives that are self-sustaining, mostly through user fees. Since 2000, air pollution, public transport, clean energy and municipal planning are possible projects. NADBank interest rates are not subsidized, generally Treasury Rates plus 2 percent. The NADBank has a cooperative agreement with the EPA to combine its financing with EPA grants. It also has partnered with export credit agencies, border states, and the private sector in co-financings.

It is fair to say that the BECC and NADBank proceeded slowly in carrying out their missions. There have been lots of studies and strategizing. Gradually some environmental infrastructure projects were given the green light. By the end of 2003, the BECC had certified over 90 projects, nearly 70 of which garnered NADBank's approval for

leveraged financing. That said, with $2.5 *billion* to
lend, NADBank by 2004 had only lent $1.05 million.
By 2013, thousands of water or wastewater
treatment facility financings had been undertaken.
Although the pace of BECC and NADBank (jokingly
referred to as the Nada Bank) activity has increased,
their capacities to meet the challenges of border
pollution remain in doubt.

LABOR

NAFTA had virtually no coverage of labor
standards, rights or regulations. Ordinary workers
were also left out of the NAFTA provisions on
temporary entry visas. See Chapter 3. Unlike the
European Union, there was and remains no NAFTA
right of free movement for workers. The omission of
labor from NAFTA became an issue in the 1992
presidential election. As he promised during his
campaign, President Clinton negotiated a "side"
labor agreement in 1993: The North American
Agreement on Labor Cooperation (NAALC). This
supplemental agreement was helpful in securing
passage of NAFTA through the U.S. Congress. U.S.
free trade agreements since NAFTA directly
incorporate coverage of labor, as does the USMCA.

Mexico's presence drove the NAALC negotiations.
Ironically, the Mexican Constitution embraces
workers, unions, working conditions and a host of
labor-related rights. But the operational reality of
Mexican labor law is debatable, especially given the
alliance for many years between the Confederacion
de Trabajadores Mexicanos (CTM), Mexico's most

powerful labor organization, and the dominant PRI political party.

A number of commentators suggested that Mexico's employer-dominated industrial relations were more "customary" than legal. Indeed, many of the customs directly contravene Mexican labor law. For example, organization of "independent" unions (not affiliated with the CTM or sponsored by employers) is customarily opposed, sometimes by payoffs or violence, but more generally by CTM or PRI/government-controlled labor tribunals charged with registering unions. Job security, paid leave, working hours, occupational safety and even the constitutionally enshrined Christmas bonus don't always conform in reality to the requirements of Mexican law.

The NAALC agreement therefore centered on enforcement problems under Mexican law, but was not limited to Mexico. It was limited in its application to Canada because most labor matters in that country were governed by provincial not federal law. Canadian provinces could opt in or remain outside NAALC. For NAALC to apply, the matter had to be governed by Canadian federal labor law or designated percentages of the Canadian labor force as a result of provincial opt ins. Alberta, Quebec, Manitoba and Prince Edward Island agreed to respect the NAALC.

THE NORTH AMERICAN AGREEMENT ON LABOR COOPERATION (NAALC)

The right of each NAFTA nation to establish different but "high" labor standards was preserved by NAALC. However, eleven "guiding labor principles" were recognized in Annex 1. These are reproduced at the end of this chapter. Annex 1 specified that these principles were not to be construed as creating common minimum labor law standards for the region.

Under NAALC, each member state promised "effective enforcement" of its labor laws. This commitment extended to laws governing the eleven areas cited in the guiding labor principles: Occupational safety and health; equal pay for men and women; labor rights to organize; the right to strike; forced labor; employment standards; collective bargaining; child labor; workers' compensation; employment discrimination; migrant workers; and collectively bargained agreements. As we shall see below, NAALC remedies varied with the subject matter under dispute.

Procedural guarantees to support fair, transparent and equitable legal processes of concern to laborers were also established under NAALC. These included promises to ensure due process of law, open meetings, the right to be heard, reasonable fees, time frames and procedures, written decisions based on evidence in the record, impartial review and effective remedies.

Much of NAALC's cooperation on labor matters was educational in focus. Conferences, seminars and workshops abounded on everything from child labor to gender issues, the right to organize and occupational safety, and employment and job training. Just exactly what impact all these educational programs had is hard to measure.

THE NAALC COMMISSION AND SECRETARIAT

The NAALC created a North American Commission for Labor Cooperation. This Commission had a Council of Ministers and a Secretariat located in Dallas, Texas. Perhaps most importantly, in sharp contrast with NAAEC (above), the Labor Secretariat could review individual or organizational complaints concerning effective labor law enforcement. The Commission's functions were largely monitoring, study and report.

The Commission's comparative Report on Plant Closings and Labor Rights (1997) is quoted below regarding union organizing. Other comparative Reports covered Labor Markets (1997), Employment of Women (1998), Income Security Programs (2000), the Garment Industry (2000), Labor Relations Law (2000), Migrant Agricultural Workers (2002), Nonstandard Workers' Rights (2003), Labor Markets since NAFTA (2003), Work Violence (2006), and Migrant Workers (2011).

CITIZEN, UNION AND NGO
SUBMISSIONS, NAO REPORTS

Individual and organizational submissions about labor law, its administration or labor market conditions in a member state could be filed with "National Administrative Offices" (NAO) in each country. The U.S. NAO was located in the Bureau of International Affairs of the Department of Labor. All submissions had to allege a failure to enforce national labor law in *another* member state. For example, complaints about Mexican labor law could only be filed with the Canadian or United States NAO. The three NAOs consulted one another, but whether to review and report was a matter of discretion for the NAO receiving the complaint. See U.S. NAO Submission No. 9801 (handling of AeroMexico strike, dismissed as not furthering NAALC objectives) and No. 9804 (collective bargaining for rural mail carriers at Canada Post, dismissed as not raising issues of application or enforcement of labor law). Two NAOs could and did review the same submission concerning labor law enforcement in the third NAFTA nation.

Under NAALC there were no structured complaint and response procedures as in the Environmental Cooperation Agreement. Even so, there was a reasonable amount of NAO activity. See https://www.dol.gov/agencies/ilab/trade/agreements/naalcgd. Most NAO reports followed public hearings and ended up recommending ministerial consultations (below).

MINISTERIAL CONSULTATIONS, EXPERT REPORTS

NAFTA nations could at any time request ministerial consultations on all labor principles (see the attachment to this chapter) covered by the NAALC. If ministerial consultations failed, a three-person Evaluation Committee of Experts (ECE) could be created in most trade-related instances, but not if the issues concerned collective bargaining, strikes or union organizing. This meant that the numerous disputes about union organizing (below) could never proceed to an ECE report.

The Labor Ministers Council selected the Committee which reported back with recommendations to the Council. Comparative assessments of the enforcement "patterns of practice" of NAFTA nations on mutually recognized labor laws were the focus of ECE reports. In the end, the ECE report was published unless the Council decided otherwise. But no Evaluation Committee of Experts was ever created under NAALC!

LIMITED LABOR LAW ENFORCEMENT ARBITRATIONS, MONETARY PENALTIES

For certain issues, publication of the ECE report was all that could be done under NAALC. This was the case for issues of employment discrimination, equal pay, occupational safety, worker compensation, minimum employment standards, migrant workers, forced labor and protection of children and youth. When, however, the issues concerned enforcement of occupational safety and health, child labor or minimum wage laws, further consultations could occur. The Labor Ministers Council could attempt to mediate.

Ultimately a two-thirds vote of the Council could send the persistent pattern of enforcement failure issue to arbitration. That would have been be hard to find since Article 49 of the NAALC specifically provided that a Party had not failed to effectively enforce its law where the action or inaction by agencies or officials: (a) Reflects a reasonable exercise discretion with respect to investigatory, prosecutorial, regulatory or compliance matters; or (b) results from *bona fide* decisions to allocate resources to enforcement of other labor matters determined to have higher priorities. No such arbitration, conceivably to be followed by monetary or tariff penalties, ever took place.

SUMMARY

In sum, the NAALC labor law enforcement system was a calibrated four-tier series of dispute resolution mechanisms. *First*, the NAOs could review and report on eleven designated labor law enforcement matters that correspond to the NAALC Labor Principles (below). *Second*, ministerial consultations could follow when recommended by the NAO. *Third*, an Evaluation Committee of Experts could report on trade-related mutually recognized labor law enforcement patterns of practice concerning eight of the NAALC Labor Principles (excluding strikes, union organizing and collective bargaining). *Fourth*, persistent patterns of failure to enforce occupational health and safety, child labor or minimum wage laws could be arbitrated and awards enforced by monetary or tariff penalties.

LABOR LAW ENFORCEMENT SUBMISSIONS—UNION ORGANIZING

Early U.S. organized labor submissions to the United States NAO alleged the firing by U.S. and Japanese maquiladora subsidiaries of Mexican workers due to union organizing activities, U.S. NAO Submission Nos. 940001, 2 and 3. Public hearings were held at which Mexican workers, their attorneys and U.S. union supporters gave testimony. Honeywell, General Electric and SONY boycotted these hearings. The NAO Report in the Honeywell and GE cases was generally uncertain as to the legality of the firings under Mexican law, particularly because some of the dismissed workers accepted severance pay which indemnified the employers. No ministerial consultations were recommended, but some employees were reinstated and both Honeywell and GE made it clear to their managers that they did not want a reoccurrence of these events.

With SONY, the NAO Report cited "serious questions" about the legality of the firings and recommended ministerial consultations. These consultations resulted in a series of workshops, conferences, studies and meetings (including SONY representatives) on union registration and certification (especially of independent unions) in Mexico. In due course, the U.S. Secretary of Labor requested a follow-up NAO report. This report put a positive spin on developments in Mexico concerning union organizing, a topic that NAALC did not allow to proceed to the next dispute settlement tier (an Evaluation Committee of Experts).

On the other side of the border, the Telephone Workers Union of Mexico (collaborating with the Communications Workers of America) (CWA) filed a submission with the Mexican NAO about worker dismissals and a plant closing at Sprint's La Conexion Familiar in San Francisco, OAN Mex. Submission No. 9501. Again, the allegation involved denial of labor's right to organize. The NLRB eventually ruled against Sprint and ordered rehiring of the workers. See 322 NLRB 774 (1996). On appeal, the D.C. Circuit found that the claim that plant was closed because of union organizing activities was not substantiated. *LCF, Inc. v. NLRB*, 129 F.3d 1276 (1997).

In the *Sprint* submission the Mexican NAO found "possible problems" in enforcement of U.S. labor law and recommended ministerial consultations. These consultations resulted in a public forum, a special report by the NAALC Commission on *Plant Closings and Labor Rights* (1997) in all three NAFTA nations, and monitoring of the pending NLRB proceeding based upon Sprint's actions. The NAALC Commission report, quoted below, highlights widespread use of anti-union plant closing tactics in the United States (but not Canada or Mexico):

> "U.S. labor law authorities actively prosecute unfair labor practice cases involving plant closings and

threats of plant closing. They demonstrate a high level of success in litigation before the NLRB and the courts. However, despite this effective enforcement, the incidence of anti-union plant closings and threats of plant closing continues with some frequency. There appears to be significant variation in the types of statements employers are permitted to make about plant closings in connection with a union organizing effort.

The Secretariat examined all 89 federal appeals court decisions in cases involving plant closings and threats of plant closing published between 1986 and 1993. Of the cases, 70 arose in the context of a new union organizing campaign. Closings or partial closings prompted 32 cases, and 57 cases involved threats of closing. Courts of appeals upheld NLRB determinations that employers unlawfully closed or threatened to close plants in 84 of the 89 cases.

The Secretariat studied 319 decisions of the NLRB between 1990 and 1995 involving plant closings and the threats of closing. Of the total, 109 cases involved closings or partial closings, and 210 involved threats of closing. New union organizing campaigns in non-union workplaces were involved in 275 of these cases, while 44 involved existing unions. The NLRB found a violation by the employer in 283 of the 319 cases.

The Secretariat also looked at case files in two regional offices of the NLRB to determine the volume and disposition of cases that do not reach the level of a published determination by an adjudicator. Findings suggest that for every case that reaches a published decision, 10 cases are initiated at the regional office level. More than half of these are withdrawn or dismissed.

In more than 40 percent of cases where the regional office found merit in the charge, the NLRB General Counsel took the case to trial before an ALJ. This is 10 times the rate of enforcement in other cases of meritorious unfair labor practice charges against employers. These findings indicate that the NLRB takes plant closing cases very seriously and actively pursues them to a litigated conclusion. The General Counsel prevails in nearly 90 percent of such cases.

In the United States, resources were readily available to conduct survey research for information that could not be gleaned from administrative and judicial records. Union representatives surveyed reported what they believed to be plant closing threats occurring in half of the sampled union organizing campaigns during the 3-year period studied, with a higher incidence in industries more susceptible to closing such as manufacturing, trucking, and warehousing. Perceived plant closing threats were the largest single factor identified by respondents who decided to withdraw an election petition they had earlier filed, thus discontinuing the organizing campaign. When unions proceeded to an election, the overall union win rate where plant closing threats were reported to have occurred was 33 percent, compared with 47 percent in elections where no threats were reported to have taken place."

The fourth submission to the U.S. NAO was made by labor and human rights groups and a Mexican lawyers' association. They claimed that an independent public sector Mexican union lost its representation rights to a rival union when the government merged the Fisheries Ministry into a larger Ministry of the Environment, Natural

Resources and Fisheries, U.S. NAO Submission No. 9610 ("Pesca Union"). After a public hearing at which many testified, the NAO Report recommended ministerial consultations on the effect of International Labor Organization (ILO) Conventions (No. 87 was cited) on Mexican labor law, particularly the prohibition against more than one union in a governmental entity. The independent union subsequently had its registration restored by Mexican court order.

The Mexican NAO also accepted submissions challenging U.S. labor law enforcement concerning workers in a solar panel plant in California, the Washington State apple industry, a Maine egg farm, migrant workers in New York, H–2B Visa workers, and the North Carolina ban on public sector collective bargaining, OAN Mex. Nos. 9801, 9802, 9803, 2001–01, 2003–1, 2005–01, 2006–1.

Another union organizing case came to the U.S. NAO in 1996, Submission No. 9602. The Communications Workers of America and its Mexican ally (the STRM) alleged that Taiwan-owned Maxi-Switch had a "protection contract" with a CTM union that was not employee approved. CTM was closely allied with the ruling PRI party. After scheduling public testimony, the complaint was withdrawn when registration was granted to a STRM-affiliated "independent" union in the Maxi-Switch maquiladora plant.

Other submissions accepted by the U.S. NAO concerning union organizing in Mexico involved the Itapsa export processing plant in Ciudad de los Reyes (also filed with the Canadian NAO), and TAESA flight attendants, U.S. Submissions 9801 and 9901. A rare Canadian-oriented submission challenged Quebec law enforcement on union organizing at a McDonald's restaurant in St. Hubert, U.S. Submission 9803.

Perhaps the most bitter of all the union organizing complaints was that filed against Han Young, a Hyundai Corporation maquiladora making truck chassis in Tijuana, Mexico, U.S. NAO Submission No. 9702. Unions and labor groups from all three NAFTA nations alleged a brutal and blatant pattern of employer-CTM opposition to an independent union organizing effort. The U.S. NAO report documented threats, bribes, harassment, intimidation and dismissals.

Moreover, the independent union's election victory was inexplicably nullified by the local Mexican labor Conciliation and Arbitration Board (CAB). At this point, with outrage and embarrassment evident in the NAO investigation, the Mexican federal and state governments intervened and negotiated a settlement allowing a second supervised election which the independents also won. The local CAB then delayed notifying the election results to Han Young which in turn refused to collectively bargain. Indeed, Han Young hired a large number of new workers just in time for the CTM to petition for a third union representation election, which not surprisingly succeeded.

For a complete review of NAO submissions and reports in all three countries, see https://www.dol.gov/agencies/ilab/trade/agreements/naalcgd.

NAO SUBMISSION STRATEGIES

One pattern that emerged in NAALC dispute settlement was the cross-border alliance of U.S. organized labor with Mexican labor groups, particularly those that are part of the "forista" movement for independent unions. Another factor of note was the absence of any need to exhaust national administrative remedies, which was required under the NAAEC. Indeed, there were essentially no "standing to complain" requirements under NAALC. The NAOs could investigate and report at their discretion.

One example of creative use of the NAALC involved double barrel submissions. In at least two instances, organized labor and NGOs filed complaints with both available NAOs. In one case, the U.S. NAO and the Canada NAO received essentially the same submission concerning union organizing and occupational safety at an auto parts plant in Ciudad de los Reyes, Mexico, U.S. Submission No. 9703 and Canada Submission No. 98–1. Each NAO then proceeded to review and report on inadequate Mexican labor law enforcement. Both NAOs recommended Ministerial Consultations.

Likewise, in 1998, a coalition of NGOs headed by a Yale Law School group filed submissions with the Canadian and Mexican NAOs alleging ineffective enforcement of U.S. minimum wage and overtime pay laws against employers of foreign nationals, Submission Nos. Canada 98–2 and Mexico 9804. These complaints challenged U.S. Labor Department reporting of suspected immigration violations to the U.S. Immigration and Naturalization Service. They alleged that such practices deter immigrant workers from filing wage and hour complaints under U.S. law. On the same day that the Mexican NAO accepted the submission (Nov. 23, 1998), the U.S. government announced that a Memorandum of Understanding had been signed with the intent of dealing with these issues.

THE PREGNANCY DISCRIMINATION COMPLAINT

As the number, scope and creativity of the submissions and reports grew in the first decade, NAALC appeared to be something more than the toothless tiger many alleged it to be. For example, the U.S. NAO investigated allegations of widespread state-tolerated sex discrimination against pregnant women in maquiladora plants, Submission No. 9701. This complaint could have resulted (but did not) in a report by an Evaluation Committee of Experts (discussed above).

Human Rights Watch/Americas, the International Labor Rights Fund and the Association Nacional de Abogados Democraticos (the same complainants in the *Pesca Union* case above) filed this submission. They maintained that employers regularly used pregnancy tests to avoid the six weeks paid maternity leave required under Mexican law. The

Mexican NAO challenged these complaints as beyond the scope of the NAALC, asserted that Mexican law adequately protects women from gender discrimination, and argued that there was no Mexican law against pre-employment pregnancy screening. The U.S. NAO hired an expert on Mexican labor law and gender issues and held public hearings in Brownsville, Texas at which workers and expert witnesses testified.

The U.S. NAO, in its report, reviewed Mexican constitutional and labor law, their enforcement bodies, the Alliance for Equality (the Mexican National Program for Women, 1995–2000), the Mexican Human Rights Commission and relevant international conventions. Post-employment pregnancy discrimination is clearly illegal in Mexico. On pre-employment law, one decision of note that emerged from the investigation was that of the Human Rights Commission for the Federal District which found pre-employment pregnancy screening a violation of Articles 4 and 5 of the Mexican Constitution. Below is the U.S. NAO analysis on point. Note especially its implications concerning the credibility of the Mexican NAO submissions in response to the complaint:

> "[T]he Human Rights Commission for the Federal District offers a markedly different interpretation to that of the Mexican NAO on the legality of pre-employment pregnancy screening. The Commission found (1) that the federal agencies it investigated did, in fact, conduct pregnancy screening and, (2) this practice violated Mexico's Constitution.

The Mexican NAO has asserted that the recommendations of the Commission are not binding and do not establish jurisprudence. The enacting legislation for the Commission, however, imposes an obligation on the responding agencies to comply with the recommendations once they accept the findings of the report. Additionally, the Commission was created pursuant to the Mexican Constitution and implemented by Federal law. It is composed of prominent jurists, appointed by the President and confirmed by the legislature, and their recommendation, in this case, was complied with by Federal Government agencies. Further, though the case involved public sector agencies, in its recommendation the Commission made no distinction on the application of the appropriate constitutional guarantees between the public and private sectors.

The position of the Human Rights Commission on the legality of pregnancy screening is markedly different from that expressed by the Mexican NAO. Moreover, the *Alliance for Equality* recognized pregnancy screening as a problem and outlined a plan of action to address such discriminatory practices. That pregnancy screening occurs and is of concern is supported by information from companies conducting business in Mexico, women workers, and the submitters. It also appears that the intrusive nature of the questioning described in the submission goes beyond what is necessary to determine if an applicant for employment is pregnant.

An additional question is raised with regard to the lack of any legal procedure by which to bring cases of pre-employment gender discrimination. The Mexican NAO asserted that the FLL [Federal Labor Law] does not provide for the adjudication of cases involving pre-employment discrimination. CAB officials interviewed by HRW [Human Rights Watch] also indicated that the CABs had no jurisdiction over these cases as they involved issues that occurred prior to the establishment of the employment relationship. The Mexican NAO's position appears to go beyond the question of pre-employment pregnancy screening to also include the lack of a legal procedure for bringing any pre-employment discrimination issue. Since Mexican law clearly prohibits employers from discriminating in hiring for a variety of reasons, the Mexican NAO's response creates a question as to what process exists for bringing such pre-employment discrimination claims."

The U.S. NAO report issued in Submission No. 9701 recommended ministerial consultations. These resulted in a U.S.-Mexican agreement on an improved "action plan" to combat pregnancy discrimination in the workplace, which seemed to have somewhat reduced pregnancy screening prior to employment in Mexico.

After a flurry of NAO submissions during the first decade of NAALC, the numbers dropped significantly. NAALC as a labor law enforcement "remedy" was increasingly perceived to be largely cosmetic and not worth pursuing.

TRADE ADJUSTMENT ASSISTANCE

There was a second Clinton Administration approach to labor issues and NAFTA. Worker training and trade adjustment assistance for persons displaced by NAFTA 1994 was adopted unilaterally as part of U.S. law. These provisions can be found in the NAFTA Implementation Act, Title V, entitled the "NAFTA Worker Safety Act" (now merged into the Trade Adjustment Assistance program, below).

Under this Act, workers could petition the Secretary of Labor for assistance if a significant number of employees were threatened with job losses. NAFTA imports had to have "contributed importantly" to this result. Assistance was also available if production of like or directly competitive articles had been shifted to Mexico or Canada. Income support (extended beyond regular state unemployment benefits) and job search and relocation reimbursements were possible, but only if job training was undertaken.

In the first three years of operation, the Secretary of Labor certified nearly 100,000 U.S. workers as being "at risk" because of NAFTA imports or job shifts. Not all of these workers actually lost their jobs. Mexico was the source country in 60 percent of these certifications, Canada 23 percent and 17 percent involved no single source. Of these 100,000 workers, only slightly more than 12,000 applied for NAFTA trade adjustment benefits. Another 20,000 certified workers opted for regular (non-NAFTA) trade adjustment benefits where job training requirements could be waived. By 2002, more than half a million workers had been certified for NAFTA trade assistance.

The NAFTA program was merged into a consolidated Trade Adjustment Assistance (TAA) policy under the Trade Act of 2002. The TAA program covers workers displaced by NAFTA 1994, CAFTA

2005, bilateral U.S. free trade agreements, the Andean Trade Preference Act, the Caribbean Basin Recovery Act or the African Growth and Opportunity Act. Such workers no longer need prove that increased imports are a factor in their displacement. See *Former Employees of Tesco Technologies v. U.S. Secretary of Labor*, 30 C.I.T. 1754 (2006) (software designers eligible). Presumably, it will apply under the USMCA.

NAALC 1994

Annex 1

LABOR PRINCIPLES

The following are guiding principles that the Parties are committed to promote, subject to each Party's domestic law, but do not establish common minimum standards for their domestic law. They indicate broad areas of concern where the Parties have developed, each in its own way, laws, regulations, procedures and practices that protect the rights and interests of their respective workforces.

1. Freedom of association and protection of the right to organize

The right of workers exercised freely and without impediment to establish and join organizations of their own choosing to further and defend their interests.

2.   The right to bargain collectively

The protection of the right of organized workers to freely engage in collective bargaining on matters concerning the terms and conditions of employment.

3.   The right to strike

The protection of the right of workers to strike in order to defend their collective interests.

4.   Prohibition of forced labor

The prohibition and suppression of all forms of forced or compulsory labor, except for types of compulsory work generally considered acceptable by the parties, such as compulsory military service, certain civic obligations, prison labor not for private purposes and work exacted in cases of emergency.

5.   Labor protections for children and young persons

The establishment of restrictions on the employment of children and young persons that may vary taking into consideration relevant factors likely to jeopardize the full physical, mental and moral development of young persons, including schooling and safety requirements.

6.   Minimum employment standards

The establishment of minimum employment standards, such as minimum wages and overtime pay, for wage earners, including those not covered by collective agreements.

7. Elimination of employment discrimination

Elimination of employment discrimination on such grounds as race, religion, age, sex or other grounds, subject to certain reasonable exceptions, such as, where applicable, bona fide occupational requirements or qualifications and established practices or rules governing retirement ages, and special measures of protection or assistance for particular groups designed to take into account the effects of discrimination.

8. Equal pay for women and men

Equal wages for women and men by applying the principle of equal pay for equal work in the same establishment.

9. Prevention of occupational injuries and illnesses

Prescribing and implementing standards to minimize the causes of occupational injuries and illnesses.

10. Compensation in cases of occupational injuries and illnesses

The establishment of a system providing benefits and compensation to workers or their dependents in cases of occupational injuries, accident or fatalities arising out of, linked with or occurring in the course of employment.

11. Protection of migrant workers

Providing migrant workers in a Party's territory with the same legal protection as the Party's nationals in respect of working conditions.

CHAPTER 5

NAFTA: ITS ECONOMIC AND BUSINESS IMPACT

International trade has been going on for a long time. If, as some critics suggest, trade is "bad" for America it would have likely died a quiet death sometime in the past. Most economists and trade experts probably agree with the statement, "Trade is good for America but not necessarily all Americans."

When attempting to assess the impact of NAFTA since 1994, it is important to recognize who is doing the assessment. There are pro-trade organizations and anti-trade groups. Probably the most objective analysis is provided by the Congressional Research Service (CRS). In early 2017, with President Trump threatening to withdraw from NAFTA, Congress asked the CRS to analyze the impact of the agreement to date. As stated in their byline, the CRS's mission is "Informing the legislative debate since 1914". What follows largely draws on their analysis (CRS 7-5700).

MACRO PREDICTIONS AND RESULTS

The overall impact of NAFTA is difficult to measure since trade and investment trends are influenced by numerous other economic variables including economic growth, inflation, and currency fluctuations. The agreement likely accelerated and also locked in trade liberalization that was already taking place in Mexico, but many of these changes may have taken place without an agreement.

Nevertheless, NAFTA was significant because it was the most comprehensive free trade agreement (FTA) negotiated at the time and contained several groundbreaking provisions. A legacy of the agreement is that it has served as a template or model for the new generation of FTAs that the United States later negotiated, and it also served as a template for certain provisions in multinational trade negotiations that led to the creation of the WTO in 1995. See Chapter 3.

When first proposed, NAFTA was controversial mostly because it was the first FTA involving two wealthy, developed countries and a developing country. The political debate surrounding the agreement was divisive with proponents arguing that the agreement would help generate thousands of jobs and reduce income disparity in the region, while opponents warned that the agreement would cause huge job losses in the United States as companies moved production to Mexico to lower costs. In reality, NAFTA did not cause the huge jobs losses feared by the critics or the large economic gains predicted by supporters. The net overall effect of NAFTA on the U.S. economy appears to have been relatively modest, primarily because trade with Canada and Mexico account for a small percentage of U.S. GDP.

However, there were worker and firm adjustment costs as the three countries adapted to more open trade and investment. Some proponents argue NAFTA helped strengthen economic relations with Canada and Mexico and act as a counter weight to China's rising presence in Latin America. They contend NAFTA helped create more efficient production processes, increased the availability of lower-priced consumer goods, and improved living standards and working conditions. Opponents argue that the agreement caused disappointing employment trends, a decline in U.S. wages, worker displacement and the loss of "good" jobs in the United States.

THE NORTH AMERICAN MARKET PRIOR TO NAFTA

The concept of economic integration in North America was not new when NAFTA negotiations started. In 1911, President Taft signed a reciprocal trade agreement with his Canadian counterpart but, after a bitter election the Canadians rejected free trade and ousted then Prime Minister Laurier. As discussed in an earlier chapter, in 1965 the U.S. and Canada signed the Automotive Products Agreement liberalizing trade in that industry and establishing the North American content requirement often challenged in the 2018 negotiations. In the 1980s Mexico began moving away from its protectionist import-substitution industrialization trade policy and unilaterally initiated trade liberalization efforts. And, as discussed in an earlier chapter, the groundbreaking U.S.-Canada Free Trade Agreement of 1989 was, at the time, probably the most comprehensive bilateral FTA in existence.

Average Applied Tariff Levels in Mexico and the United States (1993–1996)

	PRE-NAFTA		POST-NAFTA
	1993	**(percent)**	**1996**
Average Mexican tariffs on U.S. imports	10.0		3.5
Average U.S. tariffs on Mexican imports	2.0		0.7

Prior to NAFTA, of the three countries Mexico remained the most closed market with a trade weighted average tariff of about 10%. By contrast the U.S. average was 2 percent and Canada's less than 1 percent. Mexico used import licenses on hundreds of products from the U.S., and numerous nontariff barriers. As the CRS study observed:

"For Mexico an FTA with the United States represented a way to lock in the reforms of its market opening measures from the mid-1980s to transform Mexico's formerly statist economy. . .An FTA with the U.S. was a way of blocking domestic efforts to roll back Mexican reforms, especially in the politically sensitive agricultural sector. NAFTA helped deflect protectionist demands of industrial and special interest groups in Mexico. One of the main goals of the Mexican government was to increase investment confidence in order to attract greater flows of foreign investment and spur economic growth."

For the United States, NAFTA represented both an opportunity to expand exports and an opportunity to resolve some of the political tensions between the two countries. U.S. trade representatives had not forgotten the 1970s Mideast oil embargoes and also recognized that imports from Mexico would likely include higher U.S. content than imports from Asian countries.

NAFTA'S IMPACT ON TRADE, GDP AND INVESTMENT

Estimating the economic impact of trade agreements is a daunting task due to the lack of data and important theoretical and practical matters associated with generating results from economic models. In addition, such estimates provide incomplete accounting of the total economic effects of trade agreements. Numerous studies suggest that NAFTA achieved many of the intended trade and economic benefits. Other studies suggest that NAFTA has come at some cost to U.S. workers. As stated earlier, most economists maintain that trade liberalization promotes overall economic growth among trading partners, but there are both winners and losers from adjustments.

TRADE

U.S. trade with its NAFTA partners has more than tripled since the agreement took effect. It has increased more rapidly than trade with the rest of the world. Since 1993, trade with Mexico grew faster than trade with Canada or with non-NAFTA countries. In 2011, trilateral trade among the NAFTA partners reached the $1 trillion threshold. In 2016, Canada was the leading market for U.S. exports, while Mexico ranked second. The two countries accounted for 34% of total U.S. exports in 2016. In the same year, Canada and Mexico ranked second and third, respectively, as suppliers of U.S. imports (China being number one). Combined the two countries accounted for 26% of U.S. imports.

U.S. Goods and Services Trade with NAFTA Partners 1993–2016		
(billions $)		
1993	2005	2016
$300	$800	$1,100

As stated in an earlier chapter, a major NAFTA motivation for the United States was access to Canadian and Mexican oil production. Ask Americans in their fifties to recall where and when they first learned "curse" words and they may tell you it was in the back seat of their parent's car as they waited in incredibly long queues at gasoline stations during the 1973 and 1979 oil embargoes! Until very recently, the U.S. has consistently imported more energy resources than produced domestically. Some economists suggest that oil imports from NAFTA partners should be excluded from NAFTA trade analysis because of the volatility of oil prices and the fact that the U.S. would have had to import those resources from another source anyway. The CRS study found that, over the last twenty years, excluding oil and petroleum trade reduced the U.S. trade deficit with both Canada and Mexico and in some years resulted in a net positive balance of merchandise trade with the two partners.

While trade deficits were a major part of the rhetoric in the USMCA negotiations, a new study from the Bureau of Economic Analysis (BEA) suggests that the present accounting methods overstate the value of imports and understate the value of exports. Using the example of an iPhone, the authors assume the phone sells for $750 in the United States and Europe. If it is assembled in China for $250, Apple's profit is $500 per phone but that profit is often attributed to a subsidiary in a low-tax country like Ireland. If most of the research and development for the phone took place in California, much of the $500 represents American production and should be included in U.S. Gross Domestic Product and only the $250 as an import from China. Also, when the iPhones are sold in Europe the $500 value should count as an export from the United States. Using their logic, the BEA economists argue the trade deficit would be slightly less than the 2017 $500 billion figure.

Stated another way, more than half the value of the goods and services counted in the U.S. trade deficit actually were produced domestically. Of course, that "value" was produced largely by high-skilled technology workers and the companies that employ them and does not address the problem of reduced numbers of well-paid industrial jobs.

Using the BEA methodology, Samsung LCD televisions assembled in Mexico and exported to the United States "count" as U.S. imports from Mexico increasing the United States' bilateral trade deficit. The value of LCD research and development is probably an export of Korea and the screen, an export of Vietnam or Indonesia. All of which suggests that political focus bilateral trade deficit figures are likely to represent an "unfocused" picture.

GROSS DOMESTIC PRODUCT

Gross Domestic Product and percent change in GDP are the standard measures of economic and/or political "success". Given the size of the U.S. economy, the overall net effect of NAFTA on the GDP has been relatively small, primarily because total trade with both Mexico and Canada was equal to less than 5% of the U.S. GDP at the time NAFTA went into effect. Since the U.S. and Canada had already liberalized trade relations, NAFTA's economic impact was mostly associated with U.S.-Mexican trade. As stated in the introduction, it is difficult to separate the impact of a free trade agreement from a host of other factors and changes that have transpired in the last twenty-five years. Also, since U.S.-Mexican trade was growing prior to NAFTA, and would have likely continued to do so without the agreement, measuring NAFTA's impact on GDP is a difficult challenge. A 2003 CRS report found that the agreement increased U.S. GDP "probably no more than a few billion dollars, or a few hundredths of a percent."

The report also stated that "in some sectors, trade-related effects could have been more significant, especially in those industries that were more exposed to removal of tariff and non-tariff barriers, such as textiles, apparel, automotive, and agricultural industries."

INVESTMENT

Foreign investment includes both portfolio investment and direct investment (FDI) which both vary in risk, control, and attractiveness to host countries. Foreign portfolio investment is the purchase of stocks bonds and other financial instruments. Usually there is no intention on the part of the investor to be involved in the management of the company. In recent decades, many Americans have been encouraged by their financial advisors to diversify their financial investments beyond U.S. companies in order to reduce risk. In fact, if your portfolio includes U.S.-based multinational corporations like Ford, Apple, or Coca-Cola you are internationally diversified. Foreign portfolio investment tends to follow current perceived opportunities and can be transient. In an attempt to stabilize investment flows, some countries have considered a tax on international portfolio investment transfers.

Both types of foreign investment incur risks including currency, political, diplomatic, and information risk. More important to policy makers is direct investment and foreign direct investment which are both critical to economic growth and a statement/commitment to expand economic relations across borders. Investors generally prefer stabile, predictable business climates. Part of the economic impact of NAFTA was to reduce investment uncertainty and risk. A major NAFTA motivation for Mexico was to make their investment climate more attractive to FDI. Though rarely mentioned in USMCA debates, the largest percentage increase among the NAFTA partners has been Mexican FDI in the United States. The Table below shows the dramatic increase in FDI among the NAFTA partners.

Foreign Direct Investment Among the NAFTA Countries

(billions of dollars)

Year	Can. FDI in U.S.	U.S. FDI in Can.	Mex. FDI in U.S.	U.S. FDI in Mex.
1993	40.3	69.9	1.2	15.2
2015	268.9	352.9	16.5	92.8

NAFTA'S IMPACT ON INDUSTRIES AND MARKETS

Twenty-five years ago, we wrote:

"For trade economists one of the unanswered questions is whether NAFTA will increase or decrease competition? At first glance the answer seems obvious. Opening markets to new competitors should increase competition. Of the three NAFTA countries Mexico has been the most closed. Therefore, NAFTA should have its greatest impact on competition in Mexico."

Similarly, when NAFTA was being negotiated, others suggested that the agreement would result in a strange paradox, the country that gave up the most in terms of control over international trade (protectionism) would gain the most from competition and scale economies.

AGRICULTURE

In NAFTA negotiations, like other trade agreements, agricultural goods and food products were a sensitive subject. Most nations, including those of NAFTA, have government-supported agricultural sectors. The long-running U.S.-Canada timber dispute is basically a debate over which country subsidizes their industry more and how, in defiance of what was agreed upon. Even in industrial societies, cultural and political ties to the land remain powerful and the desire not to be dependent upon food imports has national security implications.

With NAFTA, roughly half of all Mexico-U.S. agricultural trade became tariff-free. In addition, the United States and Mexico "tariffied" the agricultural quotas, import licenses and other nontariff trade barriers each traditionally applied. "Tariffication" converted trade restraints into equivalent temporary restrictive tariffs or tariff-rate quotas which adjusted the level of applicable tariffs according to the volume of imports. Generally, the more imports the higher the tariff. Most agricultural tariffs were removed by 2003 and all removed by 2008. The 15-year phase out was reserved for the most politically sensitive categories, corn and dry beans going into Mexico and orange juice and sugar going into the United States.

NAFTA negotiators anticipated many of the standard Sanitary and Phytosanitary (SPS) regulatory issues, requiring SPS regulations be based on scientific principles, agreed to avoid arbitrary or unjustifiable SPS discrimination, and not use SPS regulations as a disguised restraint on trade. The agreement encouraged (but did not require) use of international SPS standards and created another working group, the Committee on Sanitary and Phytosanitary Measures.

In the USMCA negotiations, agricultural trade disputes were a "sticky" issue but some of the most vocal supporters of retaining the agreement were U.S. agricultural interests. Before NAFTA, U.S. agricultural exports Canada were approximately $7 billion annually, and yearly agricultural imports from Canada averaged $5 billion, creating a small surplus of $2 billion. For most of the last twenty years U.S./Canada agricultural trade has been almost equal but by 2015, agricultural trade with Canada had risen to $25 billion U.S. exports and $23 billion imports. U.S. agricultural trade with Mexico has followed a similar path with slightly lower volume.

While NAFTA contributed to increased agricultural trade among the three countries other international trade agreements, rulings, and changes in domestic farm policies, and changes in exchange rates all impacted agricultural imports and exports.

NAFTA has aided numerous major U.S.-based agricultural sectors. By 2017, Mexico had become the largest market for U.S. corn, dairy, poultry, and wheat. By 2016, Mexico had become the third largest destination for American agricultural exports valued at nearly $18 billion, including $2.6 billion worth of U.S. corn. Although overall trade between the U.S. and Mexico exceeds $500 billion annually, corn is probably Mexico's most important agricultural commodity and the volume of U.S. imports is symbolic of NAFTA-influenced codependence.

One of the most frequently cited agricultural "success" stories has been U.S./Mexico avocado trade along the border near San Diego. For 80 years prior to NAFTA the United States banned Mexican avocados even though orchards literally cross the Tijuana/San Diego border. Under NAFTA, the ban was initially relaxed and then fully removed in 2007. Avocado imports surged, yet at the same the number of U.S. orchards and production expanded to meet increased domestic demand.

Even though NAFTA included provisions for a special Working Group on Mexican/U.S. Agricultural Grade and Quality Standards and a Working Group on Agricultural Subsidies, twenty-five years later, disputes remain a lively issue. During USMCA negotiations, Wisconsin dairy farmers complained about lack of access to Canadian markets, Mexican sugar exports created political conflict, and U.S. poultry exports were challenged by Mexican counterparts.

ENERGY

Without question, the industrial sector that has changed most dramatically since NAFTA is energy. While, twenty-five years ago, access to Canadian and Mexican energy resources was a major motivation for American business leaders, politicians, and trade negotiators few, if any, leaders would have predicted Mexico would open its constitutionally protected energy resources to multinational energy corporations and, though hydraulic fracking existed back in the 1860s, and experiments improved it in the 1940s, only in the 1990s, when combined with horizontal drilling was its potential to open and access huge new supplies of oil and natural gas understood by the energy industry.

NAFTA included provisions on investment that exempted the energy sector in Mexico from foreign investment. In CUSFTA 1989 and NAFTA, energy chapters contained a so-called "proportionality" provision, a restriction preventing Canadian producers from reducing the proportion of exports delivered to the United States and prohibiting price discrimination between domestic consumption and exports to the U.S. Some Canadians found these provisions particularly intrusive on domestic policy and there was speculation that Canada would attempt to change this in USMCA. But, as stated at the beginning of this section, the dynamics of energy economics and politics have changed.

For most of NAFTA's existence, PEMEX, the Mexican national petroleum company shipped crude oil to the U.S. and in return bought refined petroleum products. Which country had an energy trade deficit or surplus often depended on the world price of oil. The amount of energy trade also depended on ups and downs in the U.S. economy with both imports and exports declining during recessions. But, U.S. imports of crude oil peaked in 2011 and have declined significantly since then. And, in 2015 the overall U.S./Mexico energy trade flipped with U.S. exports of petroleum products and natural gas greater than Mexican exports of crude oil to the United States. The energy trade balance shifted from a deficit of $20 billion in 2011 to a surplus of 11.5 billion in 2015. U.S. based multinationals earned almost as much from exporting hydrocarbons to Mexico as from cars and trucks.

In addition to the shale oil fracking boom, Mexico's slumping oil output and energy liberalization in 2014 contributed to this dramatic change. Analysts expect continued new energy investment and doubling of natural gas pipeline capacity by the end of the decade. Collectively, the NAFTA partners were predicted to achieve energy "independence" by 2020, with significant supplies of low-cost energy as a driver for industrial competitiveness. But, analysts noted, this all depended on resolution of USMCA.

MOTOR VEHICLES AND PARTS

Automobiles and parts were widely seen as potentially the most contentious issue in the USMCA negotiations. Even before NAFTA, many of the major automobile manufacturers had set up operations in Mexico. Since the 1965 Auto Pact, Canada and the

United States had substantially embraced free trade in new automobiles and original equipment maker (OEM) parts. Early manufacturing plants locating in Mexico often required their own infrastructure including sewer, water, and communications systems in regions unprepared for industrialization. With NAFTA this quickly changed and, in addition to lower-cost labor, Mexico became an export platform as their leadership expanded the number of Mexican bilateral trade agreements while the United States did not.

China's ascension to WTO resulted in many labor-intensive, and initially low-skilled jobs leaving North America. Auto manufacturers integrated their NAFTA operations. Reflecting the supply chain integration argument U.S. industrial leaders universally expressed during the USMCA negotiations, one of the largest categories of U.S. imports from and exports to Mexico and Canada is automobile parts in various stages of the automobile production. In the last decade U.S. motor vehicle parts imports and exports with NAFTA partners have both averaged about $30 billion annually. One report cited manufacturers transferring automobile components across borders up to fourteen times in the process of completing final goods.

Another argument for not increasing North American content rules and initiating an American content rule was the high percentage of American content in Mexican made automobiles, having risen from 5 to 40 percent since NAFTA was ratified. Industry leaders contended increased content rules would be difficult to comply with and make production out of North America more competitive even with paying the 2.5 percent vehicle duty.

By 2017, the "Big Three" U.S. based automobile manufacturers plus Honda and Toyota had production operations in all three NAFTA countries. BMW, Daimler, and Tesla only had production facilities in the United States, while Renault-Nissan, Hyundai, and Volkswagen each had production facilities in the U.S. and Mexico but not Canada.

According to the Center for Automotive research, one of the main reasons for Canada's loss of auto assembly: Mexico. With its significantly lower wages, aggressive incentives, free trade agreements with other countries, lower manufacturing costs and a growing skilled workforce, the country beat out Canada and the U.S. to win at least eight of nine North American vehicle assembly plants announced between 2011 and 2016.

OTHER INDUSTRIAL PRODUCTS

NAFTA chemical industry trade has tripled since 1994 and U.S. chemical companies currently run a $16 billion chemical trade surplus with Mexico and Canada. Chemical industry leaders worried that terminating NAFTA would hurt American companies most of all. As the American Chemistry Council director stated:

> "North America has become so integrated, throwing up tariffs or taxes would be like putting a toll booth in the middle of a factory. More than 70 percent of U.S. chemical imports and 50 percent of exports are intra-

company trade. That's why we're making the
argument that tariffs are basically a pure tax."

The industry advocated reduced USMCA rules of
origin requirements and a more efficient regulatory
environment allowing the industry to increase supply
chain synergy.

LABOR MARKETS

Anyone old enough to recall the 1992 presidential
debates will remember independent candidate Ross
Perot's use of the phrase "giant sucking sound" to
forecast the NAFTA's impact on American jobs and
labor markets:

"We have got to stop sending jobs overseas. It's pretty
simple: If you're paying $12, $13, $14 an hour for factory
workers and you can move your factory South of the border,
pay a dollar an hour for labor, . . .have no health care—
that's the most expensive single element in making a car—
have no environmental controls, no pollution controls and
no retirement, and you don't care about anything but
making money, there will be a giant sucking sound going
south.

. . .when [Mexico's] jobs come up from a dollar an hour to
six dollars an hour, and ours go down to six dollars an hour,
and then it's leveled again. But in the meantime, you've
wrecked the country with these kinds of deals."

Perot argued NAFTA would lead to equalization of
wages in the United States and Mexico, even stating
the equalization would occur when U.S. wages fell to
$7.50 per hour and Mexican wages rose to the same
amount. This is known as the "pauper labor"
argument. The pauper "theory" rests on the

assumption that labor is the only factor that determines output. Using that logic, China and India would be the biggest economies in the world. What escaped Ross Perot was the fact that labor is ultimately paid based on its productivity. Higher wages in the United States were the result of the productivity of labor, which is in is attributable to labor skills and capital equipment.

For decades prior to NAFTA, when the Mexican government pursued import-substitution-industrialization, investment in both labor skills and capital equipment lagged. For Mexico, NAFTA was designed, in part, to attract new foreign investment, which, if combined with improved labor skills would increase productivity and wages. As reported in the CRS study, one of the main arguments in favor of NAFTA was that the agreement would improve economic conditions in Mexico and narrow the income disparity between workers there versus the U.S. and Canada. It would lead to "economic convergence."

But the CRS study authors found that NAFTA failed to fulfill the promise of closing the development gap. They attribute this failure to a variety of factors including; lack of deeper forms of regional integration or cooperation, stating neither country "adopted complimentary policies after NAFTA that could have promised a more successful regional effort. These policies could include education, industrial policies, and more investment in border and transportation infrastructure." Similarly, a World Bank study found that while NAFTA brought economic and social benefits to the Mexican economy, it was not enough to help narrow the disparities in economic conditions. Their analysis also contends Mexico needs to invest more in education, innovation, infrastructure, and in the quality of national institutions.

As USMCA negotiations progressed, various groups offered their assessment of how workers have been affected by the agreement. Often quoted is the Economic Policy Institute study which determined that over 850,000 jobs, mostly industrial, were lost in the United States. Other studies found that, when adding in jobs created by increased trade, the pact had little or no impact on overall employment in the United States. The NAFTA trade pact (along with China's ascension to WTO) had the most impact on low-skill factory jobs.

A 2016 U.S. International Trade Commission (USITC) study reported that NAFTA "led to a substantial increase in trade volume for all three countries; a small increase in U.S. welfare; and little to no change in U.S. aggregate employment." The study also stated that "some studies find that trade with Mexico depressed U.S. wages in some industries and states, while wages in other industries increased."

In Mexico, as the agricultural restrictions gradually were eliminated, small-scale farm operations declined and workers were displaced. Many found jobs in the rapidly growing automobile manufacturing sector and other industries. Because the Mexican labor force is, on average, ten years younger than that of the United States or Canada, the supply of labor expanded over the last twenty-five years while stagnant in the partner countries. This reality, along with global competition from lower-wage countries and lack of worker-controlled unions have kept Mexican industrial wages low. In USMCA negotiations, Trump administration representatives stated they would push for higher wages in Mexico offering they represent "an unfair advantage".

In "Promises Kept and Promises Broken—NAFTA at Twenty" Vanessa Humm summarized:

"[The NAFTA] treaty has been in force for twenty years. . .However, as with most things that have a multi-national impact, especially an economic one, NAFTA has always been surrounded by controversy and clouded by disagreement. The arguments made both for and against NAFTA remain much the same today as they did when the trade pact was being proposed and debated. . .NAFTA was motivated by a desire for economic growth. The member countries aimed to accomplish this goal through NAFTA by making it easier for goods and services to move between Canada, Mexico, and the United States. . .While it was President Clinton who signed NAFTA. . .the push for a North America with free trade was initially a Republican initiative. . .a bi-partisan product, having been "conceived" by Ronald Reagan, negotiated by George H. W. Bush, and pushed through the US Congress by Bill Clinton in alliance with Congressional Republicans and corporate lobbyists.

But NAFTA's bipartisan birth did not insulate it from criticism; all areas of the political spectrum criticized the agreement. Environmental and agricultural groups were split in their support and criticism for the agreement. Further, while most business groups supported NAFTA, it received opposition from labor, civil rights, human rights, certain businesses, and other groups.

NAFTA proponents also claimed the agreement would improve efficiency. U.S. exporters would find great advantage in exporting to Mexico because NAFTA would lower the tariffs on goods from the United States and Canada, but not goods from other countries the United States competes with, like European and Asian competitors. NAFTA would also open Mexico's markets to U.S. services, allowing U.S. services to grow operations in Mexico. It was predicted this would benefit entities like U.S. banks, securities firms, and insurance companies by giving them the opportunity to invest in Mexico for the first time in a long time. With all of these arguments supporting NAFTA, however, its proponents were sure to always state that the benefits gained by U.S. companies by being able to do business more cheaply with and in Mexico would in no way jeopardize jobs in the United States.

Ultimately, the supporters of NAFTA won the battle and the agreement came into force. . . But the criticism and the support continues. . .NAFTA has certainly helped increase consumer choice in its twenty years of life. Most would agree that it has had a positive impact on trade. Trade among the three NAFTA countries has "soared" since they agreed to the trade pact. . . But the second decade of NAFTA's existence did not have the excitement of the first decade. Events like the terrorist attacks against the United State, the rise of China as a global competitor, the Great Recession, and the like, meant the trade gains seen in the first decade were not as evident or impressive in the second decade. The momentum seen in the early years of NAFTA's life has waned recently.

But just as the case was when the agreement was being proposed over twenty years ago, harsh critics of NAFTA remain...They argue that it has actually caused a decrease in U.S. shipping and manufacturing jobs. They argue that "NAFTA has also displaced Mexican agricultural workers into other sectors or forced them to immigrate illegally to the United States." NAFTA also failed to keep its promise to close the wage gap between Mexico and the United States. While the Mexican auto sector has increased its jobs by about 50 percent since the enactment of NAFTA, the average Mexican manufacturing wages were about 15 percent of those in the United States in 1997, and only increased to 18 percent by 2012.

Regardless of the criticism of NAFTA, the simple truth remains that it is impossible to prove what would have happened with trade policy without the agreement...Despite NAFTA's alleged failures and alleged successes, and regardless of the proponents and critics of the agreement, most agree that NAFTA needs to be reinvigorated." (20 Law & Business Review of Americas 363 (2014)).

Whether USMCA represents a reinvigorated NAFTA is debatable, but economists and political analysts are taking up the challenge of predicting the future! See Chapter 7.

CHAPTER 6
THE USMCA AGREEMENT

NEGOTIATIONS

Early in 2017, the Trump administration notified Congress of its intent to re-negotiate NAFTA 1994 with Canada and Mexico under "fast track" as authorized in the Trade Promotion Authority Act of 2015. President Trump's prior tweets called NAFTA 1994 the "worst trade deal ever". He threatened to withdraw from NAFTA or impose high tariffs on Mexican goods in light of that country's sizeable trade surplus ($69 billion in 2017) in goods and services with the United States. The U.S. states most involved in NAFTA trade were Texas, North Dakota, Michigan, Indiana, Kentucky and Vermont. They let their views be known vociferously in the re-negotiations.

Including merchandise and services, the U.S. actually had a small trade surplus with Canada in 2017, but President Trump continued to deny that reality, focusing only on a small goods deficit. This approach is about 100 years out of date: Some 150 million U.S. private sector jobs are in the services/ technology sector, with tourism and intellectual property rights payments heading the list, followed by finance, insurance, telecommunications, information technology and professional services. U.S. jobs in manufacturing are dwarfed by comparison.

On balance, the initial Trump Administration NAFTA re-negotiation notice was remarkably moderate, as were the subsequently released U.S. negotiating objectives, which partly borrowed from the Trans-Pacific Partnership (TPP) agreement. NAFTA 1994 it seemed at first blush would only undergo a tune-up.

Many attribute this outcome to lobbying by major U.S. exporters to Mexico, especially farm products. Under NAFTA, Mexico has become the largest foreign market for U.S. corn, dairy products, pork, poultry and wheat. Overall, Canada is the number one buyer of U.S. agricultural and food products. Manufacturers, fearing disruption and added costs, were quick to point out the high degree of supply chain integration among the NAFTA countries. Some components cross NAFTA borders repeatedly before a final product is finished. About two-thirds of all U.S. imports from Mexico involve internal company trading.

When negotiations commenced in August 2017, the fundamental relationships between the three NAFTA partners had changed from 1994. Mexico and Canada were still heavily dependent on the U.S. market for their exports, and for technology and foreign investment capital. The United States, however, had become noticeably less dependent on foreign oil imports, but hardly self-sufficient. Mexico, contrary to its strong reservation of oil and gas rights in NAFTA, at its own initiative had amended its Constitution and significantly opened oil and gas exploration to foreign investors. Meanwhile, Canada was still having trouble accepting the reality that satellite and Internet broadcasts, and WTO remedies, had rendered its cultural industries exclusion almost meaningless. See Chapter 2.

By 2017, principally as a result of WTO negotiations, Mexico's average MFN tariff on manufactured goods had fallen to approximately 8%, Canada to 4% and the U.S. to 3.5%. All three countries maintained generally higher tariffs on agricultural goods, and selectively higher tariffs on particular manufactured goods such as the 25% U.S. tariff on pick-up trucks, a legacy from a 1960s "chicken war" with Europe.

These national tariffs were, of course, not applicable to "North American goods", those goods meeting the NAFTA rules of origin. See Chapter 3. But tightening up the existing 62.5% auto rules of origin quickly became a focus in the U.S. approach to re-negotiation. The U.S. sought an 85% North American auto content rule, *plus* a 50% U.S. content rule. Tighter auto rules of origin, however, could cause manufacturers to move elsewhere, then pay U.S. tariffs (2.5% for passenger autos) upon entry.

The U.S. also wished to re-think the rules on NAFTA trade remedies, such as safeguards, that could result in tariffs on Mexican and Canadian goods. Removal of the waiver for Buy American preferences enjoyed by Canada and Mexico under NAFTA also surfaced as a goal, along with a "balancing" of procurement opportunities as between the U.S. and Mexico and Canada combined. Stronger labor and environmental provisions than offered through the NAFTA side agreements were also on the negotiating table, with relatively little conflict.

The U.S. sought to open up its neighbors' duty-free rules for cross-border online sales, think Amazon. Canada started with an unbelievably low online tariff exemption of only $20 CDN (compared to $200 per day CDN for shopping in the USA and returning to Canada with the goods). Mexico had $50 US online limit, while United States buyers could import online up to $800 in duty free goods from either Canada or Mexico.

Other items on the U.S. agenda included improved protection of intellectual property rights, facilitation of cross-border data flows and a ban on forced localization of computer data on servers, opposition to Canadian dairy "supply management" restraints, better customs clearance procedures, tariffs on seasonal agricultural goods (berries for example), expanded coverage of state-owned enterprises, vague references to policing currency manipulation, and dispute settlement.

The U.S. focused particularly on elimination of NAFTA binational panel arbitration of dumping and subsidy disputes, which would return appeals to national courts. Arguing that it promoted outsourcing, the United States also wanted to make NAFTA 1994's controversial investor-state arbitration of disputes optional, forcing such disputes back into national courts or state-to-state negotiations.

Mexico and Canada also came to the table seeking change. Mexico, for example, emphasized its desire for coverage of security, narcotics and migration issues. Little attention was given to investor/trader/professional visas created under NAFTA 1994, but many talented Canadians and Mexicans working lawfully in the United States put their immigration lawyers on speed dial.

Canada reiterated that continued binational panel arbitration of trade remedy disputes could again be a deal-breaker, noting it had been involved in over 70 such proceedings since 1994, and that a previous Prime Minister had walked out of negotiations with the United States in order to obtain this unique appeal system. Canada also indicated it would like to see reduced application of Buy American procurement rules and a more "progressive" trade deal.

The NAFTA re-negotiations that commenced in August of 2017 were pushed by critical deadlines: The elections for the U.S. House of Representatives (November 2018) and the election of a new President of Mexico (July 2018). Nevertheless, negotiations proceeded at a slow pace, and deadlines for their conclusion were repeatedly extended. In the end the United States employed a divide and conquer strategy by first agreeing to a deal with Mexico, then inviting Canada to join in, which it did.

After a thorough "legal scrub", the leaders of Canada, Mexico and the United States signed a finalized USMCA deal on November 30, 2018, one day before Andres Manuel López Obrador took office as President of Mexico. He had won in a landslide, mostly keeping quiet about his views on the agreement re-negotiated by his predecessor, President Pena Nieto.

The signature date was also important to President Trump. It was the last day he could submit the new agreement for Congressional review under U.S. "fast track" procedures that mandate a Yes or No approval vote by Congress, no amendments allowed. See R. Folsom, *International Trade Law including Trump and Trade* in a Nutshell.

THE USMCA AGREEMENT

The first issue was what to call the new trilateral agreement. The Trump administration, wishing to disassociate from the NAFTA title, prefers USMCA. Canada prefers New NAFTA and/or CUSMA in English or ACEUM in French. Mexico calls it T-MEC in Spanish. For purposes of this book, we primarily call the trilateral agreement USMCA.

The 2018 agreement was subsequently amended in late 2019 primarily as a result of pressure from the U.S. House of Representatives controlled by the Democratic Party. The USMCA incorporates a mixture of provisions from CUSTA 1989, NAFTA 1994, and the 2016 Trans-Pacific Partnership (TPP-12) agreement signed by President Obama but denied ratification by President Trump. Overall, as economist Gregory Daco has noted: The benefits of the USMCA "are not what [it] brings, but rather what it prevents".

For texts of the individual USMCA chapters, 34 in number, plus individual annexes and side letters, see: https://ustr.gov/trade-agreements.

A consolidated, edited version of the USMCA 2018 Agreement is reproduced as an Appendix to R. Folsom, *Free Trade Agreements: From GATT 1947 through NAFTA Re-Negotiated* (West Academic Publishing, 2019).

USMCA PROVISIONS WITH LITTLE CHANGE FROM NAFTA

Trade Remedy (AD and CVD) Dispute Settlement. Replacement of national court review of AD and CVD determinations with binational panels was retained under strident insistence by Canada in USMCA Chapter 10.

Safeguards (Escape Clause Proceedings). Despite considerable controversy and pressure, little change was made in 2018 to the NAFTA provisions on this trade remedy. The exclusion of NAFTA partners from global safeguard actions was retained.

Telecommunications. Expanded to allow regulation of mobile service roaming rates.

Temporary Business Visas. Minor changes to NAFTA coverage are contained in USMCA Chapter 16.

Textiles. Small changes in USMCA Chapter 6 tighten up required North American sources.

Canada's   Cultural   Industry   Exclusion.   See
Chapter 2 for details. Fully retained under USMCA
Chapter 32.

NEW OR NOTABLY REVISED USMCA
PROVISIONS COMMON TO ALL PARTNERS

Intergovernmental   Dispute   Settlement.   The
Chapter   20   government   dispute   settlement
provisions of NAFTA 1994, including the option to
take most disputes to the WTO, was largely
replicated in USMCA Chapter 31. Unlike NAFTA,
each side cannot block use of the Chapter 31 process
by refusing to name panelists. In addition, for the
first time ever in a trade agreement, rules of evidence
are created for these proceedings. Chapter 31 is
particularly critical to the USMCA labor and
environment provisions (below), and topics not
covered by the WTO agreements. See Chapter 3.

National Security. The NAFTA "essential security
interests" exception (Article 2102), resembling that of
the GATT/WTO, references actions member nations
consider necessary relating to: (1) Information
disclosures; (2) traffic in arms and the supply of
foreign militaries or security establishments; (3) war
time or international relations' emergencies; (4)
nuclear weapons proliferation; or breaches of UN
Charter peace and security obligations.

USMCA Article 32.2 provides a more ironclad
"national security" exception than found in the
GATT/WTO and NAFTA rules:

"Essential Security 1. Nothing in this Agreement shall be construed to: (a) require a Party to furnish or allow access to information the disclosure of which it determines to be contrary to its essential security interests; or (b) preclude a Party from applying measures that it considers necessary for the fulfilment of its obligations with respect to the maintenance or restoration of international peace or security, or the protection of its own essential security interests".

In May of 2019, President Trump, seeking Congressional ratification of USMCA, lifted application of the U.S. steel and aluminum tariffs to Canadian and Mexican exports. Those two partners in turn removed their retaliatory tariffs on U.S. exports. However, the U.S. reserved the right to re-impose its steel and aluminum tariffs if surges beyond historical U.S. imports occur. Canada and Mexico further agreed to monitor and stop diversions of shipments from other nations seeking to avoid U.S. tariffs on steel and aluminum.

The Trump administration has threatened to apply global national security tariffs to U.S. auto and auto parts imports. The USMCA anticipates just such action by creating quotas, noted below, to shelter Mexican and Canadian autos and parts from such tariffs if they should emerge.

Autos and Parts. Arguably, the most notable and contentious changes to NAFTA undertaken in the USMCA, concern the rules of origin for vehicles and their parts. To be free traded, passenger vehicles and light trucks after a three-year phase-in must contain

75% regional value content, up from 62.5%, both measured using the net cost method. In addition, 70% of the steel (slab steel to be "melted, smelted and poured" in North America within seven years) and aluminum content of such vehicles must originate in North America. The automotive tracing and "deemed originating" rules of CUSFTA 1989 and NAFTA 1994 were terminated in favor of regional content rules for key vehicle components such as engines and transmissions.

Furthermore, 40% of the value of autos and 45% for trucks must be produced by workers earning an average of $16 or more per hour (not including benefits and not indexed for inflation), well above prevailing Mexican wages. This "labor value content" rule favors U.S. and Canadian sourced parts and components, and eliminates the possibility of free trading entirely Mexican sourced vehicles. Note that it requires two calculations: Production line wages and labor value content percentages. A useful figure appearing in the U.S. International Trade Commission 2019 Report on the Likely Impact of the USMCA on the U.S. economy diagrams the rules of origin for vehicles. This diagram is reproduced in Chapter 7.

The complex, micromanagement rules governing auto rules of origin calculations are detailed in the USMCA and explained by Professor Matthew Schaefer in the 2019 edition of Folsom, Van Alstine, Ramsey and Schaefer, *International Business Transactions 13th, A Problem-Oriented Course Book*, as follows:

"[T]he value from workers making $16/hour [must] "consist of at least 25 percentage points of high wage material and manufacturing expenditures, no more than 10 percentage points of technology expenditures, and no more than 5 percentage points of assembly expenditures." USMCA, Article 4–B.7(1)(d). The technology expenditures can include software (i.e., may "include expenditures on software development, technology integration, vehicle communications, and information technology support operations"). With autos becoming "smart" vehicles and more and more autonomous, software inputs are rapidly increasing and Canada believes this will help its producers meet the new labor wage content rules in auto rules of origin. * * * The USMCA provides that "the production wage rate is the average hourly base wage rate, not including benefits, of employees directly involved in the production of the part or component used to calculate the LVC, and does not include salaries of management, R&D, engineering, or other workers who are not involved in the direct production of the parts or in the operation of production lines." USMCA, Ch. 4, fn. 104. These new rules will essentially be phased in over three or more years."

All of these provisions were driven by the Trump administration's goal of bringing vehicle and parts production back home. A grace period ("alternative staging regime") of up to five years can be applied regarding compliance with the USMCA auto rules of origin. As a practical matter it is estimated they will generate compliance costs estimated at between 3 to 5% and likely favor GM, Ford and Fiat-Chrysler over foreign rivals. About a third of the autos produced in Mexico were thought unable to comply in 2018 with the USMCA rules of origin.

Studies by the USITC and Federal Reserve Bank concluded that roughly 28,000 auto industry jobs would be created in the USA. But the USMCA rules could also raise the cost of cars to consumers in all three countries and make North American automakers (such as BMW based in South Carolina) less competitive in the global marketplace. An IMF study reached a similar conclusion, anticipating that although the USMCA auto rules of origin would create jobs, the cost increases stemming from those rules would lead to 140,000 fewer vehicles sold, with a corresponding reduction in automotive-related jobs.

An alternative to compliance with the new automobile rules of origin is to pay the U.S. passenger auto import tariff of 2.5%, assuming no new U.S. national security or other U.S. tariffs are applied to autos. The authors are surprised there no public plans within the auto industry to engage this seemingly cost-effective alternative. The 2.5% alternative is not an option for manufacturers of pick-up trucks, vans and SUVs, all of which face a 25% U.S. tariff. These vehicles are consequently produced primarily in the USA.

Side letters to USMCA anticipate that the United States may, as threatened, impose "national security" tariffs on autos from anywhere in the world, including its North American partners. Quotas in the side letters exempt 2.6 million Mexican passenger vehicles and light trucks and $108 billion in Mexican auto parts from any such future tariffs. Canada has an exemption for 2.6 million vehicles and $32.3

billion in auto parts. These quotas are currently well above 2018 Canadian and Mexican export levels.

These quotas are not indexed for inflation, and hence in time are likely to be reached. In a backhanded way, they support the threat of U.S. national security tariffs on autos from Japan, the EU, China and Korea.

Currency Manipulation. Limited transparency and notification obligations regarding currency manipulation have been added to USMCA. Each country must disclose government foreign-exchange transactions. None of the NAFTA partners have in the past been considered currency manipulators. This provision was included mostly as a model for future U.S. FTAs where currency manipulation may be an issue. Disputes regarding currency manipulation which are not associated with any of the North American partners are not subject to USMCA dispute settlement.

Non-Market Economies. Under USMCA Chapter 32 any party may terminate the agreement if a partner enters into a free trade agreement with a non-market economy (NME). This provision is clearly targeted at Canadian and Mexican relations with China, which the United States continues to treat as a NME for trade law matters, treatment that China has contested before the WTO. It could also apply to Cuba and North Korea, but not Vietnam as a pre-existing partner with Canada and Mexico in the TPP-11 agreement that took effect in 2019. See R. Folsom, *International Trade Law including Trump and Trade* in a Nutshell.

Labor. Unlike the labor and environment "side agreements" to NAFTA 1994 (see Chapter 4), the USMCA incorporates these areas into the core agreement making them "enforceable" thereunder. This follows the pattern of the G. W. Bush administration's U.S. free trade agreements with Korea, Peru, Colombia and Panama, as well as TPP-12. An "Annex on Worker Representation in Collective Bargaining in Mexico" explicitly requires labor law amendments to better protect independent union organizing rights in Mexico, which did not notably improve under the 1994 side agreement. These amendments were undertaken by Mexico with substantial enforcement funding in May of 2019.

Hundreds of thousands of existing employer-friendly union "protection contracts" (often unknown to workers) need to be re-examined and validated by worker votes in Mexico. An early review of union contracts at Cemex, Mexico's multinational cement giant, was not encouraging. Some workers were clueless as to what the vote was all about. Others asserted union officials made false statements that benefits would be lost if the contract was rejected.

All Parties agreed to adopt and maintain in law and in enforcement practice labor rights recognized in the International Labor Organization's Fundamental Principles. Imports of goods from forced labor are banned. Protections for migrant workers and protections against violence targeting workers were included.

Critics, notably the post-election New Democrat Coalition and AFL-CIO, argued that enforcement of labor and environment commitments under USMCA 2018 was inadequate. In 2019, significant amendments to the 2018 agreement on labor were undertaken. A presumption that labor violations affect trade and investment, a NAFTA requirement retained in the USMCA, was added. U.S. government Dept. of Labor personnel will be based in Mexico to monitor that country's labor practices, but will not serve as "inspectors".

The 2019 amendments require creation of a U.S. interagency committee to oversee Mexico's labor reform implementation and compliance with USMCA benchmarks. Benchmark failures can lead to enforcement action. A new facility-specific "rapid response enforcement mechanism" was added in 2019 to the USMCA via Annex 31–A. Three independent labor experts will serve on Panels to evaluate asserted violations covering manufactured goods or services traded between the U.S. and Mexico. Tariffs, fines and possibly embargoes may apply to goods or services not produced in compliance with freedom of association and collective bargaining obligations. Watch for complaints regarding Mexican compliance to be filed by U.S. labor unions.

USMCA Article 23.9 broadly recognizes the goal of promoting equality in the workplace for women, and eliminating employment/occupation discrimination on the basis of sex, sexual harassment, pregnancy, sexual orientation, gender identity and care giving responsibilities. Footnote 13 states that no additional action is required by the United States in order to be in compliance with this Article, disregarding the fact that no federal statute protects U.S. workers from gender identity and sexual orientation discrimination.

Environment. On the environment, USMCA borrowed and expanded upon TPP-12 with coverage banning subsidization of illegal, unreported and unregulated (IUU) fishing and shark finning. New provisions concern invasive alien species, whales and sea turtles, wild flora and fauna, forest management, ozone depletion, environmental impact assessments, as well as cooperation on air quality and marine debris. A side agreement preserves the Commission for Environmental Cooperation (CEC) created under NAFTA 1994. The CEC can continue to receive environmental compliance complaints from the public. See Chapter 4.

Unlike the Japan-EU FTA of 2018, no mention of climate change is made in the USMCA. Amendments to the USMCA in 2019 created a presumption that an environmental violation affects trade and investment. Commitments were undertaken to adopt and maintain seven multilateral environment agreements (MEAs, including future amendments thereto) taking priority over the USMCA:

(a) The Convention on International Trade in Endangered Species of Wild Fauna and Flora, done at Washington, March 3, 1973, as amended;

(b) The Montreal Protocol on Substances that Deplete the Ozone Layer, done at Montreal, September 16, 1987, as adjusted and amended;

(c) The Protocol of 1978 Relating to the International Convention for the Prevention of Pollution from Ships, 1973, done at London, February 17, 1 978, as amended;

(d) The Convention on Wetlands of International Importance Especially as Waterfowl Habitat, done at Ramsar, February 2, 1971, as amended;

(e) The Convention on the Conservation of Antarctic Marine Living Resources, done at Canberra, May 20, 1980;

(f) The International Convention for the Regulation of Whaling, done at Washington, December 2, 1946; and

(g) The Convention for the Establishment of an Inter-American Tropical Tuna Commission, done at Washington, May 31, 1949.

Under the 2019 USMCA amendments, a U.S. interagency committee will assess and monitor Canadian and Mexican USMCA environmental obligations. A new U.S. customs service verification mechanism will ensure that only legally harvested and taken flora and fauna are traded through Mexico. Additional funds are authorized for the North American Development Bank, the Trade Enforcement Trust Fund, and EPA grants under the Border Water Infrastructure Program.

Digital Trade/Internet Providers. Digital trade, then in its infancy, was not covered under NAFTA 1994. USMCA Chapter 19 follows TPP-12 in banning data localization requirements (Canada has such rules), disallowing customs duties on digital commerce (think Netflix, social media, search engines, data storage, e-books and software), limiting cross-border restrictions on data flows, requiring anti-spam rules, and protecting consumer privacy. Source codes and algorithms are protected, as are e-signatures and electronic authentications. Internet service providers (ISPs) are protected under a "safe harbor" from copyright and criminal liability connected to unauthorized actions of their users, provided the ISPs take down copyright infringing material in a timely manner. Canada retained its "notice-and-notice" system requiring ISPs to notify customers of copyright infringement allegations.

Intellectual Property. Copyright protection is extended to life of the author plus 70 years, which will change Canada's 50-year rule, and 75 years for films and other collective works. Trademarks for sounds and scents must be allowed. Concerning geographic indicators, attempts are made at protecting trade between Mexico and the United States in arguably generic product names such as parmesan, feta and champagne. Trade secret theft must be subject to civil and criminal penalties. IP exceptions to promote medicines for all and compulsory patent licensing in national emergencies were retained. IP enforcement exceptions to protect public health and nutrition, and to promote development are recognized.

Pharmaceuticals and Biologics. Under the 2018 text, biologic (made from living organisms) medicines were to receive 10 years safety and efficacy test data exclusivity protection, adding two years to Canada's eight-year rules. This provision was _removed_ by the 2019 amendments. Such provisions typically delay market entry by generic biosimilar firms.

Pharmaceuticals also lost linkage and patent term extension or delay benefits originally in the 2018 text. Generic and biosimilar firms are to obtain marketing approval on the day after patent expiration. In addition, the 2019 amendments removed provisions requiring patent availability for new uses of known pharma products ("evergreening"). These changes focus on expanding and accelerating the growth of generic pharmaceuticals.

Greater transparency in pharma pricing and reimbursement rules, plus independent review procedures, are required. These provisions target single payer health care systems, such as that of Canada. They were in TPP-12 but dropped completely from TPP-11. Disputes regarding pharma transparency are excluded from USMCA dispute settlement.

Financial Services and Information. The USMCA on financial services generally tracks TPP-12, including a narrowing of national treatment and MFN treatment duties in "like circumstances". In addition, USMCA governments are prohibited from preventing financial institutions from transferring personal and other information across borders by electronic or other means. Also, the governments may not restrict financial institutions from locating computing facilities abroad. In either case, regulatory authorities must have immediate, direct, complete and ongoing access to information for regulatory and supervisory purposes. Each nation must adopt or maintain "a" legal framework that provides protection for personal data, and have online consumer protection and anti-spam laws.

On dispute settlement, financial services obligations are subject to USMCA investor-state arbitrations between Mexico (but not Canada) and the United States.

Trucking Services. Cross-border long-haul trucking by Mexican carriers is restricted under a Chapter 15 Annex, altering NAFTA provisions and a unanimous NAFTA dispute panel in Mexico's favor. See Chapter 3. In the event of "material harm" (including to American drivers), the U.S. may limit new Mexican cross-border, long-haul trucking services.

Provisions Borrowed from TPP-12. New provisions in the USMCA, not found or heavily augmented compared to NAFTA, were primarily borrowed from TPP-12. These include largely aspirational coverage of "good" regulatory practices (Chapter 28, transparency, notice and the like), advancement and protection of the interests of small and medium businesses (Chapter 25), macroeconomic policies and exchange rates (Chapter 33), competition policy (Chapter 21), and anti-corruption law (Chapter 27). More concrete provisions concern competitive neutrality for state-owned enterprises (Chapters 22 and 26), customs and trade facilitation procedures (Chapter 7), and development of sectoral industry standards (Chapter 12) via Annexes to the USMCA.

"De Minimis" Customs Duty and Tax-Free Shipments. Customs duty free shipments to Canada

rise to $150 CDN, and to Mexico to $117 US, with the U.S. remaining at $800. The tax-free thresholds are lower: $50 US for Mexico, $40 CDN for Canada, and $800 US for the United States. In both cases, the U.S. amounts could be reduced to match the Canadian and Mexican sums. These duty free and tax-free shipments, employing "simple" customs forms, are expected to boost cross-border e-commerce and small business trading but are hardly a victory for online trading.

Investor-State Dispute Settlement has been notably changed by Chapter 14 of the USMCA. See the coverage of Canada and Mexico below and Chapter 3.

Sunset Clause. The United States withdrew its pressure for a five-year sunset clause. Instead, the USMCA will last for 16 years. It will be reviewed every six years, triggering another 16-year period unless rejected by a partner.

As under NAFTA, any Party may withdraw from the USMCA agreement with six months' notice.

CANADA UNDER THE USMCA

Canada has for many years been the largest U.S. trade partner for goods. Before NAFTA, most Canadian exports went to the USA, with significant U.S. trade in services, investment and technology flowing north. By 2018, broadly speaking, Canada's economic dependence on the USA remained substantial, a bargaining lever exploited by U.S. negotiators. In the run-up to the finalization of USMCA, Canada reached out for alternatives. It completed a major free trade agreement with the European Union (CETA 2017) and was a leader in developing TPP-11. See R. Folsom, *Free Trade Agreements: From GATT 1947 through NAFTA Re-Negotiated* (West Academic Publishing).

Cultural Industries, AD and CVD Disputes, Progressive Goals, Energy. From the Canadian perspective, on the success side of the ledger, Canada retained from CUSFTA 1989 and NAFTA 1994 its cultural industry exclusion (see Chapter 2) along with utilization of binational panels (instead of judicial review) to resolve antidumping and subsidy disputes (see Chapters 2 and 3).

Canada also secured recognition of the rights of indigenous peoples. The USMCA agreement further requires policies against employment discrimination on the basis of gender identity, sexual orientation, sexual harassment, pregnancy, and caregiving responsibilities, all reflecting Canada's "progressive" perspectives. Footnote 13 in USMCA Chapter 23 appears to exempt the U.S. from these duties.

Canada's much debated promise under CUSFTA and NAFTA to proportionally share energy resources (see Chapter 2) with the USA in energy crises was removed.

Agricultural Goods, Wine. On the negative side of the ledger, Canada made limited concessions allowing greater entry of U.S. dairy (milk, milk powder, milk protein, cream, butter, and cheese), margarine, whey, chicken, egg, turkey and grain products into its market, concessions broadly similar to those it had made under TPP-12. In return, Canada gained small market openings to increase exports to the U.S. of dairy, peanut and processed peanut, and sugar and sugar containing products. Dairy tariff rate quotas commitments on both sides are to be reciprocal based on tonnage. All sides committed to protecting agricultural biotech, including gene editing.

Canada also agreed to open up British Columbia grocery stores to sales of U.S. wines.

Procurement. Canada and the United States have no procurement obligations under the USMCA. Hence procurement as between those countries is governed by the Enhanced WTO Procurement Agreement. Mexico (which does not participate in the optional WTO Agreement) and the United States largely retained their NAFTA federal/special entity procurement obligations under Chapter 13 of the USMCA agreement.

Investor-State Dispute Settlement. By agreement in Chapter 14, apart from legacy NAFTA claims (presented no later than three years after the new USMCA agreement enters into force), Canada and the United States *completely* removed the availability of arbitrations to resolve investor-state disputes. Compare Chapter 3. In the future, such disputes will presumably be resolved by state-to-state dispute settlement or the courts of either nation.

MEXICO UNDER THE USMCA

Before NAFTA, about most Mexican exports went to the USA, with significant U.S. trade in services, investment and technology flowing south. By 2018, broadly speaking, Mexico's economic dependence on the USA remained overwhelming, a major bargaining lever exploited by U.S. negotiators. In the run-up to the finalization of the USMCA. Mexico also reached out for alternatives. It completed a much-expanded free trade agreement with the European Union, and is a member of TPP-11. See R. Folsom, *Free Trade Agreements: From GATT 1947 through NAFTA Re-Negotiated* (West Academic Publishing).

Investor-State Dispute Settlement (ISDS). Investor-state arbitration of disputes for damages continues in full as between Mexico and Canada under TPP-11 effective Jan. 1, 2019. Such arbitrations continue under revised terms as between Mexico and the United States. U.S.-Mexico claims involving *government contracts* are limited to specified capital-intensive sectors (oil and gas, telecommunications, power generation, and infrastructure contracts for roads, railways, bridges or canals but not apparently dams, seaports and airports). Such government contract disputes may assert the full range of NAFTA investor rights (direct and indirect expropriation, fair and equitable treatment (minimum standard), national and MFN treatment, and more). See Chapter 3.

For claims *not* involving government contracts, limitations are placed on investor-state arbitrations by the USMCA. Such claims are limited to national and most-favored nation treatment, and expropriation grounds, notably dropping out fair and equitable treatment claims. In addition, borrowing from post-NAFTA U.S. free trade agreements and the TPP-12, "indirect" expropriation claims are also limited. Indirect expropriations are defined in the USMCA as situations "in which an action or series of actions by a Party has an effect equivalent to direct expropriation without formal transfer of title or outright seizure".

Further, "non-discriminatory regulatory actions by a Party that are designed and applied to protect legitimate public welfare objectives, such as health, safety and the environment, do *not* constitute indirect expropriations, except in rare circumstances." This USMCA language addresses criticisms of NAFTA investor-state arbitrations challenging environmental measures as regulatory takings and/or indirect expropriations. For examples, see Chapter 3.

Furthermore, borrowing a TPP-12 rule, investor claimants under USMCA, must first exhaust local remedies or attempt to do so for 30 months prior to seeking arbitration. This rule does not appear to apply to the select government contract claimants noted above. Investors owned or controlled by non-market economy states are barred from using arbitration remedies. Establishment claims prior to actual investment are generally excluded.

Energy. Mexico's top priority in negotiating NAFTA, protection of PEMEX as a state monopoly over oil, gas and most petrochemicals is obliquely referenced in the USMCA. Explicit reference is made to Mexico's direct, inalienable and imprescriptible ownership of hydrocarbon resources (which conceivably could facilitate the return of PEMEX as an absolute monopoly).

The numerous major oil companies with new wells and drilling rights in Mexico as of 2019 await with some anxiety the policies of its new President López-Obrador (known as AMLO). Prior to taking office, AMLO announced a three-year moratorium on new bidding for oil and gas exploration/exploitation blocs. He forced renegotiation of natural-gas pipeline contracts, directed Pemex to construct a new refinery, and gave Pemex over a billion dollars in tax cuts.

That said, buried in USMCA Article 32.11, is an obligation for MFN treatment in the energy sector. Since Mexico agreed under TPP-11 Annexes to preserve the market opening reforms of its prior administration, Article 32.11 could be construed to bar backtracking on energy rules already in place that benefit U.S. and Canadian parties. (I am grateful to Professor David Gantz for this insight).

RATIFICATION

Thirteen "side letters' that accompanied the signing of the USMCA on Nov. 30, 2018 took effect immediately. These include: Mexican and Canadian exclusions from any future U.S. tariff-rate quotas on the importation of autos (threatened by the Trump administration as a matter of national security), U.S.-Mexico agreements on biologic drugs, cheese names and auto safety standards, and U.S.-Canada agreements on wine, water and energy.

Approval and implementation of the USMCA by the U.S. Congress was complicated by the takeover in November of the House of Representatives by the Democrats. Apart from not wishing to give the President a "victory", the sizeable New Democrat Coalition and the AFL-CIO quickly let it be known that the USMCA's enforcement provisions on labor and the environment were, in their opinion, inadequate. Additional concerns were expressed about access to biologic medicines under the new agreement, the ability to block intergovernmental USMCA dispute settlement by failure to name panelists, and continuance of U.S. national security steel and aluminum tariffs on Canadian and Mexican exports, subsequently removed in May 2019. Republican conservatives opposed the progressive social provisions (above) secured by Canada in USMCA.

President Trump threatened to withdraw from NAFTA (with six months' notice) in order to pressure Congress to approve and implement the USMCA. In early June 2019, he commenced U.S. "fast track" procedures under U.S. trade law that anticipate up or down Congressional votes on USMCA as negotiated. No Congressional amendments are permitted under fast track procedures, but new side letters or side agreements can emerge. See R. Folsom, *International Trade Law including Trump and Trade* in a Nutshell.

A few days after commencing fast track, in the name of national emergency, President Trump announced, effective June 10, 2019, a 5% tariff on ALL Mexican goods absent satisfactory Mexican efforts to reduce the flow of Central American asylum-seeking immigrants into the USA. He further threatened to raise this tariff each month to 25% by the Fall of 2019. All this just as Mexico and Canada surpassed China to become the top trading partners of the USA.

Mexico quickly promised to move its National Guard to its Southern border with Guatemala, accept more immigrants returned from or denied asylum by the USA, and generally cooperate on migration issues. Mexico did not, as the U.S. wished, designate itself as a "safe third country", though apparently promised to do so if its immigrant restraints failed to measure up to U.S. goals. Such a designation would render migrants passing through Mexico ineligible to claim asylum in the USA. President Trump removed his national emergency tariff threats.

Meanwhile, formal ratification of the USMCA was undertaken first in Mexico in June of 2019. Negotiations between the Trump administration and Democrats in Congress generated changes on labor, environment, enforcement and pharmaceutical USMCA rules that formed the basis for an amendment protocol that all three countries signed in December of 2019. Ratification commenced shortly thereafter in the Mexican Senate and overwhelming approval vote in the U.S. House of Representatives.

USMCA OVERVIEW

On balance, especially considering the rhetoric and sometimes vitriolic positions of President Trump, there are relatively few provisions of major consequence in the USMCA. Apart from auto rules of origin, removal of investor-state arbitrations between the U.S. and Canada, restricted entry for long-haul Mexican trucks, and closer scrutiny of Mexican unions, most of the agreement contains predictable updates largely derived from TPP-12. In sum, the USMCA makes relatively modest to minor changes and additions to NAFTA 1994.

In other words, the USMCA is not exactly groundbreaking. It primarily repackages free trade rules found elsewhere. That said, the USMCA constitutes an FTA model acceptable to President Trump. Of course, no U.S. trade partner enjoys being "bullied" into a deal with a leader they distrust. The President seems to ignore or not understand that how you negotiate trade agreements can have long-term relationship costs. Whether the USMCA represents America First, Second or Third remains to be seen.

If NAFTA was the "worst trade deal ever," what are the business and economic implications of the USMCA? Distinguished Professor of Economics Davis Folsom addresses this question in Chapter 7.

CHAPTER 7

USMCA: ITS ECONOMIC AND BUSINESS IMPLICATIONS

Given three years of anti-NAFTA rhetoric from the campaign trail and then the White House, there was considerable time and debate among NAFTA experts and vested interest groups regarding what U.S. trade policy should be and the potential damage if the agreement was terminated. Similarly, in fall 2018, as election deadlines in each country pressed politicians and negotiators to find "a deal", lobbying and bargaining intensified resulting first in a U.S.-Mexico agreement and then USMCA.

At various times, President Trump seemingly contradicted himself, calling for higher tariffs on imports from countries whose trade practices he considered "unfair" but then saying "I'm absolutely a free-trader. I'm for open trade, free trade, but I also want smart trade and fair trade." He also stated he wanted to achieve "fairness and reciprocity." Numerous U.S. presidents have articulated similar goals but interpreted the terms differently. Until USMCA negotiations, U.S. presidents generally attempted to achieve fairness and reciprocity in terms of the rules of the game not a particular outcome; balance of trade with a particular nation.

The goal of fair trade goes back to colonial America when one of the grievances in the Declaration of Independence was a complaint about Britain's use of mercantilist policies to ban colonial trade with the rest of the world. Post American Revolution, Britain resisted U.S. attempts to establish free trade and, in 1793, Secretary of State Thomas Jefferson, while supporting free trade doctrine, reported many restrictions imposed by trade partners of the new country. Jefferson unsuccessfully proposed achieving reciprocity through retaliation. For the next hundred years or so, the U.S. set tariffs, often as a source of central government revenue, largely without regard to trade partner policies culminating in the infamous Smoot-Hawley tariffs during the Great Depression.

The goal of reciprocity in trade did not reappear until the Franklin D. Roosevelt years, when the Reciprocal Trade Agreements Act of 1934 gave the president the authority to negotiate changes in trade agreements with other nations. When Donald Trump won the election, trade law experts were quickly in demand and confirmed that, yes, the president does have authority to negotiate and end trade agreements. Often stunned political and industry leaders delved into the various statements made during the election campaign trying to discover what direction the president would take future U.S. trade policy.

Early into his presidency, Mr. Trump withdrew from the Trans-Pacific Partnership (TPP) promising, instead, to negotiate and re-negotiate many bilateral agreements particularly with Asian nations. In spring 2018, after authorizing unilateral increases in tariffs on steel, aluminum, and products from China, with little media attention, the U.S. and Korea reached an accord, signaling to some NAFTA watchers that the White House could engage in and complete bilateral agreements. Others waited, knowing new elections were coming in each of the North American countries, wondering what if anything would come of USMCA.

In this confusing, often contradictory political trade environment, investment and policy analysts offered their assessments of what would happen if USMCA negotiations had failed or if the draft agreement was not ratified. Even in early 2019, the President suggested that if the treaty was not ratified, he might withdraw the United States from NAFTA. Let's first examine the death of NAFTA economic predictions.

DEATH OF NAFTA: MACRO-MARKET PREDICTIONS

One NAFTA headline read "Leaving NAFTA Would Cost $50 Billion a Year", where the author, after reviewing dozens of academic and policy studies, concluded that NAFTA increased U.S. GDP by 0.2 to 0.3 percent annually. This does not sound like much of an impact until it is compared to current GDP which is over $20 trillion. Another headline read "U.S. Bid to Exit NAFTA Arbitration Panels Draws Business Ire." While U.S. Trade representative Robert Lighthizer had called the investor-state dispute settlement system (ISDS) an infringement on U.S. sovereignty, more than 100 U.S. trade associations sent a letter to the administration supporting the system as a "core element to protect the United States against theft, discrimination and unfair treatment of U.S. property overseas." Though the U.S. has never lost a NAFTA ISDS decision, the existence of the system was of sufficient value to business groups that they challenged the administration's stance on the issue.

The U.S. Chamber of Commerce was an early voice critical of withdrawal from NAFTA ("A NAFTA Exit Would Be a Rotten Deal") stating "quitting NAFTA would be an economic, political, and national security disaster." Their experts predicted tariffs on all products would snap back to an average of 3.5 percent for the United States, 4.2 percent for Canada, and 7.5 percent for Mexico. The Chamber noted that current areas cooperation; anti-terror, antinarcotics, and Central American immigration, would likely end "overnight." Echoing the U.S. Chamber of Commerce, a Peterson Institute for International Economics analyst concluded "Repeal of NAFTA would be a damaging economic blow to the United States but it would be a far more serious threat to U.S. homeland security."

A 2017 ImpactECON analysis concluded that if NAFTA ended some production would move north from Mexico, but the U.S. would still incur a net loss of over 250,000 jobs in the next three to five years. They predicted Mexico would be the biggest loser, over 950,000 jobs and Canada losing 125,000 jobs. Their model estimated U.S. GDP would decline by 0.1 percent, with Canada's GDP declining 0.5 percent and Mexico's nearly 1.0 percent. Within the overall impact of a NAFTA exit, ImpactECON predicted there would be small gains in some machinery, chemical, and metals sectors but large losses in services, food, and motor vehicles. Approximately thirty percent of the U.S. job losses would come from increased tariffs and their impact on demand, while seventy percent would come from reciprocal increases in tariffs by Mexico and Canada. On a non-quantitative level, the ImpactECON authors noted NAFTA's collapse would raise broader doubts about U.S. support for the international free-trading system.

In response to U.S. demands during USMCA negotiations, Canada pursued a fascinating strategy labeled a "charm offensive" by the *Wall Street Journal*. After the 2017 U.S. inauguration, Canadian officials held nearly 300 meetings with U.S. leaders other than President Trump including governors or lieutenant governors in all fifty states. "Ottawa is betting that friends in high places across the U.S. will recognize the damage tearing up NAFTA could do to supply chains and growth-and pressure the Trump administration to leave the pact alone."

DEATH OF NAFTA: MICRO-MARKET PREDICTIONS

Agriculture. In "Playing Chicken," *The Economist* magazine assessed which states and industries would be most adversely affected "were NAFTA to disappear in a renegotiation-gone-wrong." Assuming U.S.-Mexico trade would then follow WTO rules, they found Texas, particularly chicken producers, would be especially hard-hit since trade with Mexico represents a larger part of state GDP and poultry exports would then be subject to stiff Mexican tariffs. Their analysis found that farm states would face the highest charges, and auto manufacturing states would also be subject to increased tariffs as parts and vehicles passed back and forth between the countries.

A U.S. Chamber of Commerce analysis predicted if NAFTA ended Mexico would likely cut its tariffs on agricultural imports from South America substituting Brazilian and Argentinian grains and other products for commodities now entering Mexico from the United States duty-free.

Since NAFTA, the United States has entered into few new trade agreements while Canada and Mexico have continued to expand their trade relationships. One small part of the new Canada-European trade pact eliminated an eight percent European tariff on live lobster imports. U.S. lobster producers still face the tariff giving their Canadian counterparts a distinct competitive advantage.

Energy. In the anti-USMCA rhetoric little mention was made about energy trade. That may reflect the fact that, since NAFTA, the United States has dramatically reduced its energy dependence and even has a surplus in energy trade with Mexico. In 2016, U.S. gasoline, diesel, and natural gas exports to Mexico exceeded $20 billion while crude imports totaled less than $9 billion. In addition, Mexico imports almost all of its energy production equipment from the U.S. and uses U.S. electrical power as part of its burgeoning industrial production. The U.S. remains a major importer of energy from Canada, most recently expansion of the controversial Trans Canada pipeline bringing heavy crude oil from the western provinces.

Former World Bank president and U.S. trade representative Robert Zoellick offered an energy-related insight regarding USMCA. First, that in enacting the 2013 energy amendments to the Mexican Constitution, Mexico protected American investors from a populist reversal of Mexican policy but only as long as the U.S. is part of NAFTA. A Peterson Institute analysis echoed that concern, noting a rise in nationalism and criticism of the new Buy American rules as applied to border pipeline construction.

Motor Vehicles and Parts. One of the early negotiating positions taken by the Trump Administration was a call for 50 percent U.S. content and 85 percent North American content in automobiles covered by NAFTA. As negotiations first stalled and then approached looming political deadlines, parties agreed to broaden the definition of what could be counted toward U.S. content, including items such as software, technological components, research and development, and some raw materials like steel. The goal was to discourage further erosion of U.S.-based auto manufacturing without a defined American-made content requirement. But, a 2018 Business Roundtable study estimated that withdrawing from NAFTA could cost the U.S. automobile industry more than 20,000 jobs plus another 50,000 jobs in the auto parts industry while adding $330–$440 to the cost of new vehicles sold in the United States.

Similarly, industry group, the Alliance of Automobile Manufacturers, stated "Disrupting this integrated supply chain would increase prices, lower sales, threaten exports and endanger American workers' jobs." As USMCA negotiations rushed to completion, auto manufacturers cautioned not to make the content rules too complex, where compliance costs would outweigh the benefits and make non-North American production more attractive.

Also looming over the failure of USMCA negotiations was the re-imposition of the so-called "chicken tax." Back in the 1960s, the U.S. imposed a 25 percent tax on all pickups and some work vans imported into the country. The tax was a response to a dispute when U.S. farmers flooded European markets and countries including then West Germany, taxed U.S. chickens. President Lyndon Johnson responded by putting a tariff on foreign made pickups entering the country. By 2016, however, General Motors, Fiat Chrysler, and Toyota produced a total of nearly 800,000 trucks annually and exported $18.5 billion worth of vehicles that, without NAFTA, would be subject to the chicken tax.

Other Market Impacts. With the passage of NAFTA, Tijuana became a television capital as global manufacturers shifted production there to take advantage of duty-free entry into the United States. Initially, manufacturers had to produce the picture tube in North America to qualify for NAFTA entry but, as flat screens replaced tubes manufacturers, mostly Asian firms, shipped LCD panels through California ports, assembled and packaged the TVs in Tijuana and currently ship 40 million televisions yearly to the United States. In the process 15,000 workers are employed in the industry and the 5 percent tariff other manufacturers face is avoided. If USMCA negotiations had failed, one analyst predicted these jobs would move to Vietnam or other low-cost labor sources.

The Peterson Institute for International Economics provided a detailed analysis of a potentially significant issue, *de minimis* taxes imposed on consumer purchases shipped among the three countries. The United States recently raised the amount exempt from duties to $800 while Mexico has a maximum of $50 on courier and $300 on postal shipments. Meanwhile, among the developed countries, Canada had the lowest level of exemption from duties, just $15. The Peterson study suggested raising the Canadian minimum would increase consumer welfare through increased choice and lower prices. Canadian critics countered, arguing it would allow a backdoor entry into their country for competition from low-cost countries including China.

Virtually all participants beyond the White House viewed the five-year sunset clause as impractical and dangerous to long-term investment planning. Similarly, critics viewed a U.S. proposal to cap Canadian and Mexican government procurement awards in the United States to an amount equal to that awarded to U.S. corporations in their countries as unrealistic and potentially counter-productive if it then added to contracts awarded to non-NAFTA based corporations.

Labor. Not long after NAFTA was ratified, Harvard economist Dani Rodrik warned that globalization was driving a wedge between workers who had the skills and mobility to prosper in a global economy and those who did not. At that time, the United States was still benefitting from the "brain drain" as eager, technology-focused young people flocked to the U.S. and never went home. They had the mobility, in part because educational visas provided relatively easy access to opportunities, "in the States."

Exactly when the brain drain reversed is hard to determine but forces including post-9/11 education and security policy changes, increased opportunity and incentives for talented students in their home countries, and growing global prosperity and communications encouraged "brains" to return home shifting the global labor market for workers with skills. In the United States leading economists, including Princeton's Alan Blinder, later confessed surprise regarding the importance of mobility or the lack there of, in affecting towns and workers left behind in the race for globalization.

Professor Rodrik observed the key challenge would be to make globalization "compatible with domestic social and political stability." He said it would not be easy as trade "unleashes forces that undermine the norms implicit in domestic practices." In the U.S. increased trade, both a result of NAFTA and expansion of the WTO, weakened the explicit and implicit contract between workers and employers. Autobiographies including *Deer Hunting with Jesus*

(2006) and *Hillbilly Elegy* (2017) described the pain, anger, and fear among workers who had "played by the rules," but were being left behind as technology and globalization changed their reality. As stated in an earlier chapter, most economists recognized there would be winners and losers but surmised that the benefits of trade would outweigh the personal and social costs. Belatedly, trade experts noted that business leaders and free trade advocates in Congress supported trade deals but opposed even modest trade adjustment assistance for displaced workers and abandoned communities.

Almost lost in the USMCA negotiations were early statements by the Trump team to try to enhance parts of the labor agreement. Before the U.S. bailed out of TPP, Mexico had agreed to labor reforms including changes to protect collective bargaining. While seemingly incongruent with the current Washington agenda, if Mexican collective bargaining increased workers' wages it would, in theory, reduce the cost differential and reduce corporate incentives to move work to Mexico.

Leaders of many multinational corporations have strongly supported USMCA based on supply chain synergies that have evolved over the last several decades. One analysis found that a 10 percent increase in employment at a U.S. multinational's Mexican affiliate led to a 1.3 percent increase in stateside employment, along with a 1.7 percent increase in exports and a 4.1 percent increase in R&D spending. Robert Scott, author of the widely cited anti-NAFTA study which predicted NAFTA would cost hundreds of thousands of American jobs, said during USMCA debates that killing NAFTA would not bring the jobs back. With the higher costs, "multinationals like GM, Ford, and Toyota may just decide to shift production to Asia or Europe. The U.S. benefits from having that production in North America, even if it is in Mexico."

THE ECONOMIC AND BUSINESS IMPLICATIONS OF USMCA

Years ago, a U.S. trade assistant described the flurry of NAFTA negotiations as the "Watergate 300", referring to the fact that the final negotiations took place on the third floor of the Watergate Hotel and an analogy to a car race frenzy. Similarly, finalizing USMCA could be described as somewhere between hostage negotiations and the final lap at Indianapolis 500. The Trump administration's imposition of steel and aluminum tariffs on materials from NAFTA partners surprised many people, angered others, and led to a stand-off where Mexico was the first to capitulate and Canada later complied. The process was not pretty and often shuffled to the sidelines as China disputes/ negotiations took primacy, but somehow, in spring 2019, a tentative agreement was reached and, later that year, a final accord was agreed upon.

In the end, numerous changes and additions were made to NAFTA. Headlines suggested major "winners" included the three political leaders: President Trump for re-negotiating NAFTA, Prime Minister Trudeau for keeping the Chapter 19 dispute resolution mechanism and largely maintaining the Canadian dairy supply management system, and President López Obrador for avoiding the termination of NAFTA. Organized labor, with the $16 per hour minimum wage requirement in automobile production and language directing Mexico to make it easier to form unions, North American steel and aluminum with new content rules, and online shoppers with higher *de minimis* allowances were also predicted to benefit from USMCA. "Losers" were predicted to be car buyers in the United States with higher prices and reduced selection among small cars and big business facing increased compliance costs. Within weeks, industry groups and analysts began to assess the implications of USMCA.

In April 2019 the independent and generally well regarded U.S. International Trade Commission (ITC) published its economic assessment of the likely impact of USMCA: **The *United States-Mexico-Canada Agreement: Likely Impact on the U.S. Economy and Specific Industry Sectors*** (Investigation No. TPA–105–003, USITC Publication 4889, April 2019) available at: https://www.usitc.gov/publications/332/pub4889.pdf. The Commission used a combination of detailed quantitative and qualitative industry analyses and an economy-wide computable general equilibrium model to assess the likely impact of USMCA on the U.S. economy and industry sectors.

USMCA MACRO-MARKET PREDICTIONS

With the stock market near an all-time high, unemployment at record lows, an economy still digesting a trillion-dollar tax cut and an election season looming, USMCA received relatively little attention in Washington. The agreement will reduce uncertainty and, as such, facilitate trade and investment decision-making. Numerous North American CEOs were reported as "breathing easier" when the agreement was announced. The Mexican economy would likely have incurred the greatest negative impact if NAFTA had been terminated.

The macro 2019 ITC Report analysis estimated that:

"USMCA would raise U.S. real GDP by $68.2 billion (0.35 percent) and U.S. employment by 176,000 jobs (0.12 percent). The model estimates that USMCA would likely have a positive impact on U.S. trade, both with USMCA partners and with the rest of the world. U.S. exports to Canada and Mexico would increase by $19.1 billion (5.9 percent) and $14.2 billion (6.7 percent), respectively. U.S. imports from Canada and Mexico would increase by $19.1 billion (4.8 percent) and $12.4 billion (3.8 percent), respectively. The model estimates that the agreement would likely have a positive impact on all broad industry sectors within the U.S. economy. Manufacturing would experience the largest percentage gains in output, exports, wages, and employment, while in absolute terms, services would experience the largest gains in output and employment."

Given the importance of automobile parts and assembly in Mexico, the new content rules and minimum labor wage requirements will likely, over time, negatively affect Mexican economic activity.

USMCA MICRO-MARKET PREDICTIONS

Agriculture. While some farm organizations quickly applauded increased access to the Canadian dairy market, analysts described the change as "symbolic." The ITC analysis concurred that the USMCA agricultural provisions were generally minor. There are no market access provisions in USMCA that address food and agricultural products trade between the United States and Mexico, so most of the change will likely be in trade between the United States and Canada.

Most trade in agricultural products among the United States, Canada, and Mexico was duty free under NAFTA and would continue to be duty free under USMCA. However, some restrictions on agricultural trade remain. The United States maintains tariff-rate quotas (TRQs) on sugar and sugar-containing products (SCPs) and dairy products. Restrictions on trade in these products would be slightly eased under USMCA. Canada maintains a supply management system including TRQs that protect its domestic producers of dairy products and poultry and egg-containing products from imports. USMCA is likely to lead to slight increases in U.S. exports of dairy products, poultry meat, eggs, and egg-containing products to Canada, and to a slight increase in Canada's exports of dairy products to the United States and a minimal increase in Canada's exports of sugar and SCPs to the United States. Additionally, USMCA provisions address nontariff measures that will likely increase exports of U.S. wheat and alcoholic beverages to Canada.

While supporting USMCA, most U.S. agriculture interests remained more concerned about U.S.-China trade disputes and the removal of Mexican and Canadian agricultural restraints initiated after the U.S. imposed steel and aluminum national security tariffs.

Digital Trade and E-commerce. USMCA is likely to have a positive impact on U.S. industries that rely on cross-border data flows and digitally enabled trade, including e-commerce. Key provisions in USMCA's digital trade chapter require the parties to ensure free movement of data cross-border, and also forbid them from adopting restrictive data measures in the future.

In particular, the USMCA will benefit North American computer services and digital platform services firms by ensuring that data flows remain unencumbered, proprietary source codes and algorithms are protected, and intermediary liability protection is provided. The U.S. telecommunications industry will benefit from increased access to telecom networks and interconnection provisions. Exporters of low-value shipments (including e-commerce exports) and express delivery services will likely experience faster shipping and lower-cost customs processing. U.S. payments services would likely benefit from greater market access and national treatment.

USMCA will be the first U.S. free trade agreement to include a chapter on digital trade. Thus, nearly all of the digital trade and e-commerce-related provisions in the agreement are new relative to NAFTA. The digital trade provisions will impact traditional data-intensive, internet-based firms, but also firms in the services, manufacturing, and agricultural industries that rely on data and information flows in their business models and have strong competitive advantages globally. The USMCA Digital Trade chapter builds on the TPP framework which would ensure that data restrictions are not enacted in the future, and would establish trade commitments on other digital trade matters that have emerged since NAFTA was enacted.

Though the USMCA Telecommunications chapter allows greater access for competitors analysts anticipate the USMCA will affect the business segment of the telecom services markets of Canada and Mexico more so than the consumer segment which are either already facing competition (Mexico) or dominated by existing firms (Canada).

While widely discussed among USMCA analysts, changes in De-Minimis Thresholds (DMT), raising the minimum value of a cross-border purchases (usually business to consumer B2C) subject to duties, will likely have a modest, positive economic impact. Mostly this is because both Mexico and Canada made relatively small changes in their DMT levels when compared to the United States. If, as allowed under the agreement, the United States reduced its DMT to match Canadian and Mexican limits, it would likely have a greater impact on cross-border sales. Assuming no further changes are made in DMTs, major U.S.-based e-commerce companies will increase North American shipments and delivery service firms will respond accordingly. As in the United States, Mexican and Canadian consumers will benefit from expanded competition and choice.

Energy. Initial reactions among energy industry interests to the USMCA agreement were positive with the American Petroleum Institute (API) supporting the continued tariff-free flow of energy products among the three countries. API President Mike Sommers was quoted as saying: "We urge Congress to approve the USMCA. Having Canada as a trading partner and a party to this agreement is critical for North American energy security and U.S. consumers. Retaining a trade agreement for North America will help ensure the U.S. energy revolution continues into the future." (Mr. Sommers comments were made during the period when Mexico had agreed to the new NAFTA but Canada had not yet committed to USMCA). The API statement noted:

"Key provisions of the agreement related to the U.S. natural gas and oil industry include: continued market access for U.S. natural gas and oil products, and investments in Canada and Mexico; continued zero tariffs on natural gas and oil products; investment protections to which all countries commit and the eligibility for Investor-State Dispute Settlement (ISDS) for U.S. natural gas and oil companies investing in Mexico; requirement that Mexico retain at least current level of openness to U.S.

energy investment; additional flexibility allowing U.S. customs authorities to accept alternative documentation to certify that natural gas and oil have originated in Canada or Mexico upon entering the U.S."

Over the lifespan of NAFTA, the North American energy industry has experienced substantial change. The volume of petroleum and other liquids produced in the United States increased by 66 percent, and by 112 percent for Canada. Yet petroleum output declined by 28 percent in Mexico. In 2017, the United States produced 15.6 million barrels per day of petroleum and other liquids; Canada, 5.0 million barrels per day; and Mexico, 2.3 million barrels per day, placing the three countries 1st, 4th, and 11th in the world, respectively.

Increased unconventional production of crude petroleum supported the growth in the U.S. and Canadian industries, while limited investment and declining output from mature fields constrained the Mexican industry. The rise in crude petroleum production in Canada is largely due to growth in oil sands output. At the same time, Mexico's national petroleum company, Pemex, which has exclusive control over the country's industry, was prohibited, until fairly recently, from sharing ownership of crude production with foreign companies, limiting its ability to invest in exploration and production.

Several years ago, Mexico's constitutional reforms opened its energy sector to private investment. The resulting influx of new investment, including $100 billion in oil investment commitments (March 2018) have not reversed production declines but did challenge the status of Mexico's PEMEX monopoly. Before even taking office President López Obrador announced a three-year moratorium on new bidding an in the final 2019 USMCA negotiations, Mexico did not sign a side letter recognizing the importance of "the integration of North American markets based on market principles, including open trade and investment among the Parties to support North American energy."

The side letter was intended to acknowledge the fact that North American energy industries are tightly integrated. In 2017, Canada and Mexico accounted for 43 percent of all U.S. imports of energy-related products and 31 percent of all U.S. exports of those products. Canada's heavily discounted crude petroleum and extensive network of cross-border pipelines and rail make it the largest foreign supplier to refineries in the United States. Canada's share of U.S. crude oil imports has risen significantly in the past five years, replacing declining exports from Venezuela and Mexico. Mexico's declining production has severely affected its ability to export crude to the United States.

As stated in an earlier chapter, one of the major incentives for U.S. NAFTA negotiators was to gain commitments from Mexico and Canada to prioritize exports of petroleum to the United States. The large increase in U.S. production of petroleum and other liquids, attributable to improved technology such as horizontal drilling and hydraulic fracturing, caught many trade administrators, oil industry and political leaders by surprise. For USMCA, the prevailing sentiment seemed to be "leave this sector alone."

A Canadian analyst noted the absence of the emergency energy proportionality clause in the new agreement. This clause had required Canada to export a set amount of energy to the United States, and its removal was considered a "victory" for the Canadian energy industry.

Motor Vehicles. Easily the most contentious part of USMCA negotiations involved motor vehicles and parts. Industry representatives argued raising North American content rules above 65 percent (from the 62.5 percent NAFTA standard) would be difficult to achieve and undermine supply chain relationships and efficiency. Yet, when the 75 percent rule was announced, there was little opposition. Adding the 40–45 percent content must be made using $16 (USD) per hour or more labor requirement seemed a difficult rule to document but, again, there was little comment from affected companies. Less frequently cited was a clause requiring 70 percent of the steel and aluminum used in auto production to be of North American origin. The USTR described the goals of these rules as to: Preserve current domestic vehicle and parts production, increase U.S. content, and decrease incentives to use low-cost labor.

USMCA's automotive provisions have seven major components (See Figure 3.1 below from the 2019 ITC Report). The first four components are regional value content (RVC) requirements for (1) vehicles, (2) core auto parts, (3) principal auto parts, and (4) complementary auto parts. The other three components are (5) labor value content (LVC) requirements for vehicles, (6) steel purchase requirements, and (7) aluminum purchase requirements. For a Personal Vehicle (PV) or Light Truck (LT) to qualify for duty-free treatment, the vehicle must meet RVC, LVC, and steel and aluminum requirements. USMCA provisions are more complicated and require more regional content than those under NAFTA. They also require more parts manufacturer input into vehicle manufacturers' RVC and LVC calculations.

For the first five years under USMCA, a manufacturer can continue to meet a 62.5 percent RVC for up to 10 percent of its vehicles produced in North America. Unlike NAFTA, USMCA does not permit any parts to be "deemed originating," and it has eliminated "tracing" as well. Automotive RVC requirements are slated to be staged in over three years, and vary for different categories. At least 70 percent of both the steel and the aluminum purchased by manufacturers for use in producing PVs and LTs must originate in North America.

U.S.-Mexico-Canada Trade Agreement

Figure 3.1 Components of USMCA automotive rules of origin

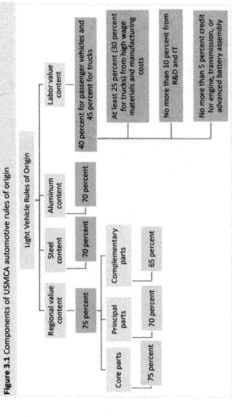

Source: Produced by USITC based on USMCA text.

Some reactions to the unbelievably complex micromanaged USMCA rules of origin for vehicles and parts were surprising. A Ford Motor spokesperson was quoted as saying: "Ford is very encouraged by today's announcement, and we applaud all three governments for working together to achieve free and fair trade in a strong regional agreement. We stand ready to be a collaborative partner to ensure this agreement is ratified in all three markets because it will support an integrated, globally competitive automotive business in North America. The benefits of scale and global reach will help to drive volume and support manufacturing jobs."

Similarly, an American Iron and Steel Institute representative stated: "We appreciate the administration's hard work to reach this trade agreement between the U.S., Canada and Mexico—especially regarding measures that ensure North American steel continues to be used in automobile production. We are pleased that the agreement is trilateral, as the relationship between our three countries has been extremely beneficial for the steel industry and resulted in robust trade and investment in the region over the past 25 years. This new agreement is significant as it will keep our manufacturing supply chains strong throughout North America."

The ITC 2019 report is not as optimistic as these industry representatives. Their analysis found auto industry responses will likely vary depending on firm's current supply chain/production assembly operations with manufacturers falling into three groups: (1) Those that already comply with new rules of origin; (2) those who will likely adjust sourcing and assembly to comply, and (3) those for whom the costs would like exceed the benefit of tariff preference.

The ITC study predicts U.S. auto manufacturing employment will increase by 28,000 over five years. The ITC analysis indicates the USMCA auto rules will likely increase the costs of production and the price of cars available to consumers in the United States.

Likewise, a U.S. Federal Reserve Bank study concluded the USMCA rules could raise the cost of cars to consumers in all three countries and make North American automakers (such as BMW based in South Carolina) less competitive in the global marketplace. An IMF study reached a similar conclusion, anticipating that although the USMCA auto rules of origin would create jobs, the cost increases stemming from those rules would lead to 140,000 fewer vehicles sold, with a corresponding reduction in automotive-related jobs.

One sceptic, the Cato Institute, predicts the increasingly restrictive rules of origin will cause more firms to pay the non-preferential tariff leading to reduced North American production and lower North American content. The result they suggest is one of USMCA's "biggest trumpeted gains, the new auto rules, are actually the worst part of the new agreement." Another commentator suggested USMCA is a "protectionist success, no matter the spin from the captains of industry."

By the time the final agreement was reached, automobile manufacturers seemed relieved, with comments including the agreement "makes the investment path for the auto industry more certain," "disaster avoided," "makes it more difficult to move jobs to Mexico," and "No Carmageddon."

Services. The services sector is a vital component of the United States' trade relationships with Canada and Mexico and the rest of the world. Many years, the United States' major bilateral trade surplus is in the services sector. Most notably, USMCA introduces binding obligations on market access that build on U.S., Canadian, and Mexican GATS commitments. In addition, USMCA makes some potentially important changes to provisions affecting certain industries including financial services and long-haul trucking. Though services trade in North America is expected to rise, USMCA provisions on services trade are unlikely to have a substantial impact on output in the U.S. services sector.

Labor. NAFTA watchers and labor leaders were initially surprised to see the United States negotiators support for labor provisions in the USMCA agreement as opposed to being left to the largely unenforceable side agreement in NAFTA. Early in the negotiations, the U.S. proposed a requirement for 50 percent U.S. labor in all motor vehicles but in the end settled for a provision requiring 40 percent labor content earning at least $16 per hour (USD) which, obviously, would include both Canadian and U.S. workers but not Mexican labor. (In 2019, Mexican auto manufacturing workers were paid the equivalent of slightly under

$8.00 per hour.) The agreement requires an initial 30 percent clause by 2020, rising to 40 percent by 2023.

The $16 per hour requirement could induce a variety of responses. In theory, Mexican factories could increase workers' wages. Another response could be to shift production to U.S. and Canadian factories. A third option would be to shift production to lower cost countries and pay the import fee. Critics noted the $16 per hour requirement has no inflation adjustment which, over time, could increase the importance of this clause. Analysts predict the clause will result in increased auto parts production in the U.S. and decreased domestic production of vehicles. The agreement also contains language directing Mexico to make it easier to form unions. Analysts were skeptical about enforcement of this provision and last-minute provisions for cross-border inspections and additional U.S. labor officials in Mexico threatened to undermine the agreement.

Unlike the NAALC, The USMCA includes enforceable labor provisions that are subject to the same dispute settlement mechanism as other provisions in the agreement. While some observers contend these enforcement provisions could have a positive impact on labor conditions in Mexico, U.S. labor groups recognize that the impact of these provisions will largely depend on the parties' willingness to proactively enforce these obligations.

The USITC estimates that the collective bargaining legislation will likely increase unionization rates and wages in Mexico and also increase Mexican output. This, in turn, would be expected to increase U.S. output and employment also, resulting in a small (0.27 percent) increase in U.S. real wages to attract the new workers.

USMCA SUMMARY

The universal response to the USMCA agreement was a "sigh of relief." Most analysts suggest USMCA is not a major revision of NAFTA but, instead, is NAFTA re-branded reflecting the priorities and politics of Washington in 2019. The agreement updates many parts of NAFTA using TPP-12 provisions and revisions adapted from other trade agreements. See Chapter 6.

For economic and business leaders two critical unanswered questions remain:

(1) What will U.S. trade policy be in the future?

(2) Can we make long-term investment decisions in North America based on USMCA or should we look elsewhere?

Consider again, what has transpired since 2016: Threats to terminate NAFTA, numerous meetings among heads of state, name-calling, face-saving gratuitous statements, imposition of protective tariffs, counter tariffs, triangulation of negotiations, a threat of tariffs as a means to impact immigration issues, and somehow a USMCA. Clearly, U.S. trade policy remains uncertain and often unpredictable.

Uncertainty creates risk which tends to cause firms to reduce or postpone investment, and reconsider existing business and supply chain relationships. Current and future business leaders are being trained in "flexible" management, recognizing the norms, assumptions and relationships of even the recent past may not continue in the future. Uncertainty in North American markets may well induce business managers to search for and implement more promising and especially more stable alternatives. To a degree, this has already happened in the run up to the USMCA agreement. If this pattern continues, the likely economic impact of a ratified USMCA will, at best, be undefined.